PEACOCK DREAMS

The 'Peacock in his Pride' was the
emblem stamped on the coins
issued by the last Kings of Burma.
The mark was also incorporated in
the British-Burma flag, introduced
after the country's separation from
the Indian Empire in 1937.

The author in 1945 when serving in the Intelligence Corps, just prior to the recapture of Rangoon

PEACOCK DREAMS

by

Bill Tydd

BACSA
PUTNEY, LONDON
1986

Published by the British Association
for Cemeteries in South Asia (BACSA)

Secretary: Theon Wilkinson
76½ Chartfield Avenue
London SW15 6HQ

ISBN   0 907799 14 0

Cover: designed by Rosemarie Wilkinson

Map: by courtesy of F.S.V. Donnison (with adaptations)

Printed by The Chameleon Press
5-25 Burr Road,
Wandsworth,
London SW18 4SG

Contents

Illustrations

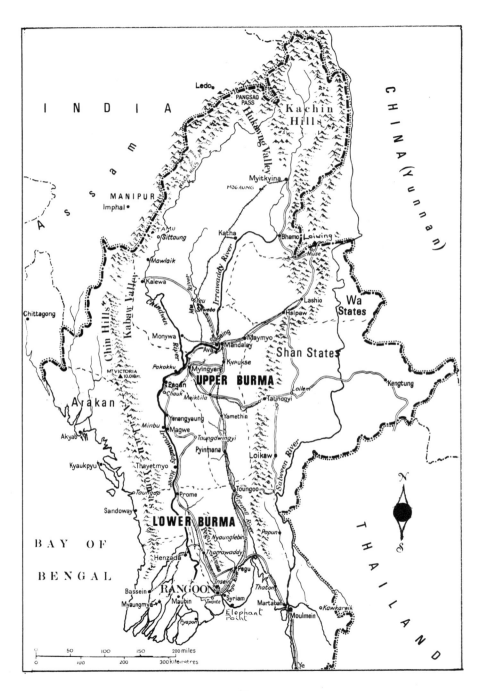

iv

Personalia

Foreword

When Bill Tydd agreed, after a good deal of prodding from his friends and family, to record his experiences in pre-war Burma, I expected a rich collection of anecdotes and some evocative descriptions. These the reader will certainly find, but if he expects no more he will be as pleasantly surprised as I was. This book is far more than 'bedside reading'. It is a most enlightened and enlightening description of a world which is already starting to fade from living memory.

The author writes in his accustomed lucid, trenchant style. His approach to his subject is, however, disarmingly modest, and it is this perhaps above everything else which gives his book, for me, its charm and indeed its subtlety.

I knew Bill most closely when he and I spent the best part of a decade at the same English public school: not as pupils but, in the 1960s, he as its Bursar and I as its Head Master. I soon came to appreciate the two sides of the man - the one which keeps us all in order, and the other which understandingly accepts our weaknesses and our foibles. This is the ideal recipe for the police officer: firmness tempered by sympathy. Thus, although Bill is still, in some ways, every inch a policeman, never does he in his book lay down the law. He certainly does not pontificate. He seldom even allows himself to make a judgement. He paints the scene and tells his story; and there are many small things to entertain and delight the reader; yet what emerges is a very subtle and indeed profound understanding of a complex and fascinating interaction of societies and systems in 'British' Burma.

The reader, then, is led on a very light rein. It is because the book is devoid of heaviness and pomposity, and full of lively anecdote and enthusiasm, that it evokes so effectively the author's early years. And one knows, with some apprehension, what the author did not know: that it is all going to come to an end, suddenly and sadly, with the outbreak of war. Thus this collection of memories of days now far away has all the freshness of the present, and none of the hindsight of a typical anecdotage. It is not a collection of bits and pieces, but a story which it is hard to abandon until one has reached its rather sad yet decisive end.

We are all familiar with what is nowadays called the 'generation gap'; namely the age-old tendency of each succeeding generation to rebel against the values of its immediate predecessor. During the period after the second world war it became the fashion to denigrate the British

Empire - lock, stock and barrel. Now, however, young people are willing and able to take a more balanced view. The perspective of history is already at work. It is to this younger generation that I think the book will most readily appeal: its vividness and directness, coupled with its lack of sermonising, will give younger readers the chance they seek to draw their own conclusions.

This book is not, nor does it pretend to be, a major work on Burma. It is more in the nature of an introduction, stimulating one to want to know more and, perhaps, to be able to travel there oneself. Nevertheless, it will be of absorbing interest to anyone who does recall British Burma, or indeed British India, or who found himself involved in that part of the world during or after the second world war. Those of us who are in that category, but who do not feel that we are yet old men, can find food for thought in much of the detail. It was not, after all, so very long ago that one relied on the heliograph for communication, or could find a local craftsmen to repair the wooden wheel-spokes of a motor car.

E.W. Gladstone
Hawarden Castle

*　　*　　*　　*　　*　　*

This is the seventh of a series of books written by a BACSA member, for BACSA members with a wider public in mind.

It follows 'On Honourable Terms' which recorded the memoirs of a number of Indian (Imperial) Police Officers in the various Provinces of India between 1915 and 1948 within a career structure, by giving a very personal account of the life of a Police Officer.

To Betty

for half a century of happiness:

steadfast in adversity and loving

at all times

Preface

My reminiscences of Burma relate to a short period in my early life, between the age of 21 and 34. The Japanese invasion of the country in 1942 shattered a way of life which had hardly changed since the annexation of Upper Burma in 1886.

My writing started as a chore, due to much prodding from my wife. Gradually, as memory revived, the task became a pleasurable pastime. I am now glad to have recorded these memories before they fade for ever. I hope that I may have been successful in illustrating the sort of life which a young man could lead in the service of an overseas Government within the British Empire.

Now, brought back to my present hum-drum life, I do get the feeling that the fulfilled, contented and sometimes exciting times of those days are just pleasant dreams.

I wish to place on record my thanks to all friends and relations for their encouragement to persevere in this my one effort at authorship. My gratitude also to my dear daughter-in-law, Liz, for her patience and determination to turn my much amended manuscript into well-typed pages.

W.H.T.

The Shwe Dagon Pagoda, seen from Royal Lakes, Rangoon, 1939

1
Initiation

The Indian Police offered a wide range of administrative and executive duties in the higher ranks of the Provincial Police Forces in British India. The career prospects attracted the attention of many young men casting around for an interesting and congenial career between the two world wars.

Recruitment to the Service was by competitive examination, conducted by the Civil Service Commissioners in London. The examination syllabus was similar to the one for entry into Woolwich and Sandhurst as Army cadets. Vacancies were few and growing less due to 'Indianisation' of all Indian Government Services; thus, competition was strong and becoming fiercer.

Successful candidates were appointed by the Secretary of State for India and allotted to the various Provinces in India. Candidates were asked to state their preferred Provinces and allocations were made according to merit in the passing-out order of the examination. I sent in my choice (we were allowed three selections) and awaited further instructions. In due course, I was summoned to the India Office for briefing. A kindly senior official initiated a general talk to probe my general knowledge about India. He then disclosed that the pundits in the office had been puzzled by my first choice of Burma (then still a Province of India), since I had passed out high enough to select any one of the more desirable Provinces for my career. Did I know that Burma was regarded as the backwater of India and not usually put first in the list of selections? I told him that I had not made a mistake and that I wished to serve where my father had been an administrator some thirty years ago.

On my voyage to Rangoon in November 1929, I received confirmation that I was going to a backwater. I learnt that members of the 'All-India' Services received an additional 'Burma Allowance' as a sort of consolation prize for having to serve in a backwater. I never did regret my first choice, even after I had had occasion to see extensive parts of India during my war service in the Army.

I doubt if anyone, now jetting in hours around the world, has any concept of the thrill and romance induced by a first long sea voyage to 'far away places'. The journey from Liverpool to Rangoon took thirty days, but could be shortened to twenty-one by travelling overland to Marseilles. My mother and sister lived in Switzerland and I caught the ship in Marseilles.

My first thrill was when the cabin steward woke me up to go on deck to see the volcano Stromboli, near the tip of Italy. Although the mountain was not in full eruption, the sight was magnificent in the night sky. Flames and lava spewed high into the darkness, the large red glow illuminating the crater and sides of the mountain, which rose straight out of the sea, thus enhancing the dramatic effect.

The most memorable stage of the journey was next. The arrival in Port Said. The newcomer was instantly overwhelmed with all the novelty and romance of the East. The bumboats with their shouting, gesticulating crews brought to life the coloured illustrations in one's child-book of "A thousand and one nights tales". These sellers demonstrated a new method of salesmanship. A rope would be thrown invitingly to any likely customer, leaning on the ship's rails, a basket full of oriental-looking souvenirs would be tied to the end and the prospective buyer begged to haul up and inspect, 'without any obligation to buy, your Honour' (or even 'my Lord'). Lady customers were all addressed as Mrs Langtry or by the name of another of King Edward's lady friends. The 'Gulli-Gulli' man, another universal character, would squat on deck and entertain adults and children with conjuring tricks, mostly by making new born chicks appear and disappear from and to the most unlikely places on himself or a spectator. Most passengers would go ashore and nearly all went to Simon Artz the department store known to thousands of travellers going 'east of Suez'. The purchase of one's first topee was an established ritual, usually to the accompaniment of unasked and contradictory advice on size and shape from 'old hands'. For those who could afford the extra cost, the ship's agents had arranged a visit to the Pyramids, entailing then an overland journey to Suez, at the other end of the canal to catch up with the vessel.

The trip through this famous man-made waterway was enthralling. Sea-going ships of every description and size would be passing through unendingly, day and night, in both directions. The canal was then not wide enough to allow large vessels to pass each other under way. Small rowing boats were towed alongside and when a ship had to stop, the boat crew would leap ashore and tie the ship's hawsers to sturdy bollards, sunk at intervals into the banks of the canal. The boat crews were all Muslims and I witnessed then for the first time the impressive devotion of these people to their religion. Prayer mats would be brought out at the appropriate times and the devotees would go through the elaborate praying ritual, regardless of surroundings or circumstances. I became familiar with this sight later on, sometimes a solitary prayer, othertimes large numbers. Whatever the size of the congregation, I never failed to be moved by the hold their religion had on them.

Then, the British Military presence in the Canal Zone was substantial, based on the 'Beau Geste' site of Ismailia, the town situated half-way along the canal. We passed through at sunset and the romantic picture was enhanced by the hauling down of the Union Jack ceremonies to the clear bugle sounds of the Last Post. We anchored briefly outside Suez to pick up our overland passengers; darkness had fallen by then but the town's white houses were reflected in the moonlight and, from a

2

distance, gave an impression of unreality. The whole trip through this narrow passage for sea-going steamers and native sailing ships was something unique for the novice traveller. The water with its busy traffic, the desert stretching to the horizon on both sides with the occasional camel and its rider ambling along the banks, produced the perfect picture one had dreamed about in picturing a typical eastern setting.

The trip down the Red Sea in a following breeze was the hottest part of the journey. I had never felt heat like it before; just lying in a deck chair, even breathing was an effort. We called in at Port Sudan, half-way along the coast; our Sudan contingent of passengers disembarked to take the train to Khartoum, which was standing on the wharf alongside; the rolling stock was first-class and as good as that of any European railways. The other remembered sight was the row of wrecked cranes. These were new and the latest in efficiency, they had been put up only a few weeks ago and then destroyed within minutes by a violent sand-storm. I can also still recollect the rhythmic chanting of the fierce looking 'Fuzzy-Wuzzies', as they were then called, handling the cargo. I was told that in the Sudan campaign, to relieve General Gordon in Khartoum, which failed and ended in disaster, the 'Fuzzy-Wuzzy' warriors were the only enemies ever to break a 'British Square'. The ship called briefly at Aden to take on Oil Fuel, we had no time for a visit ashore; the place seemed to live up to its description in the Army's repertoire of band tunes "the barren hills of Aden".

Nearly all the remaining passengers disembarked in Colombo. We had an all too short glimpse of the lovely island of Ceylon. The Galle Face hotel was a renowned rendezvous for visitors. The bare-footed Singhalese waiters looked stately and tall in their spotless white coats and long skirts; they all had distinctive half-moon shaped combs in their long hair. I committed the social faux-pas of eating the decorative seeds sprinkled on top of my slice of the papaya fruit; I wondered, at the time, why the locals could like the very bitter taste of the seeds and why I was getting curious looks from the guests at nearby tables.

The saloon bar of the ship seemed very deserted on the last lap of our voyage, due no doubt to the exodus of the many Ceylon tea planters in Colombo. As a community they were renowned for their thirst and drinking capacities. I woke early on the last day of my travels, the blue ocean had turned into a dirty brown colour. The Irrawaddy, in its long journey through Burma from the mountains on the China Border, swollen by the waters of its greatest tributary, the Chindwin, spreads itself over a wide delta and pours millions of gallons of mud and water into the Indian Ocean, polluting the surface water for hundreds of square miles. We sailed most of that last day to and up the Rangoon river; its banks, low and flat, covered with a thick crop of vividly green plants, my first sight of paddy fields at the height of their growth after the rains. Coming round a final broad sweep of the twisting river, I had a fine view of the world-renowned Shwe Dagon Pagoda, the most important Buddhist shrine in the country. The gold-covered temple, shimmering brightly in the late afternoon sun, was a marvellous sight. The pagoda looked huge from this distance, dwarfing the town and any other salient features around. I had a strange feeling that this was not my first sight. Later, when I wrote to my mother describing my arrival and my curious reaction, she replied that on leaving Burma, after my father's sudden death, she had pointed out to me the vanishing pagoda from the deck of the departing steamer; I was then four years old.

After reporting our arrival to the Inspector-General of Police at the Rangoon Secretariat (the Whitehall of the capital) we two new probationers were entertained and shown the sights in the following twenty-four hours. I retain a distinct impression of the wide clean streets, shaded by carefully planted trees and of the variety of people and their dress, jostling each other as they went about their business. The hospitality was generous and welcoming.

We caught the mail train to Mandalay in the late afternoon of our second day in Burma. During the remaining hours of daylight (night falls early and quickly in the tropics), I was again intrigued by the vivid green of the paddy fields. We were still in the rich rice-producing plains of Lower Burma and the crops spread for miles, as far as the eye could see, on both sides of the embankment carrying the railway line. Our third companion in the compartment explained that the paddy was now reaching the height of its colouring and size before beginning to dry up for the harvest in a few months time. He also told us that the high embankments, on which railway lines and roads were built, were necessary safeguards against serious flooding in the rains.

The end of the journey, next morning, seemed to have taken us to a different country. Rangoon had been a busy cosmopolitan sea port. Large sections of the community were immigrants from India and South East Asia. There was also a sizeable European business element. Although the Burmese were in a majority, the city retained an international atmosphere. Mandalay, on the other hand, was a Burmese town through and through. As the last royal capital of the Kings of Burma, the romantic old-world touch was still prevalent, especially in the old fort area with its royal palace and other regal mementoes well preserved. We were scheduled to spend a year under training at the Police school in this interesting city.

Our immediate destination was the Indian Police Mess near the compound of the Provincial Police Training School, where we would receive a year's tuition in all aspects of Police work and general administration. All officers of the Indian Police, serving in Burma, were members of the mess and could use its facilities for meals and accommodation when in the vicinity. For most of the time, the mess was more than half empty and the only permanent occupants were the young officers still under training. We were lucky to reside, at the start of our careers, in this large, comfortable, even lavish building. Later on, when we became acquainted with the more austere district bungalows, we would look back on the mess as a positive luxury hotel.

Indian Police Officers' Mess, Mandalay

The Mess living room

2
Back to School

The backbone of the Provincial Police Force was the Sub-Inspector; he did all investigation work besides more routine duties. Police Constables acted as general maids of all work to the other ranks, besides escorting and guarding prisoners. There was little or no traffic control work, except in Rangoon. The Training School was set up to teach cadet sub-inspectors all Police work prior to their posting to district forces. These cadets were recruited on an all-Burma basis by interview and written examination at various centres, after passing the set tests at the Government Secondary Schools in the Districts where English was taught as the second language. Constables were recruited on a local basis in the thirty odd districts, by interview and a written test in the vernacular. This later basis of recruitment was made possible by the excellent elementary education which all children received in the village 'Pongyi Kyaung' (Monastry) school. Every village of any size had a monastry and the buddhist monks in residence were the teachers and very good they were too, both for teaching and discipline; no nonsense about avoiding physical punishment. I hardly ever met a Burmese child who could not read or write. The Hill tribes were more backward in schooling but their other sterling qualities made them suitable material for the Police and Military forces. Many Constables showing the necessary aptitudes were promoted and sent to the Provincial Training School to blossom into Sub-Inspectors and could then take the same chances for further promotion.

We probationary Assistant District Superintendents of Police, to give the full title, were attached to the school for the advanced courses in Criminal Law, Police Procedure, Administrative procedures and, not least, the learning of Burmese and Hindustani. Members of the Indian Civil Service and of the Indian Police, serving in Burma, had to pass the 'Higher Standard' in Burmese whereas all other expatriate officials only had to pass the 'Lower Standard'. Nobody could be confirmed in his appointment until he had passed in all the prescribed departmental examinations within the prescribed period, which was normally two years.

Burmese was for most of us the most difficult subject; learning to speak, read and write the language was a daunting task. The language is largely monosyllabic and the meaning of a word can be altered by inflexion. For instance, the simple word 'la' can mean come, moon, mule, depending on the way it is pronounced. More difficult still is reading and writing, where the language contains Pali words not used in everyday speech. (Pali is the Sanskrit writing in Buddhist religious records.) The script is attractive, indeed artistic, to look at but difficult to memorise and is unique to Burma. Horoscopes are cleverly written on thin sheets of bamboo as are religious tracts recorded by the monks in their monastries.

We were lucky in our teacher of Burmese. 'Saya' (Teacher) Po Thit was an honorary Inspector of Police but had never worn the uniform nor performed any Police work. He was a self-made instructor of the language and had obtained his official teaching appointment through his private success in teaching the language to many struggling learners, trying to reach the appointed standard for confirmation in their jobs. His knowledge of English remained limited. Nevertheless he had also written his own text books, albeit rather simple and with no attempt to impart any grammatical knowledge; they proved, nonetheless, effective. The absence of notes on Grammar was not as great a handicap as it might seem; the language is not burdened with complicated declensions, or syntax; even so, most Englishmen had to work hard to achieve a good standard in speaking, reading and, particularly, writing.

Po Thit's lack of English was, in some respects, an unexpected bonus. When giving verbal explanations, he was obliged to interject, right from the start of his teaching, Burmese words between his English ones. This involuntary dual language teaching seemed to make it easier for us to memorise the strange words and their meanings. We reached an understandable elementary colloquial knowledge in an astonishingly short time. He had a much harder task in getting us to read and write. Here again, his pragmatic approach to the job enabled him to give us unusual tips to make the memorising of written characters easier. He would ask us to link the letter to the shape of some object, animal or bird. Alas, I have now quite forgotten these useful details; indeed, I would find it well-nigh impossible to read or write many words after forty years! His proud boast that none of his Police pupils failed to pass the 'Lower Standard' in Burmese before leaving after their first year's training, held good for us too. Many expatriate officers, civil and military, passed through his hands and few failed to pass their prescribed tests. I suppose he was in his early fifties when I was his pupil; I heard that he died during the Japanese occupation. I hope that he was spared the worse privations and persecutions of that unhappy time.

Besides our status as students, we 'senior ranks' under training had to act as Duty officers in rotation. On my first round of general inspection, which included the checking of the cadets' food, I noticed that the cooked rice was a suspicious brown colour instead of the usual white, which I had known all too well at boarding school. I ordered the rice to be removed as unfit for human consumption much to the consternation of the assembled cadets. Luckily, one of the Burmese Instructors was passing at the time and he drew me tactfully aside to explain that unpolished rice was always brown and that it was preferred to the polished kind, being more nutritious.

A few days later, I learnt another lesson which was not in our text books. I was inspecting the Military Police lines and at one stage walked in front of a sepoy, sitting on the ground eating some food. As I passed, I was astonished to see him pick up his mess tin and throw out the food. Again I had to be told that I had made a stupid mistake in allowing my shadow to fall across his meal. He was a Brahmin by caste and I, being of no caste, had rendered his food unclean by my shadow.

As we were a small mess at most times, we did not have to wear mess kit every evening; the dressing-up only occurred on guest nights and during the festivities of 'Mandalay Week', of which more anon. Most of our instructors were Burmese and held the rank of Inspector or Deputy Superintendent, the Principal was an officer of the Indian Police, like us, and was ranked as a District Superintendent. The instructors were all experienced Police officers who had specialised in subjects like Criminal Law, Police Procedure or Office Administration. Amongst them were several qualified 'pleaders' (lawyers entitled to appear professionally in Law Courts). A separate branch of Police officers, who elected at the training school for the course of Court Prosecuting Officers, would deal with all prosecutions by the Police in the lower courts. All of us however, of whatever rank, had to pass departmental tests at variable standards according to rank. We probationers from the Indian Police duly passed the prescribed examinations at the end of our year's attachment to the school and could now expect to be posted to a district for the second year's training. This further programme of learning did not turn out quite as expected.

My Burmese 'Saya' (teacher)

3

The Mandalay Interlude

The Kings of Burma had remained absolute monarchs right up to the abdication of the last one, King Theebaw in 1886. Nothing of any consequence was allowed to happen without the ruler's knowledge and consent. Any subject who thought himself important had to be seen frequently at court if he or she wished to become or remain powerful and influential; rather like the old French aristocracy dancing attendance on Louis XIV at Versailles. Mandalay was therefore for many years the hub of the Burmese universe. All political and social life occurred in the square mile of the fort.

The fort area was enclosed by a massive, high and wide brick wall, surrounded in turn by a wide moat covered in water lillies. At each of the four corners of the wall and at regular intervals along each mile-long stretch of wall, were large towers with intricately decorated spires, for the accommodation of a military garrison. The sentries on duty at these towers had the double task of looking out for any enemy and for keeping an eye on the activities of the King's subjects living in the town outside. It was related that when the fort walls were built, men were buried alive under each of the many towers and at each of the four main gates leading inside, as additional immortal guardians of the King's safety. Within the walls were the Royal Palace, the Royal Monastry and many ancillary buildings housing the large number of royal concubines and servants. Extensive barracks for the large garrison occupied most of the remaining ground. In spite of the many buildings, there were also large open spaces planted with many trees and lawns. Unfortunately, all these historic buildings have now disappeared, most of them were destroyed in the bitter fighting of 1945, when the fort was recaptured from the Japanese.

In my time, Mandalay was still an important administrative and military centre. The number of officials and military personnel was greater than anywhere else, except Rangoon. The social world centred around the Upper Burma club, situated within the fort area. Social habits were still governed by out-dated conventions. The quaintest of these was the Victorian-Edwardian habit of 'calling'. The caller did not walk up to the front door and ring the bell; instead he or she would 'drop cards'. Each household had a small box fixed to one of the gate posts. The words 'not at home' were stencilled in white on the front side, the top was hinged with a slit in the middle. The bachelor caller would insert two visiting cards with his rank, initials, name and Regiment or Service engraved thereon (printed cards were definitely 'lower class'); if you wished to be really snobbish and you belonged to a well-known London club, you would have that fact recorded in the left-hand bottom corner of the card. Married ladies, who had to take over this time-wasting task from their husbands, would insert an additional larger card with the word 'Mrs' or 'Lady', as the case might be, added to the husband's rank, initials and name. Cards had to be dropped within a fortnight (as far as I can recollect) of the newcomer's arrival in the station. People were also expected to leave a card when they were leaving with the initials P.P.C. (pour prendre conge) scribbled at the bottom right-hand corner. Woe betide the rebel who ignored this outdated practice. No hostess would invite him to her house until he capitulated; which was usually the case since it deprived the wrong-doer of such social entertainment as was available.

The great event of the year was 'Mandalay Week' at Christmas time. All the regimental and other main functions would be squeezed into this period, culminating with the Military Police ball at the club. Every Civil and Military Police officer, as well as members of the other senior administrative services, who could wangle casual leave, would congregate from all over Burma to participate or attend the sporting and social events of the week. The main Polo tournaments as well as the main race meetings were always scheduled for that period, and elaborate shoots on the renowned snipe grounds around Mandalay were organised by the enthusiasts.

The Ball was lavishly organised by the hosts, every officer in Burma was expected to contribute to the cost and in view of the numbers involved, the individual expense was relatively modest. The scene on the dance floor was colourful in the extreme; it was said that one would see more different mess-kit uniforms at this function than at any other in the Indian Empire. This assertion was very likely since the Military Police drew its officers on secondment from both the British and the Indian Army. Thus, it was not unusual to see fifty or more differently uniformed officers gyrating round the dance floor. Civilian guests wore full evening dress, stiff shirts and collars, white ties and gloves. The ladies were all in long evening dresses, wearing long white kid gloves and rivalled the men's uniforms for colour and trimmings. The custom for men to wear white gloves when dancing was not as silly as it now seems; it was a sensible precaution in a hot climate to protect a lady's dress or, more likely, her bare back from sticky, clammy hands.

In the early days of the Burma Military Police force, set up as an instrument of pacification, after the annexation of Upper Burma, it was rumoured that commanding officers of regular units in India would recommend for secondment to the new formation, officers of their unit who had blotted their copy-book for one reason or another and thus required banishment for a while. This practice, if it ever existed, had long since disappeared in my time. The limited number of yearly vacancies were now keenly sought and selection was strictly according to record and ability, reflected in the high quality of those who now came to serve for a while in Burma.

The geographical situation of Mandalay assured its place as a main centre for transit trade, and a circulating population added to the more permanent inhabitants. The mighty Irrawaddy river was at its doorstep; the main railway line through the country from Rangoon to Myitkyina in the far north, passed through. The branch line to Lashio in the Northern Shan States, linked with road and mule tracks leading into China and Siam. (The notorious 'Burma Road' was then not even a dream.) As a result of all this movement, the streets of Mandalay were filled with people from all parts of Burma and from beyond. This cosmopolitan eastern concourse was an admirable asset for a young man starting on his career, to acquire quickly and easily a knowledge of the different races he would probably have to deal with at one time or another. Moving around the town was always fascinating; the various crafts tended to congregate in their own streets, rather like the middle-age liveries in London. There was the street of wood-carvers, another of silver and goldsmiths, of lacquer workers and so on. The artists and craftsmen would usually sit in an open booth in front of their houses only too ready to demonstrate their skill and display their workmanship.

The most striking factor, in all these interesting activities, was the emancipation of the Burmese women. Many of them organised and ran their own businesses; they moved around quite freely and were never intimidated by the presence of men. Even if a husband had his own occupation, the wife, more often than not, ran the financial and organising side of his business. In fact they had as much liberty and independence as their western sisters. Later on, I would be charmed and pleased to find the women ready to participate unselfconsciously in the impromptu village gatherings to meet the touring official.

I was also lucky to find a more personal diversion in my wanderings round the town. I had been at school in Switzerland in my early childhood and had retained a fairly good knowledge of French and German, which incidentally stood me in good stead in the competitive examination for entry into the Indian Police. I never could work out why good marks in these two subjects were a satisfactory test of one's competence to assist in the administration of British India!

Mademoiselle Denigre was the daughter of a French silk-merchant and (I think) a Shan girl. He had come to Mandalay in the days of King Mindon Min who reigned before the last one, King Theebaw, and had established a flourishing silk trade. He had always spoken in French to his daughter, who had retained in full the vivacious and voluble knowledge of her father's tongue. I was delighted, as I think she was, to renew French conversation. I spent a great deal of time in her silk shop, which was well-known to a large tourist clientele of European women, as well as to the more permanent ones stationed in Burma. She regaled me with numerous stories of the old days at Court, which she had visited on several occasions. Most of her tales dealt with the scandals and intrigues surrounding the King and his favourite Queen, Supayalat. The only one I still recollect distinctly, is her confirmation of the fact that women were specially selected to suckle the sacred royal elephants.

Mademoiselle had a fair skin but always dressed in the old court costume and superb she looked in that style. The clothes are quite distinct from the day-to-day ones, although they consisted of the same main garments. The 'aingyi' (blouse) was longer and flared at the shoulders and at the hips. The 'tamain' (skirt) was of the wrap-around kind and long enough to cover the feet (feet were never displayed in the presence of the King as a sign of respect). The garment was tight fitting and the gap on one side occasionally displayed a shapely leg, when the wearer was walking. Mademoiselle explained that full use was made of this style of skirt by the ambitious woman or girl who wished to attract the attention of some high official or even of Royalty itself.

The shop was staffed by a bevy of well-chosen attractive young women, all dressed in the prescribed court dress and most of them seemed to have difficulty in not displaying a good length of naked limb, when going about their duties. Needless to say, this gallic touch did no harm to the business. Many young and not so young men would drop in, with or without female company, to inspect the goods so to speak.

Mandalay, like all major towns, possessed several large and many small pagodas. The principal one was known as the Arakan Pagoda and I went there during the main religious festival to see my first 'Pwe'. The Burmese love entertainment and in particular a 'Pwe', which is a combination of music, songs and acting, usually with some topical flavour. The play dealt mostly with well-known mythical stories of the past involving Kings, Queens, Princes and Princesses of olden days in the triangle of love theme. Burmese music and singing is definitely an acquired taste for a Western ear; I myself could never attune to the sounds. The eye catching attraction to a foreigner like me was the wonderful kaleidoscope of a Burmese crowd of men and women dressed up for a big occasion; they all have a very good sense of colour and, although using a great range of them in their clothing never seem to produce vulgar clashes. The artists on stage rivalled the audience, if anything looking even more gorgeous in their old-fashioned court dress and head gear. The 'Pwe' I attended was an important happening, drawing a huge crowd, which had gathered for the Pagoda's principal celebrations of the year. Subsequently I attended and even participated in many such entertainments, big and small, but regretfully remained indifferent to the music and singing. However, I could in time understand most of the dialogue and jokes, some of which were pretty broad. A nice fact was that we expatriate officials were always made welcome at such entertainments. If we showed appreciation of the dancing and jokes and were ready to take part in the fun, our participation would be much appreciated, sometimes at the expense of some good-humoured leg-pulling.

My instructive and active first year was passing all too soon. Mandalay was then just about the best place in which to gain one's first knowledge and appreciation of a picturesque people and country; the author of one of the early books on Burma gave it the appropriate title "The Silken East" and I echo his description to the full. As usual, Rudyard Kipling, that fine writer and poet of our Imperial Past, got it right, although he never actually reached Mandalay:-

"For the wind is in the palm trees,
And the temple bells they say;
Come you back, you British soldier;
Come you back to Mandalay."

Mandalay Fort, a watch tower, 1930

Mandalay shore scene

4

The Haunting .

Burma abounded, and no doubt still does, in stories of mystery and the supernatural. Superstition is by no means only restricted to the primitive hill tribes. Many Burmans believe in spirits called 'nats'; these are souls of dead people who for one reason or another, have not yet found peace and have returned to plague the living. The nats usually seek abode in a large tree and, as soon as the locals are convinced of a malign or benign presence, set up a shrine at the foot of the tree and place offerings of food and flowers to propitiate the spirit.

During my service, I met a number of British officials who could recount odd happenings which had occurred to themselves. The most susceptible, quite understandably, were those who spent long periods alone in the forests, undergoing an inevitable feeling of seclusion and loneliness which could be inducive to local beliefs and influences. I also heard many weird tales from villagers in all parts of the country during my touring days; all implicitly believed their stories. I only had one odd experience myself, which I cannot explain rationally to this day and it happened in my very first year.

The Indian Police Mess was a fine large building erected in the early days, after the occupation of Upper Burma. The downstairs was constructed in brick and the upstairs in wood. This was the universal and sensible pattern in those days, when air-conditioning was not even a dream. The brick walls retained the relative coolness of the night for as long as possible and the thin wood around the bedrooms would cool down as quickly as possible after sunset. The ground floor consisted of a large dining room, an equally large ante-room and a billiard room, all 'en-suite'. The upstairs had a dozen bedrooms also in line, each with its own primitive bathroom, with a wide covered verandah and deep overhanging eaves provided good shade throughout the day. A narrow balcony ran continuously along the back of the bedrooms, with a set of steps at each end allowing access to these for the servants; they all lived in separate quarters at the rear of the mess.

As in all of these high old buildings, walls upstairs and downstairs did not reach from top to bottom nor were there proper doors; instead, half-way wooden flaps mounted on springs, were fixed into the sides of the door frames, rather like those seen in saloon bars of Western films. These arrangements allowed for maximum circulation day and night of whatever breeze would spring up from time to time.

In our time there were usually plenty of empty rooms, except on special social or official occasions, when the place could not hold all the officers seeking temporary accommodation. Although many young men had passed through the mess over the years, only one tragedy had been recorded. A young probationer, unable to bear the homesickness which assailed us all at times, shot himself after his first four months. He stretched out on the rug beside his bed, placed the barrel of his shot-gun in his mouth and then pulled the trigger; he had occupied one of the two end bedrooms. We occupants of course knew the story and followed, by tacit agreement, the age-old custom of a succession of mess members, in leaving the fateful bedroom unoccupied.

In the middle of our training period, a young officer was sent for intensive tuition in vernacular languages. I was mess president at the time and had to allocate accommodation for the newcomer, who turned out to be a gregarious Irishman. Somebody mentioned that the Irish were said to be more susceptible to the unusual and that we should put this trait to the test. Unfeelingly I agreed and told the mess butler to instruct the newcomer's servant to put his master's belongings in the end-room which had been empty for so long. We had a convivial evening, our guest had a well-travelled past in various occupations and he kept us entertained with his adventures in many places. No doubt the tales were occasionally laced with the Irish blarney, but even so, his stories were interesting and proved that he had used his powers of observation to advantage.

We all sat down to breakfast on the following morning, nothing having disturbed the night's peace. In my capacity of official host, I turned to our Irish guest and asked him the obvious question – had he had a good night? I can remember his reply to this day:

> Yes, thank you. I slept all night but I had rather a strange dream which I cannot account for as it bears no relation to anything I have been through in the past. I dreamt that I woke up suddenly and saw a man lying on the bedside rug with a shotgun barrel in his mouth; I must have struggled to sit up because I really did wake up then and there was of course nobody on the rug. It took me some time to get back to sleep. I notice that you have a number of vacant rooms and, if you do not mind, I should like to move into one of them because I cannot get rid of the feeling that there is something odd about the one I am in.

We others then rather shamefacedly confessed to him the reason for allotting the end room to him. He took the disclosure in apparent good grace but I could see that he was upset by our callous experiment. I am positive that he had never heard about the old suicide story because he had spent the first few months of his new career in the Kachin hills, far away from our mess and from people who could have known about the sad tale.

5
Further Instruction

After my year at the school, I was posted to the Mandalay District Police for my second probationary year. Although the transfer did not involve any physical changes, I even retained my accommodation in the mess, I was pleased about the posting. I liked the District Superintendent, Dick Prescott. He and his family had shown me a lot of kindness whilst I was at the school and we had become friends. He had a reputation for efficiency and professional competence, confirmed by the fact that he had been put in charge of one of the most important districts in the country at a comparatively young age. His subsequent career justified this early assessment of his qualities, he rose to become Commissioner of Police, Rangoon, where our paths crossed again and he ended his career as the last British Inspector-General of Police, Burma, before the declaration of Independence in 1947. I knew that I was in good hands and would receive efficient further instruction under his care.

I spent the first weeks in the office at headquarters, learning the routine of administering a large force. I realised that this static period of work in my training was essential and I did my best to keep to my resolve to learn everything, dull or interesting, required to make me competent in my chosen profession. Nevertheless, I was glad when the necessary office routine work came to an end. I was then sent to one of the district police stations. The jurisdiction of this one included parts of Mandalay town and about a hundred square miles of the countryside lying to the east.

By this time my colloquial knowledge of Burmese was fair, which was just as well since the station officer plunged me immediately into an investigation conducted by a sub-inspector who had risen from the ranks. His English was limited but we seemed to understand each other quite well and I managed to follow his explanations. He may have been short on English but he had learnt plenty about police procedure. In my innocence I thought that his methods in not acting at once on positive statements implicating the suspects, too cautious. I soon learnt, however, that in this country it was very necessary to seek corroboration wherever and whenever possible.

Form-filling and other paperwork at the station was conducted mainly in the vernacular and I still had difficulty in reading the Burmese script. All the sub-inspectors went out of their way to help me in this respect. Some of them would write up their investigation notes in English but those who found this difficult would, nevertheless and in spite of pressure of work, write a short precis in English in the margin of the pages, so that I could follow progress. Thanks to this kind of extra assistance, I managed to improve my reading; I even ventured to do some vernacular writing on set forms. I remained at the Police Station for about two months and most of the reported cases during that time were of a petty nature. I do however remember distinctly two incidents.

The first, a simple case of burglary was in an unusual setting. On the outskirts of the town on the road to Maymyo, stood a large Leper Asylum, run by a religious order of French nuns. The local community, white or coloured, took little or no interest in the place and limited their support to periodical donations of money when the nuns made their periodical rounds to collect subscriptions. Few, if any, ventured to visit the place. The complaint about the break-in was made at the station by the Mother Superior herself whilst I happened to be there. I seized the opportunity to air my French, which seemed to please her. After the formalities, she talked to me about the nuns' work and invited me to visit the place; I promptly accepted. After she had left I began to have second thoughts. I shared the common dread about leprosy and contact with lepers, even at a distance. I did know, however, that medical science had made considerable progress in dealing with this disease and that those who could be persuaded to attend treatment in the early stages of the infection stood a good chance of eventual recovery. Unfortunately, people in Burma waited until the symptoms were well advanced before appearing for medical attention. The Mother Superior had warned me that some of the sights would be unpleasant.

I decided, in the end, to time my visit to coincide with the Police investigation so that I could have an excuse to break off the round of inspection and join the sub-inspector in his examination of witnesses, if I found the sights too trying. The Mother Superior was waiting for us and announced that she was going to be my guide; that neatly disposed of my alternative route of escape.

I realised, at once, that not only was the Asylum efficiently organised but that it had to cope with many more patients than I had realised. My guide told me that numbers fluctuated between one and two hundred of both sexes and all ages. The whole place was spotlessly clean, then a rather unusual state of affairs in large institutions in the East. I saw that the reason for this high standard of cleanliness was due to the nuns participating in all the most menial tasks in addition to their skilled nursing and caring duties.

My distinguished guide was quite obviously held in high respect and affection by all her nuns and by all patients, big or small. She took me all over the place, public rooms, kitchens, wards. Everywhere she had a kind word of encouragement for individual patients; I noticed that she made a point of touching those who seemed to be the greatest sufferers. However harrowing the sight, her own countenance betrayed no sign of revulsion or even pity; in short she treated every patient as a normal human being. The whole religious community was completely devoted to their self-imposed charitable work. I left the Asylum greatly impressed and indeed moved by the self-sacrifice of these long-exiled French women, and not a little ashamed of my past indifference about their exceptional and unselfish work. I did go back several times before I left Mandalay, partly to redeem my past behaviour and partly because I thought that the Mother Superior and her followers did welcome the opportunity to speak in their mother tongue to someone who could bring them news from the world outside. My distinguished hostess I found out was from an old aristocratic family, had a nice taste in wine and kept a modest but select stock. A pleasing worldly touch from a saintly woman.

The second case was tragic. A well-known bully in the town returned home very drunk one afternoon, began to abuse his family and the neighbours. When finally challenged by one of those he had insulted, he had pulled out a revolver and fired some shots in the air. A sub-inspector was sent to investigate the fracas, arrived on the scene with the bully still threateningly brandishing his fire-arm. The officer told him to throw down the weapon. Instead, the man fired straight at him. As the policeman fell he managed to draw his own pistol and fired a shot which hit the attacker; both collapsed close to each other. The station officer and I arrived on the scene to find the attacker dead and the officer seriously wounded. Unfortunately he died on admission to hospital. I attended the Buddhist funeral service with the Superintendent and many of his colleagues, together with a large number of local inhabitants; a testimony to the deceased's popularity in the area.

Gradually, I began to see how the theoretical knowledge, acquired in the Police Training School fitted into the practical work at a Police Station. After a while, I thought privately that I was now fit to supervise a major investigation. The opportunity arrived quicker than I expected. Dacoity is defined in the Indian Penal Code as an assembly of five or more persons intent on committing robbery with violence. Such crimes were still all too common in parts of Burma, a legacy from the turbulent days after the third and last Burmese war which ended in 1886. More often than not fire-arms were carried by the dacoits, mostly home-made and not very effective except at short range and for the loud noise they made when discharged.

Mandalay district had a good record for law and order and serious crime was rare, except for the unfortunately widespread prevalence of unpremeditated murder, common to the whole of the country. A dacoity was reported from an outlying village and, to my delight the District Superintendent asked me whether I felt ready to supervise the inquiries. I departed in high spirits to the scene of the crime. The Circle Inspector (the rank below that of Deputy or Assistant Superintendent) who was responsible for the work done by three Police Stations, was already on the spot when I arrived and put me in the picture.

The attack had followed the usual pattern. The robbers had surrounded the selected victim's house after dark; forced an entry (not too difficult in a village house made of wood and thatch) and tied up the inmates. After some none too gentle persuasion, they had found the hidden money and jewellery. Meanwhile, the headman had courageously collected some villagers armed with 'dahs' (long pointed knives) and spears and, carrying his Government-issued shot-gun for village protection, had arrived at the house as the dacoits were preparing to leave with their loot. As they fled, the headman fired both barrels of his shot-gun and the dacoits retaliated with several wild shots which discouraged any thought of pursuit in the dark.

The headman reported that he thought he had wounded at least one criminal because someone amongst the scattering dacoits had cried out that he had been hit. The headman's brave action, none too common, encouraged the villagers to be co-operative in the investigation. All too often villagers and the victims in particular, were very reluctant to help the Police for fear of later retaliation from the dacoit gang or their informers. On this occasion, we received useful leads. One villager stated that, when the dacoits were retreating in confusion, he thought that he had recognised one of the voices as that of a villager, who had left his house some days ago. This vital clue led to the early arrest of the suspect. He soon realised that the game was up and made a full confession, which led us to the wounded dacoit, lying up in a jungle hut near to his home village, where his wife brought him food while he waited for his leg wound to heal. A search of this isolated hut revealed some of the stolen jewellery and the second culprit also made a clean breast of the affair. The whole gang was successfully traced, arrested and sent up for trial. They were all given long sentences of imprisonment to the penal settlement on the Andaman Islands, where all dangerous criminals from Burma were banished for the duration of their sentence.

I learnt a great deal in the practice of supervising junior officers in their detailed investigation work and giving general advice and instructions. The Circle Inspector, with his years of experience, saw to it that I did not commit any blunders; I had no illusions that, but for his presence and guidance, my first important case might not have been conducted so swiftly and satisfactorily.

My next experience was to accompany my chief on his inspection tours round the district, to learn the duties of higher responsibilities. Unlike most other districts, Mandalay was compact, with rail and road facilities. On the other hand, the population was larger and more varied than elsewhere 'up country'; Mandalay was the largest town and, with the hill station of Maymyo, contained the highest number of Europeans and Military personnel in Burma with the exception of Rangoon. Consequently, our touring in the district was usually for short periods at a time and we normally put up at Inspection bungalows instead of having to travel with camping gear. I therefore did not experience the pleasure of long leisurely tours, with all the paraphernalia for comfortable camping, until later on.

Sometimes, in the remoter places, when circumstances compelled an overnight stay, we would seek accommodation in the village headman's house. The Burmese are hospitable and social people; our presence in a village was always the signal for an impromptu gathering at which people could seek interviews to air some request or grievance. Often, after the day's business, there would be an opportunity for more relaxed general conversation and even some sort of entertainment, usually a display of dancing with the discordant (to my ears) accompaniment of Burmese music and singing.

Most of the ordinary tours around the district were taken up with routine inspections of Police Stations, dealing with general administrative problems and personnel welfare, consistent with the multiple duties imposed on a Police force spread over an area usually greater than that of an average English County. I had one interesting encounter during our travels round the district. King Theebaw, the last King of Burma, was exiled to India where he died; he left a large number of descendants but relatively few recognised as legitimately royal. One of these, known as the 'Third Princess' was living quietly in Maymyo on a Government pension. My chief took me with him on a courtesy visit to her house. She lived simply and without any ceremonial, nevertheless her presence inspired respect. I suppose that she must have been in her late fifties or early sixties by then; unlike most Burmese women, who seem to age quickly after middle age, she did not show her years and retained an erect, indeed imperious, bearing. I found it difficult to follow her Burmese as she seemed to use many out-of-date expressions. She engaged in an animated discussion with my chief, I noticed that he was careful to avoid contradicting some of her obviously incorrect statements. I could also see that the Princess had an excitable manner. When she became really animated, her eyes would flash and she would use her hands to emphasise a point, rather like a roused Frenchman in an argument. She seemed pleased that we had called and gave us a cordial invitation to return, on our next visit to Maymyo, when we took our leave. On our way back to the Circuit house, where we were staying, I mentioned that I had noticed my chief's tact. He then told me that the Princess had taken a long time, understandably, to realise that her status and days of power were over. She had gradually adapted herself to her changed circumstances but she just could not accept that people now could contradict a royal statement. He added that it was a small price to pay, if by respecting the old royal privilege, he could maintain friendly and interesting contacts with the old royal family. On another occasion, I accompanied another Government officer for a second visit and he also was careful to observe the rule of no contradictions. I could not help thinking about the stories I had been told of the absolute powers exercised by the King and his chosen favourites and the apparently cruel punishments they would inflict unhesitatingly on the culprits. In my imagination, I thought that the Princess would certainly have been capable of excesses when sufficiently roused!

6
Fun and Games

As in most Eastern stations, games and sport were available in abundance in and around Mandalay.

We played team games, such as football and hockey, usually with our own men. Tournaments were popular and frequent. Football became a favourite game with the Burmese and they were soon adept at it; many of them would play in bare feet and achieve astonishing control over the ball. They derived this skill from their own national game of 'chinlon'. The ball is hollow made of woven strips of bamboo and is about one third the size of a football. The players, around six but numbers are not fixed, stand in a rough circle and kick the ball to each other in no particular order of play; the idea is to keep the ball in the air as long as possible, using feet, knees, and shoulders. Great aptitude and ball control is achieved by regular players; I have seen games in which the ball did not fall on the ground for several minutes at a time. Football matches between the town teams and those of the local garrison or of neighbouring places were keenly contested and well attended. Hockey was another favourite game, particularly with the Sikhs, who were unbeatable. They all seem to have an extraordinary good eye for a fast game played with a small ball, such as hockey and polo.

A great boon for the impecunious junior officer stationed in Mandalay, was the opportunity to learn polo. Even the poorest of us could afford to participate. Trained polo ponies could be hired, from the Mounted Infantry Lines of the Burma Military Police, at one rupee each (one shilling and six pence or seven and a half new pence!) for a whole afternoon. So the cost of playing six to eight chukkers and using only two ponies for a good afternoon's sport, could be had for three shillings plus a small tip to the syce who brought the ponies from the lines, waited all afternoon and then took them back. We always played in mixed teams with the Indian officers and soldiers who were usually better at the game than their British comrades. The former willingly taught us beginners many useful tips but we first of all arranged to improve our riding skills in training sessions at the Mounted Infantry's riding school. The distinguished looking white bearded Subadar-Major in charge, a noted polo player himself, put us through our paces and made a bit of extra pocket money on the side. He would make us place a rupee coin between each knee and the saddle flaps before going round the ring, over or round small jumps, at the gallop to improve our balance in the saddle. Every time a coin dropped to the ground, the old soldier would pick it up and put it in his pocket with a grin. Some of us parted with quite a few rupees before we learnt to keep a tight grip on the pony's flanks. I saw our Subadar-Major play on several occasions in the more important tournaments. He must have been always one of the oldest, if not the oldest, player on the field but few of his opponents ever managed to rob him of the ball once he had possession; many players of renown received some of their early coaching from our instructor.

Golf was a game which we could not play locally in my time. There was a good golf course in Maymyo, the main hill station of Burma, forty miles away on the edge of the Shan States plateau. Access was easy on an excellent well-graded, all-weather road. We thought nothing of getting on to our motorbikes on a free afternoon, for a game of golf before returning for a late dinner or staying on at the Maymyo club and coming back during the night. The other attraction of the place was the Saturday night club dance; particularly during the hot weather when the place was thronged with the young beauties from Rangoon and elsewhere, escaping from the heat in the plains. On these occasions women were for once in equal numbers, or nearly so, to the men. The early morning drive back to Mandalay as dawn was breaking, never worried us in our youth. Looking back, I suppose that we did take more risks than apparent then, on the numerous hairpin bends before the road reached the straight stretch of ten miles to Mandalay. Wild animals abounded in the jungle bordering the road and we were often conscious of large glowing eyes staring at us from the semi-darkness, lit up by the glare of our headlamps. Once my companion riding ahead, shouted excitedly that he had just seen a tiger slink from the road into the undergrowth.

We had an amusing happening on one of these nocturnal returns to Mandalay after an all night session at the weekly club dance. Four of us were driving back in an open Morris Tourer car with the hood down. These models had the petrol tank under the bonnet in front of the windscreen; a metal flap covered the screw top lid of the tank. On this car the holding spring of the flap had worn loose and made it clatter continuously. Suddenly the flap started to open slowly and a mouse emerged cautiously, sat up for a moment and then fell off into the side of the road due to the vibrations of the car. There was a long and pregnant silence from all four of us until one passenger enquired tremulously whether anyone had noticed a mouse? Great was the relief all round when we all confessed to the same strange sight!

An orthodox pastime on these trips to Maymyo and back was water-buffalo baiting. These enormous dark beasts with fierce-looking large horns would often graze in the strips of grass alongside the road. Although they did not seem to mind moving motorcars, they did not like the loud noise made by a motorbike. As soon as a rider got within a certain distance of one of these animals, it would stop grazing, raise its head and charge the enemy. To add to the excitement of the chase, we would slow down until the beast was about to gore the machine and then accelerate rapidly to top speed. Nobody was ever injured due to a stalled engine. The real danger in this kind of stupid prank was probably not as great as it appeared; it was a common sight to see a herd of these grazing animals being tended by a small child, usually perched across the neck of the largest and most ferocious-looking beast.

Some of the best snipe grounds in Burma lay around Mandalay; the birds were so prolific that even I, who never became a good or keen shot, could bring back a respectable bag at the end of a day's shoot. Well organised drives were laid on for important visitors and the subsequent slaughter of birds was immense. In my year, an all-party Parliamentary mission from London was touring India and Burma to report back on the constitutional changes then under consideration. They visited Mandalay and a large snipe drive was organised in their honour. I cannot now remember details but at least a dozen guns participated; the drive was very successful and I think over two thousand birds were shot. Some of the distinguished visitors were not all that well acquainted with shot-guns and probably most of the bag came from the local organisers; of whom one, our Civil Surgeon, a Colonel in the Indian Medical Service, held the record for the number of snipe shot in Burma. He shot as often as possible and never failed to bring back impressive bags at the end of the day. One well-known British politician seemed quite pleased with his score of three paddy-birds in amongst some snipe; these birds are slow-flying, easy to hit and not considered game birds.

I had neither the means nor the inclination to participate in the more ambitious and expensive pastime of big-game hunting. Tigers, leopards and wild elephants were still numerous in the jungles of Upper Burma, in the Shan States and in the Kachin hills. One or two local enthusiasts would, from time to time, organise hunting expeditions for those who wished to be initiated. Sometimes a known big-game hunter would be approached to go after a particular big 'cat', which had started to decimate a herd of domestic animals near some village. The most successful hunters were to be found in the Forest Service and our local Deputy Conservator, whose headquarters were in Maymyo, had a respectable collection of tiger and leopard rugs spread around his bungalow. I always thought privately how much better these trophies must have looked alive in their own environment. I did not go so far as to preach against the sport and could see that to certain people, the thrill and skill of tracking a dangerous and cunning animal was irresistible. Despite my lack of enthusiasm for this sport, I did once sit up one night over a tiger's kill, as I shall recount.

7
Unexpected Interlude

An unexpected diversion took me away from Mandalay for a few days after my first month.

I had been playing tennis at the club in the late afternoon when a telephone message summoned me urgently to District Headquarters. There I found the Commissioner of the Division, R.R. Brown I.C.S., (this official is in general control of several districts and ranks next to the Governor in executive authority), the Deputy Commissioner of Mandalay and the District Superintendent of Police in urgent consultation. News had come in that a serious disturbance had broken out in Yamethin District, some 200 miles south of us and that the Deputy Commissioner, who had gone to the scene of action with a small posse of armed police, was missing. It was decided that I should accompany the Commissioner with a Military Police detachment from the depot. Orders were issued to hold up the daily mail train to Rangoon, which was due to leave shortly, until we and the armed force could entrain.

I hurriedly changed into uniform at the mess and then dashed to the railway station; the Commissioner and the Military Police arrived shortly after, within a few minutes of each other and the delayed train left half an hour after its scheduled departure. The Commissioner kindly invited me to share his reserved compartment, which was a great deal more comfortable than squeezing into one of the fully booked ones; the armed force had been allotted an entire additional coach in which they just about occupied all the benches. As usual, we witnessed a spectacular sunset in a cloudless sky before darkness fell quickly. The Commissioner was nearing the end of his service and had spent all thirty years of it in Burma. He entertained me with tales of his various jobs and spoke with great feeling for the people and the country. I could see that, whilst he was looking forward to retirement and permanent reunion with his family, he was sad to leave this land and its inhabitants for good. One of the great drawbacks, probably the greatest for most of us, was the inevitable separation from our children after they reached the age of six; the climate and the lack of educational facilities made these breaks unavoidable and the mother was then constantly torn between staying with the children for lengthy periods and neglecting her husband or the opposite.

We arrived at our destination in the very early hours of the next day. The District Superintendent met us at the station; he briefly reported that the Deputy Commissioner was still missing and that his last message had been received in the afternoon of the previous day. The Commissioner arranged a meeting at the Circuit house (every district headquarters has one for the accommodation of senior officials visiting district officers). The local military police barracks (each district had a detachment of this armed force, supplied and relieved from the nearest battalion depot) were near the Circuit house and I marched off with the Subadar and his men. They were able to rest in the barracks, which were partly depleted because of those who had gone with the Deputy Commissioner. After settling the men, the Subadar and I went to the Circuit house meeting. The Commissioner and the District Superintendent had been joined by the District Forest Officer and the Executive Engineer for Roads and Buildings, the other two senior officials of the District. By the time I arrived on the scene, the place from which the Deputy Commissioner's last signal had been received had been pin-pointed on the map. In those days, the wireless had not yet reached mobile civil columns and the heliograph was used by the Military and the Police wherever geographical conditions were available for long distance visibility. The Deputy Commissioner's party had been thus equipped, since they were proceeding into the hilly part of the district, and messages had got back from him in this manner and then by runner.

A decision was made to send me with half of the reinforcements (one of two platoons) as quickly as possible to the place from which the last message had originated and then I was to "play it by ear". I was also told to look out for another armed police party, sent out by the District Superintendent as soon as he ceased to get information from the Deputy Commissioner; this force had been put in the charge of a young Frontier Service officer, also still under training; so it looked as if it would become a matter of the blind leading the blind! I left in two commandeered lorries; we travelled along a bumpy unmetalled road for about fifteen miles before it petered out at a large village. By then dawn was breaking and I decided to push on along a fairly wide path in open country, leading to the jungle-covered foothills. We reached the end of the path at the edge of the first rising ground in an hour or so, just as the sun, now well above the horizon, was beginning to heat up the atmosphere and the shade of the trees was a welcome sight. The villagers we had met so far were going about their usual business undisturbed and could give us no news about the trouble; I was fairly certain that they had not been intimidated and thus keeping silent out of fear. I called a halt in a clearing surrounded by trees, with a small hillock nearby, offering a good look-out for a sentry. We started to brew-up and eat some food. Suddenly, the sentry shouted that an armed group was approaching, I ran up to him and through my field glasses saw that this was the armed party sent out under the other young officer. They joined us and whilst eating, we exchanged information. Mine was meagre and the other party's not much more; they had done an extensive sweep round the area but, not having received the information about the D.C.'s last place of contact, had not visited that place. However, they did report that people, encountered during their march, seemed to be apprehensive and talked of sighting an armed gang melting into the thicker jungle in the hills further eastwards.

I had to go on to the place which had been pin-pointed on the map and suggested that the other party should continue with their sweeping operation to gather more definite information one way or another. I reached my goal after an arduous trek through scrub jungle which became thicker and thicker as we penetrated deeper into the hills. The place turned out to be a small hamlet. These forest dwellers depended on 'jungle cultivation' augmented by casual work for the Forest department and for the timber extraction firms. They moved around the forests, cleared a piece of jungle by burning all vegetation, planted their crops in the soil, richly fertilised by the burnt vegetation and then when the crops ceased to yield satisfactory returns, would move to a new site and repeat the wasteful burning process. They knew their own forest intimately and put this knowledge to good use when working for the Forest department of the timber firms.

The headman was co-operative and told me what had happened and what he had heard. The D.C.'s party had arrived soon after a large gang of armed men had left the village, where they had spent the night and consumed most of the spare food. The Government party had followed the trail after a short rest, taking with them two guides from the village. One of them had returned a day later with the news that the D.C.'s party had made contact with part of the gang and had exchanged shots before the enemy had scattered into the thick jungle; he could not tell me anything about casualties but was fairly certain that the 'Asoya' (government) had suffered no losses. He had not been told what the pursuers intended to do. The headman suggested that he should send one of his own men, who knew all the short cuts, to scout around for a day and report back. I had not been equipped for a prolonged patrol, since the original object was to mount a swift rescue operation. Taking into account the uneventful searching of the other party, it seemed obvious that the D.C. and his force were not in imminent danger, I decided to accept the headman's plan.

The scout, in fact, returned before his time with the welcome news that the D.C. had returned to headquarters, after a further difficult march in the hills, having failed to make further contact with the fleeing men. I decided, in consultation with the Subadar, to split my force so as to extend the search for one more day and then also return. The villagers were again helpful and supplied two more guides. My party was approaching the next forest settlement, a half-day's march from our point of departure, when round the bend of the jungle path we suddenly saw two armed men ahead of us. By extraordinary luck, they had not heard our approach although we had not taken any special precautions to move silently. I shouted to them to stop; startled they looked round and started to run off. The sepoy behind me, a young Gurkha, immediately raised his rifle and fired two shots in rapid succession; one man fell to the ground and the other jumped in the air clutching his ankle and then dived into the thick undergrowth beside the narrow track. The man on the ground had a nasty thigh wound, to which I applied a field dressing, whilst the rest of the party fanned out in search of the other wounded man, who had left a faint trail of blood behind him. Half an hour later, the wounded man was found hiding in a clump of giant bamboos (jungle bamboo grows high, wide and strong, some canes are several inches across and cut sections are commonly used for the storage of food and liquids). I was just in time to prevent the discoverer shooting the terrified wretch. He had thrown away his firearm, which was retrieved later on in the undergrowth; the weapon was a rather pathetic home-made imitation of a single barrel shotgun. His wound was not as serious as his companion's but the bullet had nicked the protruding part of the ankle bone which made walking, let alone running, pretty painful.

The two apprehensive prisoners were questioned separately and their stories tallied in detail. I concluded that they must have received the common indoctrination, about the dreadful fate awaiting anyone who was captured by the authorities, and had decided to tell the truth as the best way out of their dilemma. We learnt that the original gang was about fifty strong (the Burman is hard to pin down to precise figures for numbers, distance or hours) and that they had been badly shaken by the encounter with the Deputy Commissioner's force. They had then decided to split into smaller parties and make their escape eastwards into the Shan Hills and even over the border into Siam until the hue and cry had died down. Meanwhile, the capture of our prisoners had spread around by jungle telegraph and, by the time we had concluded the lengthy interrogations, a sizeable crowd had collected to pick up what gossip they could. I drew aside two or three older spectators and one of them turned out to be a headman from nearby. He confirmed the news that armed men had been seen in small groups, making their way eastwards on the jungle tracks. He also said that some of the fugitives appeared to have bandaged limbs.

Having impressed on all and sundry the importance of letting the district authorities know immediately if any further news about the raiders was received, I gave orders for our withdrawal. The wounded prisoners were loaded on to a bullock-cart and with a small escort told to follow as quickly as possible. We joined the two lorries at the head of the motorable road; we had to wait for an hour for the bullock-cart's arrival. Back at the Circuit House, the Deputy Commissioner had joined the others for further deliberations. I reported on what had occurred to us and on the information I had collected, which agreed broadly with that brought back by the Frontier Service officer and his escort when he also arrived soon after me. The general picture now was that things had again settled down for the time being.

The Commissioner decided to return to Mandalay and told me to hand over my force, under the Subadar, to the District Superintendent of Police as temporary re-inforcements. On our return journey, he told me that a rebellion, which I knew had broken out in Tharrawaddy district a month ago, was now serious and was spreading to other districts in Southern Burma. He added that the Government had issued a general warning to all other districts to be on the look-out for trouble. Subsequently, the district authorities in Yamethin collected evidence that the gang we had been chasing around had been formed by supporters of the original movement, sent northwards to foment disruption. So, what I had thought of, privately, as a storm in a tea cup had more sinister origins and aims.

I returned to what I thought would be a resumption of my interrupted training.

Native boat on Irrawaddy

Burmese bullock-cart in Mandalay

8
The Rebellion

The 'Tharrawaddy Rebellion', as it came to be called, broke out in the district of that name, just after Christmas 1930. The leader, Saya San, had been a monk who thought he had magical powers; he was in no way a political agitator fighting for political rights. Like similar cranky leaders of past uprisings, he had visions of defeating the Government of the day, whoever they were, and proclaiming himself King of Burma. He managed to gather, in the end, several thousand followers in various districts and succeeded in terrorising and looting large parts of the country before the momentum of his rising was broken by his capture eight months later.

I had just completed a week of my resumed training programme when orders came from Rangoon for my transfer to Tharrawaddy on special duty with the Military Police. By this time, the rebellion, which had been raging for two months, was at its peak in that district. On my arrival, I reported to the senior officer and was told that the Deputy Commissioner would put me up for a day or two until I could be given a specific task.

The whole place was a hive of activity, with officers, civil and military, arriving all the time, some with contingents of troops and police. All junior Assistant District Superintendents still under training like me, had also been drafted for special duty. We had a rowdy and late reunion celebration at the Circuit house with others also drafted for special duty. Needless to say, there was the usual confusion which seems inevitable in the early stages of any mobilisation, big or small. Having read a number of books on the Indian Mutiny, I could not help feeling that our general state of mild uproar and muddle must have followed an earlier pattern, albeit under much less tragic and serious conditions.

The next morning I received orders, posting me as C.O. of the armed escort on the 'armoured train'. This was a rather grandiose title for an engine, three coaches and two open trucks. The trucks were the 'armoured' part of the train, one in front of the engine and the other at the rear of the three coaches. Both trucks had parapets of sand bags on all four sides and a machine gun with crew at each corner. The coaches accommodated the personnel. The officer in charge of this outfit was an army officer seconded to the Military Police.

The train was used to patrol the line between Tharrawaddy and the disturbed area northwards, which extended into Prome district, a total distance of around a hundred and twenty miles. Most of the patrolling was done at night, usually on a specific stretch, expected to be sabotaged according to the latest intelligence reports, most of which turned out to be false. Nothing at all happened until the second night of my attachment.

We were passing near a large village, which seemed about a mile away, suddenly we saw flames rising in the village and heard the sound of shots. The train was stopped, I detrained with my escort platoon and started towards the village. Although the moon was up and the night bright, the shadows were deceptive and we had some difficulty in walking across the dried up paddy fields. We kept on stumbling over the 'Kazins', small mud walls built up by the peasants around each field to trap the rain water and thus ensure a good continuous soaking for the growing plants. The village now seemed a lot further away.

Eventually we reached the outskirts of the village; the firing, which had been steadily intermittent during our progress, had died down but we now heard shrieks and yells. In my youthful ignorance, I was all for charging straight into the place but my experienced second-in-command, a Sikh Jemadar, did not think much of my tactics. He suggested tactfully that it might be better to surround the village with a ring of sentries and then enter with the remaining force; we would then be in a position to flush out the enemy and drive them into the arms of the waiting sentries; an obviously much more sensible plan. Accordingly, we cautiously infiltrated the village in due course; in view of the poor visibility, we stayed in close formation so as to avoid any danger of cross-fire. Once inside, we advanced from house to house with startling results. Shadowy figures began to jump down from various buildings, some firing wildly and all running as fast as they could towards the perimeter fence, which surrounds every village in Burma to prevent indiscriminate access, particularly at night.

The raiders disappeared into the open fields around in a remarkably short time. We heard several shots from our 303 rifles, indicating that some of our men outside had made contact. I silently blessed my wise assistant commander for his timely advice. The upheaval in the village died down gradually and I gave orders for the sentries to be withdrawn and for the platoon to assemble outside the headman's house. The villagers had suffered two casualties only in spite of the rebels' indiscriminate firing when they attacked the village, but three good houses had gone up in flames; they were full of thanks for our unexpected intervention which had cut short any plans for extensive looting and perhaps summary justice for suspected informers.

Dawn was not far off by the time all the men had gathered together. The ring of sentries had netted four prisoners, one of whom was hit by a grazing shot on the arm; the other three had stopped sensibly, when challenged. One sentry reported that he had definitely hit another fleeing rebel and had seen him stagger after running a few yards; he had started to search for him when he was recalled. I had to return to the waiting train with my force and asked the headman to organise a search for the wounded man as soon as it was daylight. The subsequent search party found nobody and it had to be assumed that he had managed to get away, with or without help, and hide up until his wound had healed or he had died from the effects; nobody reported the presence of a wounded or dead rebel.

My attachment to the armoured train ended after a week. The authorities had by then decided to establish numerous temporary outposts, spread all over the disturbed areas, so that effective and constant patrolling could be undertaken to flush out the gangs of rebels still roaming around and attacking indiscriminately, to keep the population terrorised. At the time, the gangs were still large and did not hesitate to attack large villages; even two small towns on the railway line were assaulted, with limited success, as the armed forces were soon on the spot and drove off the rebels with effective losses. After these reverses, the gangs confined themselves to areas where access was more difficult and where Government forces were thin on the ground. Saya San, the leader of the rebellion, was still at large and his numerous followers were still convinced that he had supernatural powers. Trading on these beliefs, he organised widespread distribution of charms and having his recruits tattooed with the 'Galon' a mythical bird described in old folklore. Both the charms and the tattoo marks were supposed to make the wearer proof against the enemy's bullets. This belief persisted for some months and the rebels would charge head on into the firing troops, firmly believing in their invulnerability. Even those who were wounded retained the faith until the inescapable mounting losses made them alter their minds. When the rebellion was ended everywhere, about a year later, disillusionment was complete.

I was ordered to assume command of an outpost and an area bordering on the Yoma hills; this range, known as the Pegu Yomas, straddled the Tharrawaddy-Pegu districts and was a favourite hide-out for rebel gangs. Saya San had collected his original band of supporters secretly under the cover provided by the forests in these hills. The general situation in the disturbed areas was very much what it had been after the annexation of Upper Burma in 1886, when the country remained in a turbulent state for some time. Gangs of ex-soldiers from the royal army, joined by dacoits, roamed around, looting, killing and terrorising the population. Gradually, the Civil and Military Police, the latter a creation of those disturbed times, subdued the gangs. Following closely the methods used fifty years ago, the Government forces now slowly cleared up, area by area, the law-breakers and restored peace.

Meanwhile, only the first stage of the mopping-up operation was being established. These temporary outposts had also a contingent of civil police under an Inspector or Sub-Inspector, who set up a temporary police station, where the public could lodge complaints or report crime; the detachment also acted as an Intelligence unit for the collection and assessment of information on rebel activities. The larger posts had the use of a section of mounted infantry in addition to the ordinary contingent of military police. The total strength of the combined civil and military personnel in an outpost varied from fifty to eighty depending on the size of the area and on the population therein. Close contact was maintained with adjacent outposts and a senior officer, at a township headquarters, was in overall command of several outposts, which he visited frequently to inspect, collect and supply information.

Most of our time was spent on hum-drum patrolling, calling on village headmen and generally trying to obtain news of rebel movements. The villagers were on the whole singularly unmoved by the disturbances until brought to their doorstep. The hostile people were usually young men, who had been to the urban areas, picked up rebel propaganda and false news about rebel successes. The most trying factor was the discomfort we had to put up with from the heat. The dry season was at its peak and our abode was a barn-like building, built of thatch and bamboo, with a watchtower and annex for the C.O., also built of the same materials. As these outposts were all situated in the middle of a dried-up paddy field, the heat generated during the day-time built up to temperatures around 110 degrees, even more, under the thin thatched roof. Going on patrol and being on the move, even in the sun, was a relief from sitting or lying in the airless hut, even though the thatch walls reached only half-way up the sides to allow maximum ventilation.

Another recurring task was to carry out intermittent checks in villages to ensure that no absconding rebels were in hiding, helped by sympathetic or, much more often, intimidated inhabitants. The villagers would be assembled, the women and children on one side, the men on the other. After a quick check of the former, to ensure that no male had concealed himself in their midst, they were told to go but most of them stayed on to watch the process. The men were told to remove their shirts or jackets and squat bare-backed in rows. We then started to search for the tell-tale tattoo mark of the 'Galon' bird; the tattoo was usually punctured into the skin at the back of one shoulder or into the inside of the forearm. We did catch several wanted men in this way.

We had an amusing incident in connection with these searches. The men were squatting as usual for the inspection. Going slowly down the rows I came across a man who was still wearing his shirt and I ordered him sharply to remove it, which he did reluctantly. Instead of finding the half-expected tattoo, I saw distinct imprints of small teeth marks high up his back. This discovery was greeted with loud shouts, whistles and rude laughter from the assembled villagers. Apparently, the man was known as the local Lothario and people were delighted to see him caught out so flagrantly; the incident was made funnier when some wag shouted that not only one but two maidens were blushing!

I learnt also a further lesson which had not been in any of my text books. My military police force was made up of Gurkhas, Garhwalis, Karens, Kachins and Burmans; the first two groups are Hindus and the Garhwalis are high-caste (which I did not know at the time). All outposts always had a clear field of fire around the dried up paddy-fields. To guard against any sudden surprise assault at night, a protective ring of bamboo spikes, sharpened at each end, was driven into the hard soil at an angle of 45 degrees. This thigh-high fence was very effective; actually two of my own men suffered deep wounds in their thighs by walking carelessly into a spike at dusk. Although the spikes were driven strongly into the ground, the village cows, grazing in the paddy stubble, were constantly knocking them over with no apparent harm to their thick hides.

I issued numerous warnings to the owners of the cattle to keep the animals away from our defences; the order would be observed for a while and then the cattle would be back. Finally, when the outpost next to ours was raided one night and some casualties inflicted, because the ring of spikes had gaps caused by straying cattle, I issued a warning to the village headman that the next cow to damage our fence would be shot. Inevitably, the very next day an unfortunate cow knocked over some spikes and I shouted to the sentry in the look-out tower to shoot it. To my astonishment he flatly refused to do so, although I repeated the order.

I thought that I had a full blown mutiny on my hands because all the Garhwalis in the post turned out and joined the sentry who was, I now realised, one of them, in excited shouts. My second-in-command of the military police contingent, a Gurkha Jemadar, was absent in the village. Someone must have gone off to fetch him because he arrived unsummoned and out of breath to join me, trying to unravel the cause of the upheaval. I had meanwhile ordered the men, in my best parade-ground manner, to fall in and stand to attention, which they all did immediately to my secret relief. Calm having been restored, I was informed that my order to shoot a cow was sacrilege to Garhwalis as the animal was considered sacred. I then realised at once the enormity of my ignorance, with flashes of the Indian Mutiny going through my brain, I apologised to them all for giving an order which they could not obey. This reaction on my part had a magical effect, smiles appeared on the faces and when I dismissed them, they all came up and shook my hand in renewed friendship. I suspect that the spokesman who translated my apologies into the Garhwalis' language, probably embellished the cause of my ignorance as that of the proverbial village idiot. I got a bit of my own back out of the incident. I decreed that in future the Garhwali section would provide a cow-herd to keep the cattle off the spikes and ensure that the protective fencing remained in good order at all times. This judgement of Solomon was received with universal approval by the other sections and even the Garhwalis thought it quite just.

One happening, which was particularly tragic, in these bad times, affected me very much. A large Karen settlement was included in my area for protection. The village tract consisted of a large village and several small hamlets nearby. The head of this community and the official headman was a retired soldier, who had risen to the rank of Jemadar in the Burma Rifles. He was much loved by his people and became a valuable supporter in our efforts to re-establish peace. The Karens are a distinct race of their own; most of them had been converted to Christianity by the American Baptist Mission well-established in Burma. They were generally persecuted in the days of the Burmese Monarchy and, therefore, welcomed the arrival of British rule. Many of them enlisted in the new British-Burma army and became excellent soldiers. They proved their loyalty and courage time and again in the last war. Unlike their Burmese counterparts, who deserted in droves during the retreat into India, the Karens fought on with their British and Indian comrades until released from duty in the final stages. Many volunteered to stay on with the defeated army and returned to fight another day. Many of those who remained behind, performed yeoman service with the underground resistance when it became organised.

The whole of this Karen community established friendly contact with our men and many a hard-fought football match was played between us. I myself was honoured with an invitation to the Headman's eldest daughter's Christian wedding, celebrated by a Karen pastor in the village. The civil police Inspector, attached to our outpost, received much useful and reliable information on rebel and criminal activities from Karen sources. Although a Burman, my Inspector got on well with the Karens and had great confidence in the help they gave. We were, then again, going through a more active stage of rebel activities. Several villages were attacked, plundered and houses set on fire; those suspected of acting as Government informers were summarily executed. Our own activities increased to maximum effort and we successfully intercepted two gangs on their withdrawal to their jungle hideouts in the hills.

One night, the Inspector woke me up apologetically to report that he had received urgent information of a planned attack on a specific village on the following night. He thought the news fairly reliable but would check on it as far as he could. We agreed to make preparations on the assumption that the attack would take place. The threatened village was a good half a day's march away. I decided to leave at dawn with half of the garrison, leaving the Jemadar in charge and telling the Inspector to use his own judgement about following me later with further news. I planned to march until the hottest time of the day, then have a long break and thus arrive in reasonably fresh condition at the village before dark.

The march went as planned and we arrived in the village in daylight and made the necessary dispositions to cause maximum surprise. The villagers were glad to see us; they had been speculating more and more fantastically about the threatened attack and their subsequent fate. We spent a largely sleepless night because of the hordes of mosquitoes; not having nets under which to shelter, we were at their mercy. Apart from the odd false alarm from one or two sentries, the night passed without incident.

I split the force on the next morning, leaving half behind as a temporary garrison for twenty four hours; the rest of us made our way back. On the way, I received a hastily scribbled note from the Inspector to the effect that the Karen village had been attacked during the night and that he was going there with some men to investigate. We force-marched the rest of the way and reached the outpost in the early afternoon. I was horrified to hear that not only had the attack taken place but that the rebels had managed to abduct the headman and two village elders as hostages.

My returning force was exhausted by the fast walk back and I blessed the authorities' foresight in posting a mounted section of Military Police in the area. By a stroke of luck, half the section had called on a routine reconnoitre and were still at the post. I mounted a pony and with the remaining riders galloped off to the stricken village. The place was a shambles with villagers moving around in a dazed fashion. These were old men, women and children, the menfolk had gone with the Inspector's party to search the countryside. Besides the material damage to property, the headman's house and those on each side of it were destroyed, the fires still smouldering in the ruins, four villagers had been killed and two rebels were left behind dead.

I was given a hurried account of the tragic event by a constable left behind for this purpose. The village had been provided with five guns for protection, a common precaution taken in cases where the headman had been proved reliable. As soon as the surprise attack had started, the headman and two elders, who happened to have called at his house, ran outside to see what the commotion was about. The rebels had usually shown reluctance to attack Karen villages where arms had been provided, since the holders of guns reinforced by other villagers, always put up a stout show of resistance. The headman had snatched up his gun but the two visitors were unarmed; as they emerged into the dark night, the three of them were immediately overpowered. Meanwhile, the other trusted villagers, who had been issued with the remaining four firearms, bravely assembled and collected some men armed with spears and dahs; they counter-attacked resolutely to such effect that the rebels cut short their work of looting and destruction and fled from the village, shouting that the hostages would be killed if the villagers followed.

With this quick briefing, we mounted men joined up with the search parties in the surrounding fields. The earlier searchers had found the tracks of the withdrawing rebels, which led, as expected, into the border hills. The villagers were instructed to carry on searching in a wide arc, in case the large gang had split up later; the armed party started the pursuit, with the mounted men ahead going as fast as they could as a scouting party. Progress for riders and marchers became slower and slower as the undergrowth and trees thickened; in due course, I had to send the ponies back to the post. I had realised for some time that there was now little hope of catching up before the gang or gangs melted into the dense jungle. I decided to carry on for another hour and then order the search to be abandoned. We reached an unexpected clearing in the forest reserve and there on the ground lay the bodies of the headman and his two friends. They had been horribly mutilated before dying, presumably to avenge the stout resistance put up by the village. This sickening sight was my first, but not my last, experience of the bestiality which man could inflict on man.

Subsequent patient investigation met with some success. Several of the rebel gang were caught, identified by villagers and jailed for long periods. Owing to darkness at the time of the attack and the general confusion, positive identification of individual murders in the village was not possible. The detailed inquiries also revealed that the original information, received by the Inspector, had been false and a deliberate ruse to distract us from the real objective - to seek revenge on the co-operative Karen village. With hindsight, I blamed myself for my haste in acting on the information before it had been confirmed. But we had always, as a general rule, acted first to prevent a possible tragedy and previous false alarms had not been connected with a real disaster elsewhere. A bitter lesson and a personal loss for me.

Not long after this sad incident, the storm clouds started to gather in the blue sky, heralding the approach of the rains, when life in the midst of a paddy field would become impossible. Rebel activity was dying down to sporadic minor actions by small gangs of desperate men, wanted for serious crimes and who could not avail themselves of the general amnesty offered by the Government after the capture of the overall rebel leader Saya San. By the time the rains had set in, rank and file followers, disillusioned by the false promises of magical protection, were beginning to surrender in ever increasing numbers.

The temporary outposts were gradually withdrawn as they became uninhabitable in the flooded fields. I was ordered to set up headquarters in Letpadan, a railway town of some importance and relieve the Captain who had been in charge of several outpost areas. Headquarters was the 'dak' bungalow in the town which also possessed good stabling facilities for the mounted section, which I was allowed to retain much to my satisfaction as I did not fancy trudging about in the rain. Riding a pony was a definite improvement in all respects. After life in a native hut of the simplest design and no conveniences, living in a proper bungalow with bathroom and toilet facilities, albeit of the primitive kind, was positive luxury for all of us, even for the ponies in their purpose-built stables. The railway-line passed alongside the inspection bungalow and I was able to vary my hitherto austere diet by the purchase of imported luxuries from the main Rangoon grocers, catering for European palates. I did not even have to collect the goods from the station; the train driver would blow his whistle, stop the train whilst my servant or anyone else present would collect the package from the guard and the journey would be resumed after this momentary halt.

The odd dacoities were reported from time to time; the gangs having melted down to five or six. Thanks to the ponies, I quite enjoyed the periodical rides around to reassure the population that a presence was still available to deal with emergencies but the Civil Police, albeit still re-inforced, were coping more and more with breaches of the law. It was obvious that my days with the Military Police would soon be over and I wondered how I would settle down again to my training programme after six months of active outdoor life, not without variety and excitement. I need not have worried.

I was back in Mandalay for three days, during which time I was entertained more or less continuously by all the friends I had left behind so abruptly a few months back. People were very kind and generous to the returned 'soldier'. I began to feel a bit of a fraud since most of my hosts had exaggerated ideas about the dangers and discomforts we 'special duty' men had undergone. On the fourth day, I was quickly brought down to earth. A telegram arrived posting me at once to Thayetmyo district on the Irrawaddy, again for attachment to the Military Police.

Although the core of the Rebellion, in Tharrawaddy and Prome districts, had been destroyed, disturbances had spread elsewhere and continued to do so for some time. The latest flare-up had taken place in

*Karen wedding, Sindalin village, April 1931:
Headman, seated left, was murdered with four
other villagers by rebels a week later*

The bride and bridegroom

the hinterland of Thayetmyo, a poor and sparsely populated area. The town had a historical past; for over thirty years it was the frontier town between British Lower-Burma and Royal Burmese Upper-Burma. A strong military garrison was stationed in the town, to which the existing extensive barracks and elephant stables bare witness; the latter still had the chains, tethering the animals, rivetted in the walls. These great beasts were used by the Army to transport the field artillery guns over difficult terrain. The cannon was dismantled and then loaded on the backs of elephants and carried through jungles, rivers and along steep narrow paths in the hills and mountains.

I travelled from Mandalay to Thayetmyo in the last week of July 1931 by the Irrawaddy Flotilla Company's steamer service. These huge paddle steamers, over 300 feet long, usually had two 'flats', tied one on each side. Thus, they could carry several thousand deck passengers and many tons of cargo. The bulk of the huge riverine traffic in goods and people between Rangoon and Bhamo was carried by 'the I.F.' as the company was known to all and sundry living along the banks of this huge, long river. The boats would pull in at any sizeable village to pick up or drop off passengers and cargo. The vessels themselves and their attached flats served as floating bazaars in addition to their normal functions as carriers. In fact, the company had arrangements to hire out deck space stalls and I believe that many tenants kept their hired spaces for long periods.

This was my first trip on the Irrawaddy and very interesting and comfortable it proved to be. The first class accommodation in cabins and a main saloon was on the forward top deck with wide open deck space in front of the cabins and saloon, reaching to the bows of the steamer. Accommodation was spacious, cool and comfortable and the catering was equal to any provided by a good hotel. The rains were upon us and the river had swollen to its maximum width, in places the stretch of water was more like a flowing lake, several miles square interspersed with sandbanks. Navigation was extremely difficult in these conditions and the Company employed a large number of local pilots, all along the river's course, with intimate knowledge of the constantly shifting channels in their stretch of water. These pilots had a highly skilled task, particularly at night when they had to navigate by a single powerful searchlight in the bows. The ships' captains depended utterly on the local man's skill and knowledge; the comparatively rare occasions, on which a large steamer ran hard aground and remained imprisoned for some days, is a testimony to these men's skill. I never became bored during the two day trip, either watching the goings on at each stop, moving around the stalls on board and talking to the owners or the customers and, best of all, sitting behind the pilot at night watching the huge beam of the searchlight playing on the water and the banks, suddenly showing up a dead white pagoda, perched on a hillock at the water's edge and constantly throwing the most fantastic, coloured shadows against the dark sky or earth. My journey was over all too soon.

In Thayetmyo, I stayed at the District Superintendent's house, George Chettle, who told me that I was to relieve another Assistant

No.6 Sub-Area Post, Okposu; evening 'stand-to'

My bungalow for several weeks

Military Police; Karen, Kachin, Gurkha, Kumaon and Burman

The girls who brought my daily bath
and cooking water; Karens from Okposu

More friends from No.6 Post

Superintendent on special duty, when he returned from an extensive patrol with a troop of mounted infantry of the Military Police. This was welcome news, I was fond of riding and my bottom had now become hardened to prolonged periods in the saddle. Whilst unoccupied, I had a look round the Cantonments, which had again come to life with the arrival of Military Police re-inforcements and a battalion of the Burma Rifles. I had recently read an account about the annexation of Upper-Burma in 1885 when Thayetmyo had been the staging post for General Prendergast's assault on the royal city of Mandalay, which brought the campaign to a victorious end. The bustle, shouted orders and bugle calls revived an echo of the past in this ancient military settlement.

The District Superintendent suggested that, whilst waiting to take over my new task, I should join him on a short tour in his launch. I accepted with alacrity as the offer would give me a chance to see in comfort what the country was like. I had been feeling limp for the last two days and put it down to fatigue from my active life in the past six months. We travelled south along the Irrawaddy, stopping at all riverine villages to reassure the inhabitants and hold impromptu meetings with headmen and village elders and gathering what news we could about the disturbances inland. The District Superintendent had been in Burma for twenty years and spoke the language, as well as several hill dialects, fluently. He exuded confidence and had the happy knack of lacing his speeches with a few jokes, some pretty broad, which made the audience laugh and put their minds more at ease.

On the third day of the trip, we were going up the main tributary river to visit some inland places. I had started a fever and went to lie down in my cabin, after taking a hefty dose of liquid quinine, hoping to throw off what seemed the onset of malaria. The launch was chugging round one of the numerous bends and hugging the starboard bank, where the navigable channel had formed. Before I reached my bunk, there was a tremendous bang and the sound of splintering wood. I shot back on deck and the first thing I saw was a large gash in the wooden hull luckily above the water line, with a big irregular chunk of metal embedded in the gap. I forgot about my fever in the excitement and joined the party which was jumping ashore, as the launch grounded into the river bank.

At a short distance, in some bushes, we found the remains of a home-made cannon and four dazed men, one of whom had a deep wound in a thigh and was bleeding profusely until someone applied a tourniquet. It appeared that when the cannon was fired at the launch, as it came in sight, the muzzle had exploded as the shot left the barrel and a sharp-edged piece of the barrel's metal had hit one of the rebels standing beside the piece of artillery. The four prisoners were taken on board with the remains of the cannon and we cut short the trip. Later on, when the men had been interrogated and the bits and pieces examined, it was found that the builders had raided the local Ordnance scrap heap and some P.W.D. (Public Works Department) stores for suitable materials. As far as I know, this was the only occasion on which a cannon was fired on either side during the whole rebellion.

After this bit of excitement, I began to feel worse and worse and the local Civil Surgeon seemed puzzled. Finally, he decreed that I had to go to Rangoon for a detailed medical examination. By the time I disembarked from the steamer at Prome, to complete the journey as quickly as possible by train, I was running a high temperature and hardly aware of my surroundings. My faithful 'lugalay' (Burmese house boy) spent the night in my compartment bathing my head with iced water whilst I lay half-conscious on my bunk. I do not remember the last stages of the journey, the next thing I knew was to find myself in a nice clean bed in a lofty room, surrounded by doctors and nurses; I had arrived at the Rangoon General Hospital. The upshot of all this medical and nursing attention was a diagnosis of paratyphoid fever. I spent six weeks in hospital, very well looked after, and after discharge, the medical authorities notified the Government that I should be kept near Rangoon for some time, to undergo periodical check-ups and tests. So instead of returning, once again, to Mandalay district, I was posted to Insein district, next door to Rangoon, to complete my much interrupted second year's training. As the doctors had prescribed light work for a while, the programme was confined to administrative procedure in the Headquarters office. I still had to pass my 'Higher Burmese' examination and got down to a crash correspondence course with Saya Po Thit. I had derived one sound advantage from my roaming months; my colloquial Burmese was now fluent, which was not surprising after going for weeks without speaking much English. In due course I appeared for the examination before a Rangoon board and passed with more ease that I had expected. Subject to a clear bill of health, I could now expect my first executive appointment in a subdivision of a district.

A mode of travel when visiting villages in my Sub-Area

9
Subdivisional Police Officer

Ten days after I had been confirmed in the Service, on 3 December 1931, exactly 2 years after my arrival in the country, orders arrived appointing me Subdivisional Police Officer, Nyaunglebin, Pegu District. The history of Pegu went back a very long way. The earliest inhabitants were the Mons, who had come from further East; they expanded successfully and reached their zenith in the fourteenth century, with the establishment of the Kingdom of Pegu which lasted until the middle of the sixteenth century, when it was conquered by the Kingdom of Burma. Thereafter, the Mons people became absorbed by the Burmese.

In my time, Pegu was one of the first half dozen in importance. The district was rich in paddy fields, teak forests and cattle. The population was high and generally prosperous. Rail and road communications were good, which in turn ensured busy trading with other parts of Burma and beyond. This affluence also attracted the other side of the coin. The district, and in particular the Nyaunglebin (northern) subdivision, had the doubtful distinction of the highest crime rate in the country. I received the news of my appointment with mixed feelings. I was flattered to be considered fit to run such a heavy charge but I was apprehensive that I might be found wanting in the practical experience required to supervise a large and busy police force in all its multifarious duties. After all, both my theoretical and active training in conventional police work had been severely curtailed by circumstances beyond my control. Hoping fervently that these factors would be taken into consideration if I made a mess of my first job, I packed up, got into my newly acquired large second-hand (very) American touring car and headed for my destination, a hundred miles from Rangoon on the main rail and trunk road to Mandalay.

I was again lucky in my new chief. The District Superintendent, G.E. Banwell, was another outstanding officer in the Burma section of the Indian Police. He took a great deal of trouble to make me catch up as quickly as I could with the knowledge I had been unable to acquire during the training period. He was the kind of man who would have risen to the top of any profession of his choice. He had to retire prematurely for family reasons, joined the Police service in England and rose to the rank of Chief Constable in two different counties. I stayed with him for a night in Pegu and took the opportunity to call on the other chief district officials in Headquarters. The Superintendent informed me that I had no official residence in Nyaunglebin and that he had asked the only other

European there, the Assistant Executive Engineer for Irrigation, a bachelor, to accommodate me whilst I looked round for a suitable abode. Apparently, the official Police bungalow had been destroyed by fire some years ago and my predecessor, a Burman with a large family and independent means, had rented a large house in the town and had not pressed for official accommodation.

On my way from Pegu and nearing Nyaunglebin, I saw another open car coming in the opposite direction. As we were passing we both recognised each other simultaneously; the driver was L.B. Jack, one of the passengers in the ship which brought me to Burma, and we had become friends during the long voyage. The initial surprise was even greater when he told me that he was stationed in Nyaunglebin and I told him that I had just been posted there. We realised then that he was my host and I was his guest; my name had not been mentioned by my chief when he arranged these temporary quarters for his new assistant nor had he told me the name of my benefactor. We had a quick chat, before he went on his way; having confirmed the kind invitation, he told me to make myself at home and that he would be back in a couple of days. To complete the story, we got on so well together that he asked me to stay on permanently, on a sharing basis, an offer which I was very glad to accept. This unexpected encounter had even more lasting effects than either of us dreamt of at the time; as I shall recount in the appropriate place.

The subdivision was large, around 2,000 square miles; the size of the force under my command, 400, was as great as the total force of some districts. The trunk road and the railway line, from Rangoon to Mandalay, running more or less parallel to each other, bisected the area into two rectangles. The flat, densely cultivated land stretched for the whole length, about sixty miles, and from the Sittang river in the east to the forest reserves of the Yoma hills in the west. The Police force was dispersed in eight main Police Stations and two outposts; most of these were situated along the main lines of communication, running from south to north. One station and the outposts were off the beaten track on the edge of the forest-covered hills in the west. Even routine inspection tours took up a great deal of my time but these trips were constantly interrupted by outbreaks of serious crime, which necessitated a quick change of plans. We were all kept on our toes and things were never dull for long.

Unlike Mandalay, social life in this small station was limited in scope but not in good will; moreover, in the absence of a European community of wives, tedious out-of-date conventions about calling and seating arrangements at dinner parties, were happily unknown. There were about a dozen officials in the place, most of them Burmese. Besides us two Europeans, there were two Eurasians and an Indian doctor. One of the Timber firms employed four European Forest Assistants in the North Pegu Yoma Reserve extracting teak. These employees had their headquarters in Nyaunglebin and would swell the club's membership noticeably, particularly the profits of the bar, whenever they came in for a few weeks rest from their arduous and lonely months of work in the jungle. Despite the small size of the station, the club was active, we had

44

a tennis court, billiard table, library and bar. Tennis was played daily, weather permitting, and the billiard table was seldom out of use in the evenings. Several of us ran a regular, or as regular as work permitted, bridge four; the senior Magistrate, a Burman, was the best card player and collected most of the modest pecuniary gains; we all agreed that his obviously mis-spent youth made him quite unfit to grace the bench, where he had the power to dispense long prison sentences on others for their ill-gotten gains!

Occasionally, when the forest lads were in residence, we expatriates would call at the Railway Institute, five miles away. There were large railway works at Pyuntaza down the line and the Railway community, mainly Eurasian men and women, was large. The main event of the week there was the Saturday dance in their well-appointed Institute building, which was much grander than our little club. Anglo-Indians and Anglo-Burmese girls are attractive and have good figures when they are young but all too soon they seem doomed to acquire matronly shapes at an unnecessarily early age. However, there were always enough of the young shapely ones at these dances and nothing could hold us, particularly the girl-starved 'Jungle wallahs' from this particular honey pot. Our descent in relative strength on these dances was popular with the girls but, understandably, not with their regular boy-friends, who looked upon all of us as cursed intruders. My position as head of the police made it imperative that no serious unpleasantness spoilt these social occasions; so my own social activities were always handicapped by keeping an eye on the general situation. I was always relieved when the evening ended more or less amicably and I am glad to say that I was spared any serious incidents which could have had serious consequences, not least for myself.

We did also organise the occasional dance, on a smaller scale, at our own club and even got some of the ladies in Pegu to come up with their husbands for the night. Quite often, on these occasions, we would end the evening by bringing back to the bungalow up to a dozen unexpected guests for a midnight (more like post-midnight) dinner. The servants were marvellous on these occasions; within the hour they would produce, goodness knows how, a four course meal for all.

To get me around my 'patch' more effectively, I invested in the purchase of a good pony. I obtained this well-built, strong animal through the good offices of one of the headmen. The deal turned out to be a bargain in every sense of the word. Upkeep was cheap, since the pony was used to coarse grazing and the luxury of occasional grain supplemented a diet which kept the animal in good trim throughout my ownership. The only defect was that it had a mouth like iron, which no type of snaffle could subdue. As soon as I was in the saddle, the animal would bolt and nothing I could do would halt its headlong flight. I tried hard to stop this practice but soon learnt that the easiest and quickest way to quieten the animal was to let it have its head. Gradually, the length of the wild gallop diminished but it never lost the habit altogether and I always had to be prepared for a sudden display of assertiveness after mounting. Once the pony had had its way, it would settle down as docile and as obedient as any other horse I had ridden. The great asset was that it had been well trained to do the 'Burmese trot'. This style of riding was (presumably still is) commonly used by Burmans when riding over flat country. The horse is taught to fling its legs sideways in a sort of shallow arc, instead of straight forward as in ordinary trotting. This side-swaying movement of the legs keeps the pony's back horizontal and the rider does not have to rise and fall in the saddle, or bump along, when trotting.

My sturdy beast could keep up Burmese trotting, alternating with some walking, for very long periods and I was able to cover an astonishing number of miles in a day. Quite often, when crossing a wide expanse of paddy fields, I would drop the reins altogether and read a book at this ambling pace. On one such occasion, whilst immersed in my reading, the pony came to an abrupt halt, nearly throwing me off balance, a thing it had never done before. I looked up and right in front of us was a man tugging hard at the tail of a long snake, half-way down a hole in the ground. I watched this unusual tug of war in open mouthed astonishment. Finally, the human won the contest, lifted the snake high above his head, cracked it like a whip and broke its back. Rather out of breath but clearly pleased, the wrestler explained to me that this type of grass snake made excellent eating and that the size of this one would suffice to provide a good meal for his whole family. Whereupon he wound the dead snake round his neck and shoulders and went happily on his way.

My touring was no longer confined to the rather short and more civilised experiences of my Mandalay days. I now had to set up camp quite often on the outskirts of a village and this meant travelling with considerable camping paraphernalia, loaded on slow moving bullock carts. In this respect Forest Officers, who toured for weeks on end, had brought camping to a high degree of comfort, indeed even luxury, because they had an advantage denied to others: elephants. There was no limit to what two or three touring elephants could not carry in the way of size, shape or quantity. Even so, none of us suffered much hardship on tour, unless departure was hurried and abrupt to deal with a crisis somewhere, a situation which confronted us police officers more than others. The routine of an undisturbed tour from camp site to camp site, away from roads and railways, was a most welcome change. The district officer did then come into his own. Sitting in front of his tent or under a wide shady Banyan tree, facing a friendly gathering of country folk and listening to their requests, complaints or just plain gossip, one really did feel close to the people of the country. To me this was the part of the job I had visualised when I had first thought of going into the Service. In those days villagers were pleased for the opportunity to meet the 'Thakin' (the Burmese term for the Indian 'Sahib') and vent their views and opinions freely. I learnt most of what I know about the Burmese during these early days of my service, before the pressure of paper-work and the use of the motor-car changed the method and time spent in travelling around one's district.

The indigenous population usually took it for granted that the touring official was honest and impartial. Quite often, during impromptu village gatherings, an officer's opinion, given on some contentious matter brought to his notice, would be sufficient to solve it, even when the matter might not be his direct responsibility. It was just on one of these occasions that I was offered my one and only bribe in the Police Service. I happened to be in a part of the subdivision where a sudden violent storm had badly damaged a crop of paddy. As I was contemplating the scene, I remarked casually to the headman, who was standing next to me, that some fields looked much worse than others. Whereupon, an old man nearby sidled up to me, squeezed surreptitiously a coin into the palm of my hand and whispered "When you return to headquarters, Thakin, please tell the Land Settlement Officer that my field was the worst". I opened my hand and found a silver rupee coin (worth one shilling and six pence)! I told my seducer that I would certainly report that some fields were more damaged than others but that I could not single out his own as the worst. I returned the coin which he received with a mixture of chagrin and relief.

One of the great delights of this outdoor life was to witness the spectacular sunrises and sunsets in the open countryside. Anybody who has seen these daily occurrences in an Eastern sky knows what I mean by the riot of colour which paints the heavens in the early morning and evening. I regret that I do not possess the ability to describe scenery adequately. The cloudless night skies are equally eye-catching. Sitting in an easy chair, gazing up, the moon and the stars appear twice as brilliant, twice as large and twice as near as in a Western sky. These sights never failed to grip me with the feeling that man's futile little problems pale into insignificance besides these wonders of nature.

Sometimes touring officers' paths would meet and we would then pitch a joint camp for the night. Thus I would meet my friend the District Forest Officer, known as the Deputy Conservator, at times. He, of course, had THE camp and I never had to unload my more modest amenities on such occasions. All touring officers had to keep up with their office work and despatch boxes would follow on wherever they went. The paperwork was usually left to be dealt with in the evenings, unless the matter needed urgent attention. We all suffered from a surfeit of forms and memoranda, most of which were routine, requiring only ritual approval from the departmental head. One evening, when both my friend and I were dealing with our respective boxes, he suddenly stopped signing his papers, turned to me and said "Do you always read what you sign?" I confessed that I did not. He then told me the joke about the definition of the Government of India:-"Banerjee writing to Mukerjee with Smith and Jones signing on the dotted line". A great deal of truth is contained in this succinct sentence!

I was now in my fourth year of service and applied for home leave after the end of the 'cold weather'. I had enjoyed my first spell of authority and had never been bored for long. Unusual situations had a habit of arising when least expected. A sudden crop of dacoities somewhere, serious flooding elsewhere, even earthquakes, kept me busy and on the move most of the time. Amongst these happenings some have stuck in my mind more than others. I have recounted a few as best I can after so many years, in the next pages.

10
The Tiger Man

One of my early murder cases brought me face to face with a prevalent superstition. I was visiting my furthest Police Station, on the edge of the North Yoma Forest Reserve. A girl was brought in by some jungle villagers. She was accused of killing her lover whilst he was asleep in his parents' house in the nearby forest village. Most of the men worked for the Forest Department and, as was common in these backward tracks, the people were prone to believe in supernatural happenings and spirits.

The station officer interrogated the accompanying villagers briefly and then told me the salient facts. The parents of the murdered man had been woken by the victim's death throes and had seen a slight figure dash out of the room. Some villagers, aroused by the commotion, had caught the girl near the house, still grasping a blood-stained 'dah'. It appeared to be a straightforward case of murder. I told the station officer that I should like to hear the girl's statement. She was brought before me, seemed quite unmoved and told her story in a calm manner. I can still remember distinctly all the important details; this is what she recounted:-

Maung Ba (the deceased's name) and I were lovers. We had known each other since childhood and we intended to get married as soon as he was earning enough to raise a family. Like all courting couples we would meet in some private place to be alone, but unlike other young men he would make some excuse and leave me before it became dark. I would tease him about his apparent lack of ardour but in spite of my taunting he would never spend a night with me. One day one of my girl friends told me it was rumoured that my lover belonged to the dreaded sect of men who had the power to change into wild animals at night. At first I would not believe her and thought that jealousy had made her invent this dreadful story. I had heard my parents and other villagers discuss the habits and strange powers of this secret society. We all believed that they existed and some asserted that members of the sect also lived in our village. I then began to think about my lover's strange reluctance to spend a night with me and decided to find the reason.

One evening, after he had left me, I followed secretly to his parents hut, saw him go inside and then come out shortly,

48

carrying what seemed to be a hairy blanket over one arm. He walked through the village and then along a path, leading into the forest. I was afraid to follow beyond the village as it was getting dark quickly so I went back to his hut to wait for him. I sat down on a mat in the front room with his parents; after a while his father and mother went to sleep in the back room. I must have then dozed off myself. Some time later I was disturbed by a sort of rustling sound on the verandah outside. I peeped through the thatch walling of the room and was horrified to see a full-grown tiger; I screamed loudly, the tiger jumped off the verandah and in the next moment Maung Ba burst through the door. He was very angry to see me crouching terrified on the mat; we had a violent quarrel, he hit me several times shouting that he would not marry a girl who spied on him. I replied that he obviously did not love me or he would have shown concern about my awful experience and ran out of the room back to my parents home.

The next day Maung Ba appeared early and apologised for his bad hehaviour of the previous evening and said that he had not realised that I had been so close to the tiger. Anyhow, he seemed very sorry and I agreed to forgive him. A few days later, the same girl friend came to tell me that my lover had been seen with some other men walking in single file along a jungle path at dusk. They all had their thumbs tucked into their fists which they were holding against their ears and their heads were bowed, with eyes looking at the ground in front of them; they were chanting some strange words as they gradually disappeared into the jungle. Everyone knows that this is the beginning of the secret ritual by which they change themselves into wild beasts for the night.

I was now convinced that my lover was a 'Tiger man' and became nearly demented with worry and terror. My one thought now was to find a way to rid myself of the dreadful prospect of marrying a half-man half-beast. That very night, I stole my father's sharp long hunting 'dah' and resolved to kill Maung Ba as my only hope of deliverance from a monster. Two days later, after dark, I waited near his parents' house until they went to sleep and I then crept into the front room. As I had expected, Maung Ba was not there so I sat down to wait, but this time I hid behind a screen. In due course, I heard the same rustling noise as before but I was too afraid to look through the walling. The sound ceased and immediately afterwards, Maung Ba came quietly into the room, lay down on a rug, pulled a blanket over himself and went to sleep. I waited for a long time until I was sure that he was fast asleep and then tiptoed towards him, raised the dah as high as I could and brought it down with all my strength across his neck. He gave one fearful shriek, then groaned and lay still. I ran out of the house, still holding the dah now covered in blood. Some villagers came running and caught me near the house; later they told me that Maung Ba was dead.

Ma Shwe (the girl's name) never wavered from this statement throughout the trial which was short and decisive. She was found guilty of murder but insane. Maung Ba's parents left the village after their son's death, forced to leave by the growing hostility of the villagers, who believed in their unproved association with the secret sect.

The Pongyi (Burmese priest) who lived near my Post at Okposu

11
The Floods

The rains in my second year in the subdivision were exceptionally heavy and caused the worst flooding for some time. Two main bridges, one road the other railway, were extensively damaged and had to be rebuilt. These major damages effectively breached both the railway lines and the trunk road from Rangoon to Mandalay and all traffic was at a standstill for several days. Emergency measures restored restricted movement of goods and people, but shortages of food became widespread. All district officers, and others drafted from outside, were placed on flood relief work. The mounting level of water also scoured into the sides of the embankments on which road and rail had been built. Several sections of rail were left suspended in mid-air, causing further delay to freight and passengers, transhipped at the breached bridge; on the roads, traffic was frequently slowed down to walking pace where sections of the metalled road surface had disappeared.

My house mate, the Irrigation Engineer for the subdivision, forewarned by previous smaller floods, had managed to obtain a powerful outboard motor which he had fitted to a small shallow boat, built to his own design. The vessel's draught was only a few inches so that it could, in an emergency travel across flooded fields and its hull was strong enough to withstand heavy artificial bumps, such as the short artificial mud walls which surround every paddy field. This purpose-built design made the boat highly manoeuvreable but rather unstable.

We two carried out an early survey of the extended flooded area to assess what relief measures were required and which were the most urgent. We travelled fast thanks to the powerful engine but had to sacrifice all protection against the elements, since the craft's instability would not have supported any kind of superstructure and was just large enough to take two people. In the end, we travelled just in a pair of sodden shorts. We completed the task in two days and reported back to flood headquarters, where relief work was starting.

This scouting trip produced one unusual incident. My Engineer companion was steering and controlling the speed, I sat in the bows, looking out for snags ahead so as to warn the navigator when to alter course. I had my Winchester carbine resting across my knees; we were both armed because the criminal fraternity had seized on the pre-occupation of the Police, with flood relief work, to intensify their attacks in search of loot. Suddenly, the steersman shouted and pointed into the distance, where I could now see a violent turbulence in the water, towards which he was steering. Crouching low, I raised my carbine and aimed at the still unidentified wriggling mass in the water. The unsteady boat and the uneven course made it difficult to aim and I was concentrating on keeping the firearm's barrel on the object. Suddenly, a huge snake's head appeared in the sights, with an enormous hood beneath, flapping in and out. The snake seemed to be only inches from the end of the barrel, when I pulled the trigger. I am pretty certain that I also closed my eyes instinctively because I seemed to be so very close. The head of the advancing snake disappeared abruptly and the boat turned in a tight circle round the thrashing rings made by the writhing body in the water. We waited until all movement had ceased and then cautiously went alongside; I then saw that my 44 calibre solid bullet had nearly severed the head from the neck. This was a miracle for a poor shot like me; indeed it would have been quite a feat for a marksman. When we had towed the snake on to some high ground nearby, we realised simultaneously that we had landed a fully grown Hamadryad, the deadliest snake in Burma. Unfortunately, we had no measuring tape, but we agreed that it was over ten feet long and I had to use both hands to span the thickest part of the body, which was a beautiful dark green colour with a darker nearly black design. The Hamadryad has an evil reputation as a fast and deadly killer, attacking on sight anything it regards as a danger. My companion told me that, when he was steering towards the unknown mass in the water, he saw the snake suddenly turn and swim straight for the launch, with head raised ready for a strike.

I then told him about a Forest Officer friend who had a terrifying encounter with a Hamadryad. He was deep in the forest Reserve, 'girdling' teak trees with one of the Timber Firm's assistants. Girdling consists of ringing trees by removing a strip of bark all round, which the Forest Department considers ready for extraction. At one stage of the operation, he felt in need to relieve himself and slipped into a narrow ravine close by. Whilst he was squatting down, he suddenly heard a loud hissing noise, looked round and, to his horror, saw a Hamadryad near a nest of eggs only yards from where he was. Without his shorts, he immediately took flight but the snake was already after him and chased him along the bed of the ravine. He did not dare to lose speed by trying to scramble up one of the steep sides. The snake abruptly gave up the chase, presumably the intruder was now far enough away or she was worried about going too far from her nest. My friend was badly shaken by the incident and always took great care afterwards to avoid any likely shady damp spots favoured by snakes. I am thankful to say that this was my only encounter with the dreaded Hamadryad.

After the initial survey I went on relief work in a commandeered old steam launch, which belonged to an Indian rice miller. This vessel had been purpose built to take as many rice bags as possible in one go and little or no regard was paid to crew or passenger accommodation, let alone comfort. The only concession to the elements was a wooden roof; but this provision was of little protection in the driving rain, which swept regularly across the deck, through the open sides. We were loaded with some boxes of medicines, tins of dried milk, bags of rice, chillies and large jars of 'Ngapi', a sort of rotting fish paste, which stank to high heaven and was a popular dish amongst the Burmese. These basic commodities were all that the cultivators needed in their staple diet. The flood victims were of course delighted to receive this manna from heaven and probably hoped and perhaps even prayed for the floods to last a while, as long as they did not suffer undue damage to cattle and property. As a matter of fact, very few domestic animals were drowned and, as all houses and huts are built on stilts, flood damage in buildings was minimal. Subsequently several deaths, due to drowning, were reported at Police Stations.

On occasions, I had to walk along the partially flooded main trunk road. As usual, the P.W.D. had planted trees at regular intervals along both sides of the road to bind the embankments. When I first glanced up at one of the trees, I subconsciously noted some unusually coloured branches and leaves. On a closer look, I realised that these peculiar decorations had nothing to do with the tree; they were snakes that had climbed out of reach of the flood water and had entwined themselves round the branches. Practically every tree, on both sides, was festooned with snakes of all sizes and markings. There must have been over a hundred of them in the trees along the four mile stretch I had to walk. I knew that snakes were abundant in many parts of Burma but I had seen remarkably few in my subdivision and had concluded that this part of the country did not possess a large snake population; the floods proved otherwise.

A similar invasion of snakes occurred one night which we had to spend at a 'dak' bungalow, whilst distributing food in a badly flooded area. The bungalow, built high on stilts as usual, was surrounded by water, which had reached nearly to the level of the high verandah in front of the rooms. We were able to steer the boat alongside and unload our gear straight on to the verandah floor, where we were greeted by two swaying cobras, who had taken possession of this dry island and were ready to defend their right. We managed to despatch both after a chase around the place. Our cook managed to produce a very adequate meal under difficult conditions. Having had a long and strenuous day, we went to bed early. I had hardly gone to sleep when the servants started to shoot and rush around beating with sticks and carrying lanterns. We joined them to find that they were repelling, what in the darkness seemed to be dozens of snakes, swimming around and trying to climb safely on to the floor of the bungalow. We had to take it in turns to go on sentry duty throughout the night as the reptile invaders persisted stubbornly in their efforts.

The special relief organisation lasted for about a fortnight but it took much longer for the flood water to retreat altogether and normal communications on the railway line were not restored for weeks, until the main bridge had been rebuilt. I was again struck by the cheerful and good humoured manner in which the Burmese accepted the discomforts and losses (luckily less than might have been expected in the large area affected). They were still ready to laugh at a joke and quick to respond to words of encouragement. I again reflected on the contrasting traits in the national character, cruelty mixed with compassion, uncontrolled anger mixed with patience; contrasts which of course exist elsewhere, but not to the same degree of obviousness.

Government launch with shallow draught for touring Sittang and tributaries

12

The Christmas Camp

The eastern climate is not conducive to the traditional family gathering at Christmas. One of the most popular alternatives for a place of celebration was a comfortable camp in the jungle. The best of these were provided by Forest Officers with their equipment and transport (elephants) geared to long tours in Forest Reserves. So, I was delighted when the District Forest Officer, Jack Vorley, invited me to join his large party for Christmas 1932. Bearing in mind that some of the participants in the camp had to remain within reasonable distance and access from their headquarters, our host had chosen a very suitable site. A motorable road in the dry weather, reached to within a few miles of the camp, which was in a forest clearing next to a forest rest house. We even had running cold water provided by a hill stream nearby. Although within easy reach of modern communications, we might as well have been miles inside the Yoma hills. Our party was large; as far as I recollect there were nine men and six ladies (of the latter number I am certain). Our host had provided two large double canvas tents, more like small marquees, as sleeping accommodation, one for the men the other for the women. We used the forest rest house for meals, washing and toilet facilities; most of the men preferred to bathe in the clear water of the stream, which even had a small waterfall, very handy for a quick shower. Everyone had contributed towards food and drinks and the combined amount and variety of provisions would not have put a well-stocked select village store to shame. People had taken the opportunity to indulge in some expensive provisions shopping, by post, in the large European food shops in Rangoon. The first communal meal gave a foretaste of what we could expect over Christmas. I never ceased to wonder at the extraordinary skills of a good Indian cook in producing the most elaborate European dishes under quite primitive cooking facilities. Our two cooks and their 'maties' were worthy representatives of their culinary art.

We decided on an early night, as the organiser had laid on a big jungle-fowl shoot in the reserve for the following day. We retired to our respective tents and the camp was soon silent, apart from the inevitable jungle noises in the distance. The stillness was abruptly shattered by screams and yells from the women's tent; there was no shortage of gallant and instant rescuers from the other tent and all the women were soon in comforting arms, not necessarily those of their husbands. After peace had been restored, we discovered that one of the hobbled elephants had decided to explore the camp site for delicacies, instead of sticking to its allotted feeding ground. As luck would have it, the animal poked its huge head through the loosely tied flaps of the ladies' tent and, no doubt greatly taken aback by the unusual sight of the sleeping beauties, had trumpeted loudly. The result was complete pandemonium; only the forest officer's wife had ever been quite so near to what the others had taken for a wild beast. The elephant, equally alarmed by the strident shrieks of the badly frightened women, turned tail and hobbled off as fast as it could, topping the female uproar with its own bellowing. Two of the ladies flatly refused to re-enter the tent and withdrew to the bungalow's two bedrooms for the rest of the night; which ended without further incidents.

The next morning, despite the trouble of the night before, everyone was up bright and early for a substantial breakfast, prior to setting off into the jungle. The forest workers, augmented by other villagers, had already been disposed for the extensive beat. On the initial drive, the birds were expected to break out of the jungle into a clearing where the guns had taken up position in line. The very first bird broke cover opposite the last gun positioned on the right flank, I was the last gun on the left flank. As I have already mentioned, I was an indifferent marksman. However, the very first bird to break cover was missed by the right flank gun, veered sharply forty-five degrees and flew down the whole line of guns and was missed by all, until it was opposite me. My first shot brought it down stone dead, much to the admiration of everybody; that was the end of my spectacular shooting. Thanks to the excellent ground and good beating, we ended the morning with a respectable collective bag of jungle-cocks and hens. These birds are excellent eating both as roasts or in curries.

On our return to camp, we found that news of the presence of an unusually large number of district officers, had spread around and quite a gathering of villagers greeted us with presents of poultry, eggs and fruit. Many of the visitors, being from the neighbouring forest village, were employees of our host. He in turn sprung a surprise on us all by announcing that the 'Thakins' wished to organise some entertainment for the villagers as part of their own celebrations. It became apparent to us that this sudden surprise was not altogether unexpected news to the locals. Apparently, our Forest man always provided some kind of show for his villagers as part of his yearly Christmas camps. He announced that the entertainment would take place on the next day, Christmas Eve, in the afternoon and evening; the first part consisting of sporting contests and the second of a 'Pwe' with professional entertainers.

The Forest department people had obviously received detailed orders about the 'surprise entertainment' some time ago. Local shops in the nearest railway town had supplied an assortment of articles and sweets as prizes for those winning contests, together with stacks of mineral water bottles, displaying the most vivid colours, so popular with the local young and not so young. The cultivated open ground, near the village, now barren after the harvest, was marked out for various kinds of races, humans, ponies and bullock carts. The prizes, sweets and soft drinks were stacked ready in the forest bungalow; everyone helped in all these preparations. Again, after a busy day and an elaborate evening dinner, followed by drinks and conversation round a large roaring fire in front of the tents, we retired well content with the world at large; this time to an undisturbed night's sleep.

The next day people started to arrive long before anything was scheduled to happen. Everyone had put on their best clothes in honour of the event. The small children were bouncing up and down in the parental bullock-cart or alongside their strolling parents. Burmese children are amongst the most enchanting in the world. Like their elders, they are quite unselfconscious in the presence of strangers and respond quickly to friendly advances. When the Burmese dress up for an occasion, they can compete with any other oriental crowd for elegance and colour. Young girls, in particular, with their flower decorations in the hair, their slight willowy figures and expressive hands and eyes rank high in the charms charts. By midday the area around the hastily converted sports arena was thickly strewn with parties sitting around, chattering gaily, unwrapping cold rice and condiments from large plantain (type of banana) leaves or forking the food out of large sections of wide bamboo canes. Some had also brought bottles of soft drinks and not so soft drinks (the liquid in the coconut, known as coconut milk, is a deliciously cool soft drink which turns to alcohol when allowed to ferment in the sun). Ice was still a luxury, only obtainable in larger towns, but drinks could be kept remarkably cool wrapped in wet straw and hung in an open basket or box under the shade of a tree and given an occasional swing to create more breeze.

The sporting contests started late, after the worst of the midday heat. Men and children, including the Christmas party guests, participated in the obstacle races but, with the Burmese love of betting, the pony and bullock-cart races were decidedly favourites. After the prizes had been distributed, the crowd again sat around waiting for the big event, the 'Pwe'. Our host had engaged a well-known professional group of entertainers from Pegu. They arrived more or less as the afternoon's diversions were ending and set about putting up their stage and props. These entertainments lasted for hours and this one was no exception. The show began in the early evening and lasted for most of the night. Burmese music and singing are definitely acquired tastes. Personally, I never did succeed in getting attuned and I think this defect went for most Europeans. However, we hosts sat manfully through some hours of the show; the dancing displays, interspersed with some acting, were much more to our taste. Both the male and female dancers wore gorgeous old-style costumes and performed the stylised dance movements with perfection using hands, heads and legs, all equally important in Burmese dancing. The plays were parts of well-known stories, acted and danced for generations at all the numerous Pwes all over Burma. Most of the tales dealt with mythical happenings from long ago, involving Kings, Queens, Princes and Princesses caught up in the eternal love triangle, dramatised by court intrigue.

Inevitably, as the evening progressed, the audience, fortified by more food and drink, made repeated requests for their hosts to contribute towards the evening's entertainment, to which were added the laughing invitations from the actors on the stage. The Deputy Conservator of Forests had been in the district for several years and was widely known for apt performances on such occasions. He opened the amateurs' offerings by singing, in excellent Burmese, a rather risqué song about a girl who managed to remain married to two husbands at the same time by keeping them apart at essential times. One of the younger officials was an adept at playing the saw and he gave a polished performance, much to the intrigue of the crowd. Two others daringly joined the girl dancers in an item; the contrast of their clumsy and unco-ordinated movements with the grace of the girls, brought forth some good-natured boos and whistles mixed with laughter. For a fairly obvious reason, the crowd was anxious to see the 'Police Thakin' make a fool of himself on the stage. It so happened that someone had, on a previous festive occasion, taught me to sing a Burmese version of the then popular song "Yes, we have no bananas today". I dutifully climbed on to the stage to join the other two amateurs frolicking with the girls. On the spur of the moment whilst clowning around, I tunelessly sang the translated song. I can modestly claim that this unexpected rendering (of sorts) of a strange ditty brought the house down and I had to produce an encore. Most of the Christmas party retired before the entertainment finally closed in the early hours of the morning.

By the time the camp had come to life on the big day, most of our guests the previous day had departed leaving a number of thank-you presents of the edible kind. A very nice surprise was that carved teak figurines of a Burmese dancing girl, in a traditional poise, had been left for each one of us by the headman as a combined gift from the village. I kept my carving on display until, with all my other worldly goods, I had to abandon it to the advancing Japanese.

Our host must have scoured his forests for a suitable Christmas tree. He had secured a large well-shaped pine tree,which his minions 'planted' in front of the rest house. The traditional Christmas dinner was to be held in the open near the tree. Most of the day was spent quietly; the tree was decorated, the servants moved chairs and tables and stacked logs, even small tree trunks, for a big fire. By evening the scene was laid for the traditional celebrations. The servants, as usual on big occasions, had surpassed themselves in setting out the long table, covered with a spotless white cloth and sparkling with polished cutlery and condiment sets. They had all donned their best clothes and, standing around the table, added colour and dignity to the proceedings. We Empire builders, on the other hand, had not changed into dinner jackets in the jungle, as commonly believed, but we had long white trousers and shirts with black cumberbands. The setting was really eye-catching; the moon was appearing above the trees on the edge of the clearing, the huge fire was roaring away and the candle-lit tree set off the decorated table to perfection. We had no need for any artificial lights to cope with the traditional meal of stuffed roast turkey, Christmas pudding with brandy butter and mince pies. The large fire not only kept off the evening chill (we were in the so-called cold season) but served to warn off prowling animals which might have been attracted by the smell of food. We sang the usual carols, pulled the crackers and exchanged our presents, while the fire crackled, the moon grew bigger and the stars in the sky above the clearing twinkled more brightly. We all agreed that it had been the best Christmas in Burma for all of us, and made optimistic plans to repeat the camp next year. Inevitably, as we privately knew, many of us were no longer in the district by then. In my case, it was unfortunately the only time I celebrated our important Christian festival in the Burmese jungle under a clear eastern sky.

13

The Earthquake

Earthquakes are not uncommon in Burma, most of them only last a few seconds and the tremors are light, causing little or no damage. One of the worst in this century happened in Pegu town in 1929. The tremors destroyed the well-known Shwemahaw Pagoda, one of the largest in the country, leaving only its broad base standing. Many people perished by being buried alive under the tons of debris; they had fled to the pagoda when the earthquake started, believing that the sacred precinct would be immune. Loss of life was also heavy in the subsequent fire which swept a large part of the most congested part of the town around the main bazaar. The pagoda was not re-built and the dead were left undisturbed under the huge pile of rubble. Even two years later, when I arrived in the town, much of the destruction was still in evidence.

My own experience in Nyaunglebin was much less severe but quite frightening nonetheless. I was on tour along the northern boundary of my subdivision and staying for a night in the inspection bungalow at Pengwegon, a small town on the railway line and the main trunk road. The building was of the usual pattern, two bedrooms with a passage between leading to the front dining room and a covered verandah, built on stilts. I had spent the morning inspecting the local police station, followed by a ride round some nearby villages, returning much later than I had intended. I decided to have a bath and a short rest before tackling the unavoidable office box which caught up with me on most days. Refreshed and changed, I stretched out on one of the universal pattern of easy chairs found in 'dak' bungalows; these chairs were fitted with moveable leg rests, so that the occupant could lie at ease at full length. My boy had brought me a whisky and cool bottle of soda and I had lit my pipe.

Without warning, my chair shot forward violently, my pipe fell out of my mouth and my drink on the floor. Simultaneously I became aware of a deep rumbling noise, which became louder and louder. The whole bungalow swayed and my servants, who had been chattering quietly in the background, ran out shouting "Earthquake! Earthquake!" All this had happened in a few seconds. I sprang out of my chair, ran to the edge of the verandah as some sections of the corrugated iron sheets from the roof landed on the ground in front. I then also noticed that some ominously large cracks had split the dry earth. I remember thinking "the building must collapse at any moment" and shouted for everyone to run into the open. We assembled outside, by then the noise was diminishing to be followed by a short eerie silence, quickly broken by shrieks and yells of alarm from the town beyond the compound.

Collecting my wits, I told the servants to check on the state of the building before venturing inside again and ran off to the police station nearby. The station officer was mustering his force prior to moving into the town. He reported no casualties amongst his men or their families but damage to some quarters, none of it serious. We divided up for a quick survey. This assessment revealed that neither the casualties nor the destruction were as great as I had feared and there was no sign of fire, which commonly follows an earthquake in the East, because most dwellings contain open fire in the cooking places. Luckily also, in this small town there were few brick built houses and even these were small and were completed in wood above ground floor level. Most houses were built entirely of timber and all had light sheets of corrugated iron as roofs. Some of the poorer abodes were built of wooden frames with thatch walling and entirely thatched roofs. These relatively light building materials undoubtedly saved lives on this occasion. The inhabitants were, understandably, frightened and nervous, long after the shocks and rumbles had disappeared and most of them decided to bed down in the open for the night. I checked that the station officer had increased his normal night patrols round the town and returned to the bungalow for what remained of the night.

The next morning, my first visit was to the small local hospital. The Indian Sub-Assistant Civil Surgeon had time to give me an account of casualties. The number was hearteningly small, about a dozen minor cuts and bruises, one fractured leg and two suspected broken arms. Unfortunately, there had been three deaths; one an old man sitting outside his house was struck on the head by a heavy beam fallen from the roof; another had fallen head first from a verandah and, although the fall had not been considerable, his head had struck a sharp edge of a low wall and he had received a deep wound from which he had not recovered consciousness. The last death was the most tragic, a small girl playing in the road had been run over by a bullock-cart, parked on a slight incline of the road. The wedges under the wheels had been dislodged by the first sharp tremors and the cart had, at the same time, shot forward rather like my easy chair of the night before at the bungalow; the heavy wheels had run over the little body before anyone could do anything.

The Circle Inspector of Police, who had left his headquarters as news of the earthquake had reached him, was waiting for me at the police station. We decided to ride around the vicinity to ascertain the range of the earthquake. We were again relieved to discover that the extent of the earth tremors had not been widespread and no damage had been reported in any of the neighbouring villages, nor did we hear of any injuries to people or domestic animals.

I did experience several further earthquakes in other parts of the country later on but none as violent or as frightening.

14

The Shan States Trip

An officer was allowed ten days casual leave a year, which did not count against the amount of furlough which he could accumulate towards long leave at home.

In my second year in Nyaunglebin, four of us decided to take our casual leave simultaneously in October 1932 and organise a motoring trip through the Shan States. Only one of us had ever been there and he spoke in glowing terms about the beautiful country and its people.

Even in the days of the Burmese Kings, the Shans were governed by their own 'Sawbwas' (chiefs), nominally subject to the King, but largely independent. The further the state from Mandalay, the more independent the chief. When the British annexed Upper Burma, the Shan chiefs retained their status and continued to govern their states (I think to the number of around thirty, varying greatly in size and importance) subject to ultimate control by the British - Burma Government. The Shan States and its people were quite different from Burma and its inhabitants. The country is a plateau at an average height of three thousand feet. The people speak another language, dress differently and look different; the only common bond is the Buddhist religion.

We had a look at the map and decided to travel into the Southern Shan States and, if time allowed, as far as the most eastern and largest state, Kentung, on the Siamese border; then attempt to motor into the Northern Shan States direct on an old road. Unlike our usual style of touring, servants and baggage had to be kept to a minimum, within the carrying capacity of two cars; mine and my stable companions. Both cars were tourers with collapsible canvas hoods, one a six cylinder Buick and the other also six cylinders, an Essex (long out of existence as manufacturers of cars). We took two servants, a Shan and a Burman.

The start of the journey was not auspicious. We had left the Mandalay-Rangoon trunk road at Meiktila and driven about ten miles towards Taunggyi, the administrative centre of the Southern states, when the Buick car went off the road at a sharp bend and landed upside down in the ditch at the bottom of an eight foot embankment. Luckily, the hood was down and the three occupants were thrown clear before the car turned over, nobody was injured but the end of the journey seemed in sight. In turning over, one of the back wheels must have struck a milestone embedded on the side of the road. Several of the wooden spokes had splintered or broken and the wheel looked a complete write-off. By good luck, whilst we were ruefully contemplating the havoc, the District Engineer from Meiktila arrived on the scene, on his return to headquarters. He immediately arranged for a road gang to be fetched together with a couple of carpenters from his workshops. Within a few hours, the car had been pulled out of the ditch, the smashed wheel removed and the carpenters busy on making new teak spokes. We watched these skilled men shape the wood and then fit the new spokes cleverly into the rim and hub of the wheel. The owner of the car was delighted with their handiwork and declared that the new spokes were better and stronger than the old ones. The carpenters and the rescuers were, in turn, pleased with their unexpected rewards. We departed after expressing our profuse thanks to the rescuing angel, who assured us that it would cost us dear if his next encounter with us was anywhere near a club bar.

In spite of the fortuitous encounter, we had lost several hours journeying time and decided to spend the night in Kalaw, the second largest hill station, not as fashionable as Maymyo but just as social for club life. In fact, this station was very popular with retired British civil servants, who for one reason or another, had decided to stay in the country rather than go home like the majority. We managed to get accommodated in our friend's holiday 'chummery'. We had a convivial evening at the club where the permanent elderly members regaled us with stories about the good old days of the Empire which, as far as the old boys were concerned, was now governed by a bunch of spineless egg heads! Two short accounts, picked up that evening, may serve to illustrate their feelings.

The two incidents were recounted by a retired Police Officer about his predecessor when he took over a District from him before the first world war. In the first incident, the outgoing officer had handed over and departed the day before. Our story teller was sitting in his office reading some files. Gradually, he had a feeling that he was not alone in the room; he glanced up, saw nobody and resumed his reading. The feeling persisted so he looked round more carefully and there, kneeling on the floor, was his chief clerk, head bowed, arms outstretched and across them the folded daily newspaper from Rangoon. Like all offices, the doors were flaps, fixed halfway up the door frames, to allow maximum ventilation above and below the door. The head clerk had crawled under the flaps, rather than disturb the great man in his reading by opening them!

In the second story, our narrator went on his first inspection to a Police Station, which was within half a day's riding distance of Headquarters. The journey took him along a dusty unmetalled road built, as usual, on an embankment. As he was riding along, he noticed that all the bullock-carts, in both directions, were travelling in the ditches on either side of the embankment. Rather intrigued by this preferred mode of progress, he came to the conclusion that the drivers had chosen the ditch because the all-prevailing dust was fractionally more moist than on the road itself and therefore did not rise as high or as easily. When he arrived at the Police Station he saw a constable dismount from a pony. In answer to his question about the purpose of the rider's journey, the station officer replied: "That constable, your Honour, was riding ahead of you, driving all the bullock-carts off the road so that you would not be inconvenienced by the dust".

In fairness to us successors in the game of Empire, I should point out that our story teller's predecessor had been recruited just after the annexation of Upper Burma and long before the Indian Police was established, when all kinds of people were hurriedly recruited by the recently established Civil Government and some of them, excellent as they may have been at administering a district, not yet subject to much central supervision, had very decided views about their status and the respect due to it! Readers may be surprised to read that, more often than not, officials who had very definite ideas about their dignity and the proper regard it should receive, were held in great esteem and affection because they were just and impartial, besides the people were still familiar with the arrogance displayed by royal officials everywhere as an essential and natural requisite in a representative from the King in Mandalay.

On our way to Taunggyi, the capital of the Southern Shan States, on the next day we admired the engineering feats of the Burma Railways. The original intention had been to take the railway line as far as the main town but some ten miles short of the goal, the climb up the range of hills, before dropping down to the Taunggyi plateau, proved much more difficult than anticipated and the numerous loops and counter-loops proved so costly that the budget was exceeded and a stop called, which proved final when the motorable road was constructed. We did a quick detour to Inle Lake to see the famous leg-rowers and also encountered a few giraffe-necked women, ambling along the road with their loads on their heads. They certainly had an odd look about them, with rows and rows of broad heavy bangles closely enclosing and stretching their thin necks. I could not appreciate the aesthetic value of this strange custom.

We had made good progress on the excellent all-weather road and decided to pass through Taunggyi and spend the night at Loilem, which was considered one of the beauty spots in the Southern states. We were not disappointed; the 'dak' bungalow was situated on top of a hill which gave us a long-distance view all around, with a small blue lake in the foreground. The sky was cloudless and the evening sun beginning to set behind the far-off Kentung hills, set them out in sharp relief in the usual spectacular eastern sunset. We could have happily spent several days in this idyllic spot but our time was limited and we had been warned that the old road from Loilem to the Northern Shan States, terminating at Hsipaw, was in a state of disrepair. As we discovered in due course this was quite an understatement of facts.

We therefore reluctantly loaded up the cars early next morning and drove on to Kentung. The road gradually deteriorated and our progress slowed down. We had hoped to cover the distance in the day time but we did not reach our destination until well into the night; found the rest house with some difficulty and after a swift meal out of tins were thankful to rest our shaken-up bones on the comfortable webbing mattresses of the beds. The ruler was away so we had to content ourselves with a stroll round the town and with a distant view of the palace, which turned out to be rather disappointing. I had subconsciously expected a smaller edition of the royal palace in Mandalay. The townsfolk were not so colourful as the Burmese in their dress but the women still looked attractive and were generally fairer than their Burmese sisters. The Shans are more akin to the Siamese than to the Burmese, both in looks and in habits. We were, of course, handicapped in not being able to talk the language but Burmese did get us through some halting conversations. The prevailing impression of this small, remote semi-autonomous eastern domain was one of tranquillity where nothing could ever upset the peaceful way of life of these simple, contented and unambitious people. Little did we suspect that in only a few years, the whole fabric of their existence would be torn asunder by war, followed by continual internal upheavals for years afterwards.

We had to return to Loilem for the beginning of our next, most uncertain, stage of the trip northwards to Lashio, the capital of the Northern Shan States. We left Kentung at dawn and reached the picturesque Loilem rest house on its hill before dusk. We spent the next day overhauling both cars and buying some eggs, fruit and vegetables and trying to obtain up-to-date information about the state of the road ahead. As usual, the intelligence we gathered was vague and often contradictory. We were now half way through our casual leave period and could not take too many risks of further serious delays. We decided to start the drive to Hsipaw, another of the more important semi-autonomous states, where the road joined the main trunk road from Mandalay to Lashio.

The road was surprisingly good for the first few miles and just as we began to think that the tales of woe about the lack of upkeep were probably exaggerated, the smooth surface came to an abrupt end. Speed was drastically cut and more often than not we were just crawling along, wheels precariously perched between the deep continuous ruts scoured out of the road surface by the passage of countless bullock-cart wheels. All roads in Burma, unless the surfaces were properly metalled, suffered from the havoc created by these big narrow wooden wheels, especially in the rains. To make matters worse, water buffaloes would frequently decide to have a mud bath in the middle of the road and in no time large wallows would be added to the hazards confronting the car driver.

The inevitable happened and, what was worse, it happened to both cars simultaneously. They both became firmly stuck in two separate deep patches of mud with no help in sight. We had no hope of pulling the vehicles clear without the assistance of more men and probably also of oxen or buffaloes. The only help was from a village we had passed several miles back. Whilst debating what to do, someone wound up the gramophone we had brought along as an afterthought. As by magic, and in a relatively short time, several Shan field workers appeared out of the blue and formed an appreciative audience. Quite soon we had attracted half a dozen men from nowhere. We made them understand that the free concert would only continue after the cars had been pulled clear. Two of them went off and brought back a pair of bullocks and, with the rope we had taken the precaution to bring with us, eventually pulled both vehicles out of the mud. We thankfully gave the audience some more music which seemed to meet their full approval. The mishap had cost us only a few rupees in rewards but nearly three hours in delay. We had two further interruptions in our progress, for the same reason, but not quite as bad, and again the gramophone brought the required help.

These unscheduled stops now amounted to more than half a day's travelling time and we had reached the point of no return. At the last 'bog-down' a Burman turned up with the rescuers; he told us that he had come from Hsipaw recently and that the road from the state's border to the town was in good condition and that it had been freshly tarred after the last rains. The total distance from Loilem to Hsipaw was 150 miles, we had so far travelled just over 50 miles in six hours; the border between the Northern and Southern Shan States, was about 50 miles away. It was now the middle of the day and with luck we could be in Hsipaw by nightfall. We decided to push on.

We travelled slowly and cautiously on the brim of the deep ruts in the road and managed to avoid further trouble at the periodical buffalo-wallows. After nearly two hours and, we judged, half-way to the longed-for tarmac road, disaster struck. A stone bridge over a sizeable river had been breached and parts of it swept away (presumably our late Burmese informer thought this fact of no importance to us!). The only consolation was that the river had now shrunk to a slow-moving stream. From the evidence available, it looked as if the destruction had been recent and this was confirmed when, as expected, some villagers turned up to listen to the gramophone. We were divided on what to do next, two thought it best to call it a day and go back, the other two were for exploring the possibility of fording the river. The explorers won and we all waded into the water looking for a likely way on the river-bed.

An hour or so later, we had marked out a possible track to drive along; the depth of the water in the middle was much less than we had feared from the width between the banks. The worst hazards now were the numerous large boulders strewn about the bottom. The villagers were more than willing to help; the unexpected prospect, of helping to ferry two cars through an uneven river bed, must have been an entertaining break in the drudgery of their daily existence in this remote corner of the world. One of us went in front of the car to guide the driver round obstacles and keep the vehicle in the shallowest parts as there were one or two deeper pools. Two or three villagers were perched on the back bumper of the car to add extra weight on the back axle (there were no front-wheel drives in those days). We could not run the risk of fording both cars simultaneously one behind the other; this precaution meant losing valuable time but we would have been much worse off with both vehicles stuck in mid-stream. It was late afternoon by the time we had got across.

The road on the other bank was just as bad as the one we had left behind us; in fact the ruts looked even deeper and were more threatening because it was uphill for a while. Again one of us had to walk ahead to guide the driver. I was the leading guide and, coming round a bend, I came face-to-face with a lovely Shan girl, urinating in the middle of the way. She was performing upright with her legs straddled and holding a huge bundle steady on her head with one hand while the other was holding up her 'lungyi'. She seemed quite unconcerned by our encounter, unhurriedly finished her business, dropped her skirt, stepped aside with a sweet smile and watched us drive past as if nothing had happened. I had encountered such a matter-of-fact attitude on other occasions in out of the way places, towards what are after all perfectly normal bodily functions for us all, but never had I seen it performed with such unconcern.

The climb up from the river was longer than we expected and the road started to wind in a series of sharp bends. The shade from the increasing density of overhanging branches had left slippery patches on the uneven muddy road. Without warning, one of the cars suddenly skidded sharply and, before the driver could take corrective action, slid partly off the ridge of the road, coming to a stop with the front wheels hanging over a nearly vertical drop of twenty feet into the ravine below. The driver's efforts to back away were of no avail and only served to wedge the car more firmly and a bit further over the khud. There was no hope of finding help quickly before the short evening twilight was over. We had to settle for a night on the road-side. We prepared an evening meal over a make-shift fire and laid out our bedding rolls next to the cars. We had one bit of luck whilst eating; an old man appeared walking up the road. He could see for himself the predicament we were in and by signs and some halting Burmese made us understand that he would bring help from his village as soon as it was light. This spontaneous offer cheered us up a lot and we pressed the old boy to have some food and a drink. He refused the food but eagerly accepted a bottle of beer. He was anxious, understandably, to get home before dark and departed with renewed assurance of help in the morning. We settled down as best we could to an uncomfortable night, plagued by mosquitoes and disturbed by jungle noises around us. One camper alleged that he was woken up by a large animal jumping over his recumbent form; this news was received with the scepticism it deserved by the others, preoccupied with their own discomforts.

As good as his word, our old man turned up with some men soon after daylight and the rescue work started at once but not without a great fright. In their eagerness, some of the villagers began to push and pull the stricken car without proper co-ordination, with the result that it slipped further over the edge. However, once we had got everybody organised, the car was gradually levered back on to the road and a quick inspection underneath revealed no apparent damage. We gave our usual concert of thanks on the gramophone and the audience was again appreciative; they also cheered us with the news that the 'good' road was 'just around the corner'. Even allowing for the natives' usual optimistic estimates of distance, we thought it reasonably safe to divest ourselves of our remaining silver rupee pieces and of the few tins of food we had left over. The rescuers, highly satisfied with their day's unexpected bonus, departed with smiles and friendly hand-waving. We did reach the border of Hsipaw state without further incidents within an hour's driving. After that, it was plain sailing on a nice smooth road. We drove up to the Inspection

Bungalow in high spirits, where we found the Executive Engineer, for Roads and Buildings in the North Shan States, encamped. He could not believe that we had come direct from Loilem in two days, since he knew about the breached bridge and the bad state of the road. He told us that, as a matter of economy, it had been decided to abandon the road for regular motor vehicle traffic and that, to his knowledge, no car or lorry had come that way in his time and he had been in the job for three years. We now had only three days' leave in hand so the projected visit to Lashio had to be abandoned and we headed for Maymyo and Mandalay.

The two motor-cars had by now developed a multitude of creaks and noises in the bodyworks, which had been submitted to so many unusual stresses and strains, but the engines worked as smoothly as at the beginning of our trip. I gladly give a very belated tribute to the Buick and Essex manufacturers for their robust and reliable workmanship. Maymyo looked more like an English garden city than an eastern resort, with its well-kept lawns and flower beds. On the way to Mandalay, I regaled my friends with the incidents which used to befall me on my frequent trips between the two towns. The scene was still very much the same, the girls selling pineapples and mangoes on the side of the winding road leading into the plain and then the huge water-buffaloes grazing in the fields on both sides of the highway. We arrived at the Police Mess, where we were given hospitality. After tea, I took my friends for a quick tour of the fort area. None of them had realised that they could still find a place which exuded such an unmistakable atmosphere of the old Burma. I felt quite nostalgic when I went off to pay my respects to my old 'saya' Po Thit and his family. Unfortunately, we had no time left to see the city before dark and I much regretted the inability to visit my French lady and her silk shop. We left early the next morning for our 300 miles run to Myaunglebin, which we reached without any trouble, tired but pleased with our achievement within our limited timetable.

Re-reading the foregoing account of our trip, I am aware that I have failed to describe, effectively, in the appropriate places, the pleasure for us plain dwellers to savour the panoramic views and climate amongst the hills and valleys of that temperate zone. The Shan States plateau has such a good climate that the Government had, at one time, seriously thought of setting up a scheme to assist European farmers to develop holdings in selected parts of the area to encourage variety in the cultivation of the fertile soil. In fact, several pioneers had already established sizeable pineapple and grapefruit orchards, others were growing strawberries and European vegetables. Local farmers had begun to follow these leads and had found a ready market for their products in Rangoon and other larger towns. Strawberries, pineapples and grapefruit were being exported in ever increasing quantities overseas to Calcutta for the large European communities in India. I think that if the war had not put an end to this development, as it did to so many other activities, the agricultural potential of the Shan States could have been expanded to a considerable degree, which might even have discouraged the increasing cultivation of the poppy plant of the nefarious drug trade.

Bridge in Shan States, Oct. 1932

Fording a river; the bridge swept away

Both cars stuck in the mud

15
Nyaunglebin

I have forgotten many incidents of little importance, funny or sad, but some, like the following, have remained at the back of my mind.

Nyaunglebin boasted two Circuit Houses (grander than ordinary inspection bungalows and only found at district headquarters). Why this subdivisional headquarters should have one, let alone two, was as inexplicable as the town's name, Nyaunglebin, which means 'Four Banyan Trees', when there was no such tree in sight. In practice only one Circuit House was in use. It so happened that the Deputy Inspector General of Police, Geoff Waterworth, was in charge of the range which included Pegu district, decided to inspect my humble subdivision. His visit coincided with the unusual fact that the regular Circuit House was fully booked and I had to arrange for his accommodation in the disused one. The Public Works Officer and I did a rapid inspection, had the place cleaned up, provided a temporary 'durwan' (watchman-cum-handyman) and sweeper. It was the custom for a junior officer to call formally on his superior prior to an inspection; this meant donning full service dress (khaki tunic, riding breeches, boots and spurs, Sam Browne belt and sword). Thus attired, I presented myself at the Circuit House, after allowing for the great man to recover from his long journey. Instead of finding him changed and relaxing in an easy chair, as expected, I found the place in an uproar, with servants rushing around with brooms and sticks, directed by the 'Burra Sahib' (Big Shot) clad only in a towel. I saluted smartly, standing to attention, to be told to stop acting like an idiot and to make myself useful. It transpired that when the great man was sitting in the zinc bath tub in the primitive bathroom next to his bedroom, an indignant python had uncurled its great length from around the space between the top of the walls and the roof, and had started to slide down one wall, uncomfortably close to the bather. He, quite naturally, shot out of his bath, rushed out calling for the servants to chase the snake out of the place. Pythons are not really dangerous snakes, but their great size is frightening and can lead to panic reaction when suddenly encountered. Even then their first intention is usually to get away from the nuisance. This is what happened in this case, the snake made off as quickly as it could and would even have done so without the encouragement from all of us. I had to confess that I had not thought of looking into the long disused bathroom prior to the guest's arrival.

Matters did not end there. My chief recovered his temper and sense of humour quite quickly and, after receiving my written notes for his inspection on the following day, invited me and my stable companion to dinner at the Circuit House that evening, "and don't let us have any bloody formality, both of you come in comfortable shirts and trousers". The chief had brought his own cook and stores from Rangoon and we had an excellent meal, preceded by short drinks and brandy afterwards. Our host regaled us with many good yarns of his early and later days in Burma; he knew everyone and a lot about some, who might have felt their dignity dented if they had been present. We were drawing to the end of the small talk when a large bat flew into the room; we three grabbed some curtain rods lying in the corner and started to chase the intruder round the room. In the course of the chase, I managed to hit my inspecting officer over the head instead of the bat which shortly after decided to fly out under its own volition. Although my chief's reaction to the assault seemed sarcastically restrained, I had a strong feeling that the 'inspection' had not started too well. The formal parade and headquarters' rounds on the next morning passed off without adverse incident. I rather hesitatingly invited the chief to dinner that night, quite prepared for a rebuff. However, he seemed genuinely pleased to accept. When he arrived that evening he was wearing his topee and asked, with a straight face, whether it would be safe to remove the protection. We had another convivial evening. I received a copy of his official inspection report in due course in which he made mention of the two incidents, drawing the conclusion that my police work was better than my attempts to get rid of a senior officer to accelerate promotion. He was a much liked and popular member of the force, who died soon after his retirement and before he saw his beloved Burma going through the agonising war and post-war period.

Elephants were seldom seen in the central plains. Occasionally, timber firms would transfer working elephants from the eastern to the western forest reserves. The firm which had Forest Assistants stationed in Nyaunglebin were planning to move half a dozen grown beasts from the Sittang area to the Yoma hills in the west. Police headquarters in Nyaunglebin had a very large compound, surrounding the main Police Station and the married quarters. I was asked if the elephants could be accommodated there for a rest of two days, before proceeding westwards. From the raised open verandah of the bungalow, which I shared with my Engineer friend, one had a good view of this compound. I spent a long period in the late afternoon looking at the elephants' activities, a new experience for me. The senior Forest Assistant of the firm was an experienced handler of elephants; in fact, they were his constant preoccupation and I was amazed at the way in which these elephants seemed to recognise him as a friend and allow him to give them injections or perform quite large incisions in the course of his veterinary inspection. He told me that it was a fact that elephants have long memories and that he would often be greeted by an animal he had known or doctored many months' previously; he recounted several incidents which confirmed the elephant's ability to remember kind and unkind acts. Like many people, I had also read stories about the intelligence and long memories of these animals and I had accepted some of the more unusual ones with a grain of salt. But after hearing at first hand from someone who had lived with them for years and had acquired an intimate knowledge of their habits and actions, I dismissed most of my previous doubts. I witnessed a good illustration of elephant behaviour. One female had a year old male baby elephant in the compound. The grown beasts were hobbled whilst in the compound but the baby was allowed to run free. The 'oozie' (Burmese word for the elephant's rider) had trouble in keeping the youngster inside the compound and on several occasions had to chase after him on the main road outside. Each time he brought him back, the mother elephant gave her child a smart swipe with her trunk as if to say "Now behave yourself". The baby would glance up to her with a hurt look, remain obedient for a while and then again stray out of the compound. Finally, the mother became as angry as her 'oozie' and, when he guided the truant up to the parent, she gripped the culprit firmly between her huge front legs and gave him a good beating with her trunk. The baby bellowed blue murder in a shrill trumpeting tone and did not attempt any further sorties. It was a most effective display of motherly discipline, which I would have found hard to believe in an animal, if I had not seen it myself.

I was not particularly interested in fishing and had never learnt to cast accurately. One of my police colleagues, Rex Lawson, was a keen fisherman and invited me to share the expenses of a short fishing holiday in the hills east of Toungoo, the next district north of us. He supplied me with all the gear and made me practise casting in the compound of the bungalow. We were going to use spinner spoons as bait and, after some intensive guidance, I became reasonably precise in landing the spoon on the target. We were to fish for 'mahseer', a good sporting fish of the carp family which could grow to enormous size under the right conditions. Even in the larger mountain streams, the fish could grow to ten pounds and more. Dedicated fishermen considered this fish as good a fighter as the salmon and went after him with the same dedication.

The place we were visiting was beyond the only road leading into the hills from Toungoo and terminating at the small hill station of Thandaung, which consisted of a Karen village and a rest house. We left the car there and marched a good ten miles into the jungle-clad hill before we reached our goal. Dusk was settling fast but we both went down to the river to try our luck whilst the servants set up camp. The incredible happened, with my very first cast, I hooked a fish and, by the strong reaction, a big one. In my excitement I forgot all the things I had been told about playing the fish and keeping him away from submerged rocks or trees, I simply started to reel in as fast as I could, the rod bent nearly double, but my luck held and the gear did not break or come apart. My shouting attracted the attention of my companion, who abandoned his casting as soon as he realised that I was into something big. He came to stand beside me in the water and, thanks to his direction, I finally got the fish alongside the landing net held by my friend. He weighed fifteen pounds and was the biggest catch of the expedition. We discovered later that only one heavier mahseer had ever been known to have been caught by rod in this mountain river. We were there for two whole days, my companion caught quite a number of fish but I only managed another three, weighing between two and four pounds.

The only other excitement on this fishing expedition in the backwoods was unpleasant for me. The river was fast flowing with numerous bends and many snags on which our lines were constantly caught. Often one of us would have to dive under water to free a trapped line. On one occasion my companion's hook became firmly wedged in some boulders under a small waterfall. I dived into the pool under the fall with the water pounding down on top of me; the line was caught in a space between two big boulders near the bottom. I managed to stand, with legs spread, on two large flat stones on which the top two were perched, still submerged over my head. After several hard pulls the line came free but in doing so dislodged one of the top boulders which then wedged my left foot hard under the flat surface of the lower stone. I pulled in all directions but my foot would not budge and I was running out of air. They say that in times of danger one's life flashes before one's eyes. I have no recollection of anything like that, nor was I aware of feeling badly frightened until the very last moment when, I suppose with the strength of despair, I managed to roll the holding boulder slightly but sufficiently to free my foot and shoot to the surface gasping for breath and to confront a very anxious friend who had dashed over when he realised that something was seriously wrong. Reaction after the incident was much more severe, I started to shake and went on shaking for some time; I did not fish again that day. Reflecting on the incident later, I came to the conclusion that the loud continuous roar of the falling water over my head must have had the effect of excluding all other thoughts and may thus even have saved my life, by preventing panic to set in when I realised that I was trapped.

My sharing of quarters, for over two years, was coming to an end as my friend was returning to his home in Scotland. We had got on very well together and had shared many incidents in the course of work and pleasure. We were sorry to end the happy association and I resolved to give him a good send-off with the help of colleagues. The programme consisted of a farewell evening party at the club to be followed, on the last night, by a dinner at our bungalow with his more intimate friends. The club did him proud; every member except two managed to get into headquarters for the occasion. Besides the combined presentation from the club, a fine ivory carving of a pair of Burmese dancers, friends also gave him individual presents. Liquid refreshments flowed freely and, the 'pièce de résistance', an elaborate Burmese curry with all the numerous side dishes, considered essential at an important function, kept us at the club until the early hours of the morning.

The dinner at the bungalow on the next evening, being a more intimate affair with his bachelor friends, started with the usual short drinks, followed by an excellent five course meal which would have even won approval from more discerning connoisseurs of good food. The party became more hectic as the night went on. Our chief guest, who always loved a good argument, chose as his farewell speech a fulsome eulogy of the Russians and, in particular of their leader Stalin. The audience responded in a suitable manner and he was promptly debagged and not allowed to wear his trousers again for the rest of the evening. For the final toasts, as a tribute to Russian custom, the glasses were thrown out of the window after each drink until none were left; followed by some of the crockery still on the table. Everyone felt better after this barbaric display of destruction and departed well pleased with the celebrations. The next morning, we both ruefully surveyed the damage of the night before, particularly myself, as I had agreed to buy all his household belongings for a nominal amount. My friend left in a sad mood, seen off by most of the station; the last thing he shouted to me was a reminder about his invitation to visit him in Scotland, when I came on leave in a few months' time. Neither of us could foresee the quite unexpected result of this offer of hospitality.

Inspection bungalow for touring officers: note raised 'cat-walk' in case of floods

Typical road bridge in Lower-Burma

74

16
Myitkyina

My application for furlough from May 1933 had been sanctioned and I was making ready for my departure in a few weeks time. A telegram arrived in due course, but the contents did not as expected notify the name of and date on which my successor was arriving but ordered me to proceed at once to Myitkyina. Although the move did not mean that I would officiate in the rank of District Superintendent, it was promotion of sorts. The post ranked as an independent command for a senior Assistant District Superintendent. As there were several Assistants senior to me I wondered, during the long rail journey, what had induced the Inspector-General to give me preferment.

On arrival, I discovered that my selection was not due to accelerated promotion but to administrative convenience. The officer I was relieving had applied for two months leave on urgent private affairs and, as he had only just been posted to the District, the Government had sanctioned the leave on condition that he returned to the same appointment after his absence. As my leave had been granted more or less from the date of his return, it had therefore been thought convenient all round to put me in as a stop-gap. The only snag to this arrangement affected me financially. Under the rules, an officer proceeding on long leave, had to pay travelling costs out of his own pocket from his district headquarters to the port of embarkation. This meant that, instead of the railway fare for 100 miles from Nyaunglebin to Rangoon, I was now faced with the cost of a 900 miles journey from Myitkyina to Rangoon. I drew attention to this financial outlay but received no sympathetic response from the authorities. I think that the outcome might have been better if I had omitted the final touch of sarcasm in my letter of complaint; I pointed out that it seemed hardly logical that I should suffer financial loss for someone else's private affairs.

I soon recovered from my sense of personal grievance when I realised what a pleasant change I had gained from this transfer. The majority of district officers were agreed that the further north you went in Burma the more agreeable the surroundings. Myitkyina proved the doctrine to the hilt. The hill tribes, the Kachins, inhabited the extensive high ground surrounding the plain around the main town and stretching south along the railway line occupied by the Burmese. It did not take me long to appreciate why members of the Burma Frontier Service and of the Burma Military Police became so attached to these splendid hill people.

Their tribal lives under a local chief gave them a natural feeling of loyalty to authority for as long as they believed it just and impartial. Their sense of self-discipline made them excellent material for the military and police forces.

Myitkyina district was the largest in Burma; the north and east borders formed the frontier with China and, in the west, most of the border lay alongside that of India. This isolation with the rest of Burma gave one a feeling of still living in a pioneering atmosphere where time moved slowly. Burma's principal river, the Irrawaddy, is born 150 miles to the north, at the confluence of two tributaries, the Malihka and the Nmaihka. By the time the river flows past the town, it is already wide and deep; the water is still clear, an unusual sight for someone like me who had so far only seen the muddy waterways below Mandalay and in the Delta. The Civil Station, with its pleasant old-fashioned bungalows built in the later eighteen eighties when the area first came under British administration, was situated along or near the west bank of the river, with distant views of the north-eastern hills. Thanks to the abundance of water at all times, keen gardeners had made eye-catching flower gardens around their bungalows, instead of the usual rather dusty and drab lawns so prevalent in most civil lines in the south. The extensive military cantonments were adjacent; the combined picture reminded me of the more peaceful illustrations in one of my childhood books, depicting, in colour, the country and the way of life in India at the time of the Mutiny.

The Deputy Commissioner J.K. Stanford, I.C.S., was away on an extended tour of the Kachin hills for six weeks and was not due back for another three weeks. He was a keen naturalist and, when he retired prematurely some years later, became the editor of a well-known sporting magazine in England. There was an unwritten convention that the D.C. and the D.S.P. should not be absent from headquarters simultaneously for too long a period. This meant that for the time being I had to restrict my travelling to short distances until he returned. I realised that I would be unable to fulfil my ambition of an extended visit to the Kachin hills during my short stay. The more I saw of these people the more I wished to know about their lives and customs. Later on, they proved the reputation of loyalty to the hilt, when they became our valiant allies in adversity.

I spent the first days in the office and making contact with the other officials and military commanders. In the evening I would stroll over to the pleasant little club building, with its splendid view across the clean broad river to the distant hills on the China border. For its size the club had an unusually large membership. Both Military Police battalions were large in number because they had to provide substantial garrisons in several important outposts. One of these, Fort Hertz, gained notoriety during the last war as the only military post of consequence not to fall into the hands of the Japanese. The number of officers in each battalion was therefore much above those in other similar formations. The Burma Frontier Service provided the civil administrators in the hill tracts, alongside the military personnel. All these officers were members of the club, although absent for several months at a time; together with the more permanent officials at headquarters, the club boasted a membership of several dozen; substantially more than in other outstations, except Mandalay and Maymyo. In practice, of course, the usual attendance was small.

Thanks to the large Military Police presence, I had the opportunity to renew my polo playing. Regrettably, what little skill I had acquired, in what now seemed the far distant days of Mandalay, had diminished to vanishing point and I had to start more or less from scratch. The colonel, commanding one of the battalions, was an outstanding player, some said the best in Burma. He very kindly took me in hand and his expert coaching got me going again in the few games I managed to play during my short time. At least I had the satisfaction ever after to assert that I might have been a competent player if I had had more time to practise under such expert guidance. We played tennis daily on the one and only club court, followed by billiards or bridge in the evenings. Life was really very pleasant and nobody seemed to miss the more sophisticated amusements and flesh pots of Rangoon and other more important centres. Although not a keen fisherman, I much regretted that I could not participate in a fishing expedition to 'the confluence'. This spot was renowned amongst the expert anglers of Burma for the good sport provided by the large mahseer fish inhabiting the deep pools there. The fishing record book at the Myitkyina club contained some astonishing accounts of catches. I cannot remember the record catch but I do recollect seeing two accounts of landing fish weighing over sixty pounds; catches of twenty pounds or more were relatively commonplace. Fishermen who have gone after both salmon and mahseer say that, weight for weight, the latter fish are stronger.

After my week of settling in, I thought it appropriate to visit my largest police station outside headquarters at Mogaung, an important centre for trading and, in particular, for the jade brought in from the adjacent mines. The town was on the railway line and thus within easy reach of Myitkyina. Whilst I was there, I was informed that the Hukawng Valley annual expedition was due to arrive within the next two days. The vastness of the district made it impossible for the Government to set up permanent administrative posts in all the remote areas, so annual combined military and civil forces were sent out to tour round these places for two to three months to 'show the flag' and deal with any matters which could be settled on the spot and to report back on more important issues which might have arisen.

Both the military commander and the Civil Affairs officer of this expedition were old friends of mine and I decided to surprise them by meeting the returning force at Kamaing, twenty miles east of the railway town, a small hamlet at the eastern end of the Hukawng Valley. The latter earned an evil reputation as a death trap for the thousands of Indian refugees who tried to escape on foot to India, when the Japanese invasion spread to Upper Burma. I caught the very rickety local bus for the bumpy road journey. My friends were pleased to see the bottle of whisky I had taken the precaution to bring with me. After the convivial reunion, and fortified by the alcohol, I announced rashly that I would walk with them to the railhead on the next day. The early departure next morning found me less than enthusiastic about the prospect but the loss of face in renegading was even worse to contemplate, so off I set with my friends on either side, at the head of the column. They and all the others had marched more or less continuously for over two months and the pedometer they had trailed along recorded nearly eight hundred miles. However, somewhat to my own surprise, I kept up remarkably well and ended the trek in good shape, only to be told that the marching rate had been cut down out of consideration for the poor town dweller! So, feeling rather cut down to size, I boarded the train.

When I was under training in Mandalay, I met socially one of the best known European jade dealers. I now remembered that, although he travelled frequently to Europe and America in the course of his trade, his headquarters were in a small town next to the jade centre of Mogaung. I contacted him and he promptly invited me for a week-end visit. He was a typical Somerset Maugham character from the short stories compiled by that author during his travels in the East. He was tall, always well-dressed and sported a monocle. I was surprised to find that he was living in quite a modest wooden bungalow. I had heard that he always dressed for dinner, guest or no guest, and I had taken the precaution to bring my dinner jacket. He was an excellent host, had a first-rate Chinese cook and a stock of fine wines and liqueurs. Rumour had it that his Burmese mistresses were both numerous and beautiful. Whether this was fiction or fact I never discovered as, alas, the tantalising prospect of glamorous female company did not materialise. Instead he kept me enthralled with his experiences as a jade merchant in various parts of the world.

The next day he took me to Mogaung for a jade auction. Nearly all Burmese jade is concentrated in the neighbouring mines. On arrival in a large open square, I was astonished to see large pieces of ordinary looking rock strewn around the place. He told me that these were jade-bearing stones and that the experts would recommend the purchase price of each rock, after careful examination of various cross-sections. He explained that, through years of experience, the examiners became adept at gauging the quantity and quality of jade contained in a particular piece of stone. Even so, purchases were still much of a gamble since even the best examiner could make bad mistakes. Most of the local dealers were Chinese and much of the extracted jade was exported overland to China. My guide also told me that the same rock could yield different qualities of jade; apparently, the milky green evenly coloured jade with a velvety feel was the most valuable. When we returned to his home, he showed me some of his own collection which he had assembled over the years. Invariably, the carving was exquisite; one of his choice pieces was a lovely little Chinese pagoda about ten inches high; he told me that many tempting offers had been made for this masterpiece but that, so far, he had resisted a sale. I am sorry that I was unable to visit him again during my short time in the district.

When the Deputy Commissioner returned, I decided to fulfil at least one promise I had made to myself on arrival. I undertook a week's trip down the Irrawaddy to the border of the adjoining district, Katha, where my father had been Deputy Commissioner twenty years earlier. My main reason for this pleasure trip, for that is what it really was, although I did some inspection work on the way there and back, was to see the first defile through which the big river rushes on its long journey to the sea. The second defile, between Bhamo and Katha, was said to be more spectacular but the first was the narrowest. In fact, the water flows so fast that in the rains no Government craft was then powerful enough to steam upstream. The Irrawaddy Flotilla Company, then generally regarded as the most efficient commercial river transport enterprise in the world, considered it impracticable to maintain a regular service beyond Bhamo.

The district fleet of Government launches included an unusually large double-decker launch with several big cabins and well appointed in all other ways. I invited one of the married military police officers and his wife to join me on the trip. We had a comfortable leisurely journey down stream, calling in at several riverine villages and at the only police station on its west bank. The launch crew was made up of Chittagonians, as were most of the Government crafts' crews. They always carried a supply of domestic fowls on board to ensure a supply of fresh eggs and the occasional roast. Whenever the launch was made fast along the river bank, the birds would be let loose ashore to peck for food in the sandy shore; the reigning rooster would usually select a lofty perch on the mast to keep an eye on his brood. When the launch was due to leave, the 'serang' would pull the cord of the boat's hooter and the birds would immediately stop their searching and scuttle back on board as fast as they could. The generally accepted reason for this display of obedience was the belief that crews taught this discipline by always beating the last bird back!

The Burmese are great bathers; men, women and children spent long periods at all times of the day on the banks of streams and rivers, washing themselves and their clothes, swimming and generally frolicking in the water. Children washed and swam around naked and, in remoter regions, even mature girls and boys scorned any covering. I noticed that my married companion, despite his wife's presence, showed as much appreciation for the shapely figures displayed, from time to time, on the banks as I did. In one village, where we tied up for a while, I was having the usual chat with the headman and a few elders. I remarked that there seemed to be an unusually large number of children about for such a small village. The headman laughed and replied, "Well you see we have a lot of mosquitoes here". When I looked nonplussed at the remark, the others joined in his laughter and one of them added, "You see, we have to go to bed early". The Burmese sense of humour is never far away.

The defile was as spectacular as I had expected. The dramatic effect of the dark cliffs stark against the blue sky and the dark green of the swirling water, intensified as the passage grew narrower and narrower until one felt that it would soon be possible to touch both banks from the fast-moving launch. Dazzling white pagodas, small and large, were dotted about on prominent rocks on the cliff side and, with their numerous small bells tinkling in the constant breeze, added to the unforgettable sight. The 'serang' had a full-time job in keeping the launch on a safe course in the fast, twisting current. On the way back, his task was even harder because, at times, the boat was often nearly stationary when battling against the strong current. We were suitably impressed with his professional skill; I sent him later a typed letter of appreciation on my official note paper, which seemed to delight him out of proportion to the gesture.

My predecessor returned on the due date and I regretfully packed my bags; even the prospect of seeing my mother and sister again after nearly four years did not altogether mitigate my sense of loss in missing the many interesting tours I would have made during a normal period of duty in this big, different frontier district. Although my stay had been so short, the club insisted on a farewell party and I caught the train next day with a sore head and the good wishes of friends ringing in my ears. Thus began my eventful home leave in May 1933.

17
Intermission

I embarked for my ten months furlough, in the middle of May 1933, just as the monsoon broke in all its fury in the Bay of Bengal. Unlike my voyage out, the ship was practically empty when it left Rangoon and once we had steamed out of the River, was tossed about like a toy boat. I discovered that I was not prone to sea-sickness and rather enjoyed standing on deck, watching the huge waves smash into the side of the vessel and covering me with spray in the process. There were only a handful of passengers at this stage; all men and we occupied the single berth cabins above the main promenade deck, well away from the accommodation reserved for staid married couples or single women.

I had had no spare money on my maiden voyage and thus was not able to participate in the social drinking which was an important part of the sea voyage. This time, my finances were in better shape and most of us had known each other in Burma, at one time or another, (the expatriate Government officials numbered less than four hundred in the whole of Burma, including Army officers). We were a cheerful bunch of youngsters with one or two senior, but even they were still on the right side of fifty. The prospect of long leave intoxicated us all and we helped the feeling in a practical way. Luckily most of us were good sailors and we did more than justice to the elaborate meals, three times a day, wallowing in the great variety of choice. Being the first batch of passengers, we all sat at the Captain's table but he, unfortunately, had to spend a great deal of time on the bridge in this bad weather.

A minor tragedy occurred on the third day out of Rangoon. Two young 'Jungle wallahs', Forest Assistants from one of the big teak exporting firms, decided to make a night of it. Elated by the prospect of luxurious civilisation after the long months of loneliness and discomfort in the Burma forests, they continued their drinking session after the bar had closed. They took a bottle of whisky to one of the cabins; one of them picked up a glass from the shelf above the wash-basin, saw something lying in water, tossed the contents out of the open port-hole and filled up with whisky and water. The next morning, the owner of the cabin could not find his false teeth! The poor chap was severely restricted in the choice of his food for the rest of the voyage, but the mishap did not impair his ability to consume liquid refreshment.

At Colombo, we picked up quite a lot of passengers, including some nubile young ladies, going home with their parents. Shipboard romances started to flourish in no time. I also became susceptible to the charms of one of two daughters of a business tycoon from India; the family were returning to their home in Cornwall. We danced together and lent over the ship's rail, looking at the moonlight sparkling on the phosphorescence of the ocean waves, as countless other couples had done before us. By the time I left the ship in Marseilles, I had received an invitation to visit the family home when I arrived in England (I was going first to see my family in Switzerland).

The cabin on one side of mine was occupied by a young American, who was a stranger to me when the few passengers embarked in Rangoon. We were soon ship-board friends and he told me that he and his brother were partners in their father's business in New York who traded in precious stones. Much of their time was taken up in travelling around the world buying uncut and unpolished gems for the better-known jewellers in New York, London, Paris and elsewhere. One evening, after our usual nightcaps in the bar lounge, he invited me to his cabin to see the purchases he had made on his visit to the Burma Ruby Mines in Mogok, Upper Burma. He casually pulled out a canvas bag from the chest of drawers, pulled open the string and poured out a pile of greyish nondescript stones. He asked me how much I would give him for the pile and I replied that I had no idea as the whole lot looked far from having any great value. He then told me that he had paid 35,000 rupees for these rubies of good quality and that he was pleased with the deal, which would give his firm a handsome profit. He showed me where the unpolished ruby was embedded in the stone; on closer inspection, with his magnifying glass, I was able to make out the wonderful blood-red colour of a good ruby, partially visible on the surface. I told him about my visit to the jade auction in Myitkyina district, which he also had visited. He said the buying of rubies was also something of a gamble but, unlike jade, which formed only a small part of the large piece of rock, which the buyer had to purchase, the ruby in its raw state was the main ingredient of what you bought. That was why he never attempted to buy jade in the rock; but was now sufficiently expert to judge the size and quality of uncut rubies.

In Colombo, I went with my American companion to a jeweller's in the main street, known to many hundreds of passengers passing through. My friend was greeted with the respect accorded to a well-known and esteemed customer. Without a pause we were ushered into the inner sanctum of the shop. The partner in the business went to a large safe and brought out a leather case, turned out the contents on a velvet cloth and revealed a sparkling heap of sapphires. These stones vary a great deal in quality and judging the value of individual stones is again a matter of great expertise. My American gave the heap of jewels a cursory look, picked out a couple of dozen or so, pulled a cloth bag out of his pocket, mentioned a sum of several thousand rupees and, when the partner nodded, swept them into the bag and said "Thank you, put the deal on our account", shook hands and led me speechless out of the shop. When we were outside, I expressed surprise at the speed and the superficial nature of the transaction. My companion laughed and said, "My father has been dealing with X for many years, he trusts them and they trust us. Both sides know that they are getting fair deals and that is why they always keep good stones for our scrutiny". He was a most interesting companion on this sea journey and I made him promise to look me up when he next came to Burma, which was every few years. However, war upset his and my future activities and we never met again.

The owners of the ship, in which I was travelling, maintained a fortnightly service between England and Burma. Thus, they had a large number of regular customers, travelling to Egypt, the Sudan, Ceylon and Rangoon. Life on board these one class vessels was agreeable amongst congenial company. The boats were not luxurious but comfortable, the crews were efficient and friendly and regular passengers got to know individual officers and stewards personally. In fact, there was a distinct sort of family feeling during these long sea voyages. On nearly every trip, sister ships would pass each other in opposite directions. On this trip home we were due to pass each other two days out of Colombo. One of the Rangoon passengers, a member of the Indian Forest Service, discovered that a colleague of his was on board the other ship, returning from leave. He promptly sent him a radio message to congratulate him on returning cheerfully to his duties. I happened to be standing next to him on deck, looking at the passing ship in the distance, when the radio officer came up with a reply, saying apologetically, "I am sorry, Sir, I cannot make any sense of the reply, I have checked again with other operator". The reply contained only one word 'Gwesi'. We both laughed and explained to the puzzled ship's officer that the word was Burmese for testicles!

Although the thrill of a very first sea voyage was not there, I still had plenty of new impressions to keep me interested, apart from my social activities with the opposite sex. The scene in the Suez Canal gave me again a particular thrill. The procession of ships in either direction was still unceasing. This time I was aware of a fact which had not struck me on my trip out. Not only did the royal Navy rule the waves then but so did our Merchant Marine. In the canal and in every port of call, the 'Red Duster' flew in three ships out of four and often more. English was the prevailing language everywhere and most travellers were British, going about their business all over the world. One had to be unpatriotic or quite insensitive not to have a feeling of pride and togetherness in these encounters at sea or ashore.

I spent the first part of my leave in Switzerland and then went to my old school in England. I had kept up a desultory correspondence with the Headmaster, who had shown me great kindness during my comparatively short stay at the school (I had spent my early school days in Switzerland). When he heard that I was coming home on leave, he invited me to stay with him and suggested that, if I could time the visit to coincide with the School Certificate examinations, he would like me to invigilate them. This was a tempting offer since it would mean a fortnight's sojourn in nice nostalgic surroundings, with the unforeseen bonus of an invigilating fee! I arranged my programme accordingly and also had the good luck to create a record by being the Headmaster's first guest in his new house at the school; so large that it was later converted into a boarding house for boys.

I went to London and bought a second-hand (very) six cylinder Morris Isis car for £18 which, apart from breaking the transmission shaft in the first twenty four hours, served me well for the next months, including two tours on the Continent. When my leave was up, I sold the car for £10 to a relation and I heard that he used the car for another eighteen months, before a major repair job made its further use uneconomic for him, but I believe he did manage a sale of sorts in the end!

I was thinking of visiting my ship-board girl friend in Cornwall, when my Nyaunglebin companion wrote to say that he was coming to London bringing one of his sisters on a visit to an aunt and suggesting that we meet. We had a reunion with other 'Burma hands' over the weekend and when he was going back, he suggested that I followed him after finishing my invigilation job. I decided to accept the idea and to put off my visit to the west country as I had not yet written to the parents of the girl.

My short visit to Edinburgh became longer and longer. In brief, I fell in love with my friend's sister, Betty, the one who had come to London; after four days I proposed to her and was accepted. The romantic scene was acted out one evening under the imposing arches of the Forth railway bridge (no thought of a road bridge then). My fiancée gave the finishing touch to the romantic situation by a nice old-fashioned Victorian swoon; which left me dithering and helpless. Luckily, one of her girl friends had come with us for the drive; she had withdrawn tactfully to a short distance before the goings on and was quickly to hand, laughingly helped to restore matters. Looking back at this most important event in our lives, we are still amazed that our respective relations accepted the whirlwind courting and outcome without initial opposition for what must have been to them a rash unthinking gesture. But these things do work out at times.

I took my fiancée in the old Morris car, from Edinburgh to Geneva, to meet my mother and sister. By then funds were short and we could only afford one night at an Hotel on the Continent. The result was a long journey of six hundred miles on the last lap home. I fell asleep at the wheel (my girl did not drive) the car landed in a ditch and I had to walk a mile to find help. At first, the men in the cafe were reluctant to interrupt their drinking but when I mentioned my damsel in distress, they, with true gallic gallantry, rose to a man. Even so, the car was unmovable without more help and a horse was produced in due course and some planks were brought from a newly dug grave in the nearby cemetry. With this additional help, we were once again road-worthy. After drinks all round and my last French francs in other pockets, we completed the final stretch of the journey.

To complete the story, I returned to Burma at the end of March 1934, my fiancée followed six months later and we were married in the same little corrugated iron church built by the Royal Engineers in the Rangoon Cantonments in the last century, as my parents had been thirty years earlier.

18
The Tiger Hunt

I had no ambitions to become a big-game trophy hunter. I believe wild animals are at their best in their natural surroundings. At the very least, they should now be left alive since many species are threatened with extinction by the ever decreasing amenities in their usual habitats. Myitkyina district was known to contain a sizeable number of tigers in my day. Even during my short sojourn there, I was invited to participate in a tiger shoot, but I declined the offer without regret.

One day in the office my orderly announced the arrival of a village headman on urgent business. When he was shown in, full of agitation and short of breath, it took me some time to unravel the story. He explained that he had first called at the Deputy Commissioner's office and, in his absence, had been referred to me. The gist of his story was that a tiger had killed a cow during the previous night, on the edge of the jungle near his village and had left the partially eaten carcass, presumably with the intention of returning for a further feed. The villagers were naturally perturbed at the prospect of a dangerous beast establishing a hunting ground around them which would sooner or later lead to the loss of more domestic animals or even a human being. I was ignorant of tigers' habits but the supposition seemed reasonable; so I took my visitor round to the Deputy Conservator's office, John Flint, who was an experienced big-game hunter like most of his colleagues in the Forest Service. He however had departed on tour that very morning. As time was getting short, I made up my mind, reluctantly, to deal with the problem myself.

The railway from Myitkyina ran through some dense jungle, some miles south of the town and the headman's village was about five miles west of the line. I reckoned, by using a railway inspection trolley that it should take me about three hours to reach the scene, arriving in the early afternoon, in time to make arrangements for the night's vigil. The station master provided the trolley without delay and we departed for the adventure. I had my Kachin orderly with me and had collected one of my Sub-Inspectors who had hunted big-game, although not tigers. Both seemed a good deal keener about the expedition than I was, even the headman had lost his anxiety. These railway trolleys, except for the very few motorised ones, were pushed by two men, skilfully running, side by side, on the two steel lines. Thus they could keep up a surprisingly good speed, even with occasional bouts of walking to recover their breath. We reached our dropping-off point within the hour; the march to the village took a little longer and we lost no time in visiting the site of the 'kill' nearby.

The tiger's victim turned out to be a rather skinny cow; the tiger had started to feed from the hind quarters. There were several trees nearby and I left it to the headman and Sub-Inspector to choose a suitable one on which to build a 'machan', a sort of small platform resting across a fork of branches. The villagers completed the construction quickly, which to my critical eye seemed not nearly high enough, but everyone around assured me that no tiger would try to jump or climb that high. Although my apprehensions were not really allayed, I felt that I had to preserve some dignity by remaining silent. Work completed, we all returned to the village for a meal. The headman's wife cooked us a good curry and I redeemed some standing by eating mine with my fingers with nearly the same dexterity as everyone else sitting nearby (Burmese custom made it usually impossible to persuade a village to eat at the same time and in the same place as a visiting official; this segregation extended also to junior functionaries entertaining their seniors).

The headman insisted on being one of the hunting party when we returned to the kill, presumably to make certain that we were equal to the job. By the time the four of us had settled down, it was getting dark. The headman and my orderly had to make themselves as comfortable as they could on separate branches, as the small platform was only just sufficiently wide to accommodate two people. I noticed that these two, rather tactlessly, selected branches at a noticeably higher level to us. I had equipped myself with a long electric torch, having been told sometime that it was better to tie a torch to the rifle barrel than to hold it separately. I now tested the alignment of the light beam with the barrel on the probable line of aim. We then settled down as best we could for the long wait.

At first, my companions exchanged a few whispered desultory remarks; I was too apprehensive about my competence, for the forthcoming show of markmanship, to talk. I had spent other nights in the jungle but never in such uncomfortable conditions. Most of the numerous jungle noises were unfamiliar to me but identified by my policeman. The monkeys seemed to have the preponderance of the night sounds. Time dragged on slowly and my companions fell silent. We began to be plagued by hordes of mosquitoes of a particularly vicious and bloodthirsty species. I had taken the precaution to smear citronella oil liberally over my face, neck and arms but the unction seemed to have little repellent effect and I was soon covered in lumps of mosquito bites. After what seemed hours of waiting, all jungle sounds suddenly ceased. I had been told or had read that this first silence usually heralded the approach of the beast of prey. The contrasting quietness with the previous cacophony of noise seemed to last a long time but was probably only of short duration. Again, without any warning, a frantic outburst of monkey chatter rent the air, to be followed by another period of absolute silence. This time I heard after a while a sort of low coughing sound which seemed to come nearer and nearer in a sort of semi-circle. My policeman whispered in my ear the one word 'kya' (tiger). Although by now excitement and fear, in equal proportions, had gripped me, I and the others managed to remain quiet. I remember even now how amazed I had been that such a great, powerful animal had managed to approach us who were on the alert, without disturbing the undergrowth. There had been no snapping of twigs or rustling of grass, only the low coughing.

Again time stood still, until the sudden sound of a bone cracking rent the air; the tiger had begun to feed. This was the moment of truth for me. I slowly raised the rifle to my shoulder, finger on the trigger, barrel aimed in what I fervently hoped was the right direction for the target and with the thumb of the other hand gripping the barrel, pushed the switch on the torch. Nothing could have been better from the hunter's point of view; the beam of light shone directly into the upturned face of the tiger, crouching over the cow's body. His head looked gigantic in the foresight of my rifle and he did not seem to be more than inches off the barrel. I suppose my reflexes were in better shape than my thoughts because I pressed the trigger at once and the torch went out! The sound of the shot and the tiger's roar was immediately followed by silence. I had the sense to reload but once more nothing but silence. Again I waited as patiently as I could for some indication of the tiger's whereabouts but only quiet prevailed. I decided eventually to find out why the torch had gone out at the critical moment. I fiddled with the switch to discover that, in my excited haste, I had only half pushed the switch into the 'on' position from which it had slipped back when the bullet was fired. I cautiously shone the torch on to the carcass, which seemed to be lying slightly differently; the others followed my example and shone their torches all around. There was no obvious trace of any disturbance in the undergrowth to indicate in which direction the tiger had fled.

I remembered being told that a wounded tiger would frequently lie up in the vicinity of its kill to deal with any intruder rash enough to challenge his ownership. I decided that discretion was the soundest policy and that we should remain in our tree until dawn gave us more visibility. The decision was received with evident approval by the others. At first light we climbed down and cautiously searched around in the immediate vicinity, after I had fired some shots in the air. I had no idea whether I had done a wise or a foolish thing but, if commonsense was also a tiger's attribute, warning shots seemed a reasonable precaution. In any case, I had no other ideas for driving an animal out of hiding and the noise of firing certainly inspired more confidence in us to search for signs on leaves and on the ground. My Sub-Inspector had been examining the carcass more closely and suddenly gave a shout which brought me to his side. He pointed to what was obviously a neat bullet hole in the head of the dead cow! The audience were too polite to laugh aloud but relieved grins appeared on all faces.

A great load slipped from my mind. Since the tiger's roar, after the first shot, I had become more and more worried about the prospect of following up a wounded wild beast. It was an unwritten rule that any dangerous animal, which had been wounded, had to be followed up and killed. I knew that I had neither the skill nor the knowledge to track a cunning jungle beast successfully, without the help of an experienced big game hunter and I had no idea how knowledgeable my policeman was in this respect. I had made up my mind that if the tiger had been wounded and had managed to get away, my best course was to send urgently for the Forest Officer who was touring somewhere in the area, whilst I tried to pick up the trail with the help of the villagers. I also fervently hoped that the expert reinforcement would arrive in time to despatch the wounded beast. Now, at least, there was no wounded tiger in the vicinity but the problem, of further forays by him, remained.

I had to undergo a good deal of teasing when I returned to Myitkyina, having sent word to the Forest Officer asking him to keep a look out and, if possible, visit the scene of the kill himself. He returned a few days after me, having sat over the kill two days after me. The tiger did not return and was not seen again in the area, so perhaps my tactics of shooting in the air did some good. So ended my one and only chance to acquire a tiger floor rug for the front of my fireplace in my retirement cottage.

Author and wife, just married, 1934

19

Rangoon – Western Division

On my return from leave, I was surprised to find that I had been appointed to the Rangoon City Police. I received the news with mixed feelings. Foremost, was the immediate thought that the transfer meant an end to touring around the countryside, which was the main and best part of district work. Secondly, I wondered how my fiancee would react to the news. I had told her about life away from the flesh-pots and amenities of the western world, which had more than adequate compensations (as painted by me) to make up for these losses. On the other side of the coin was the fact that, from a professional angle, a spell of service at the hub of Government was considered an indication of the officer's competence for selective appointments later on. At least, that is what I was told when I voiced my doubts about exchanging district for city life.

Unlike the district forces, the Rangoon Police was not under the general control of the Inspector-General of Police, Burma. The force was an independent one under its own Commissioner of Police. The senior officers, including the Commissioner, were seconded for varying periods, from the Indian Police, Burma section. All other ranks, including three out of the six Divisional Superintendents, were recruited directly into the city force on a permanent basis. Officers and men (including seconded officers) wore a different uniform; blue tunics instead of the district khaki. The majority of Inspectors and Sub-Inspectors were Burmese and Karen, with some Indians and Chinese. The other ranks were made up of large contingents of Burmese, Sikhs, Punjabi Hindus and Mussulmans, Garhwalis and Gurkhas; there was also a squad of 'European Sergeants' who in my time contained a majority of Eurasians. This mixture of races was a necessity to deal with the multi-national population of a large sea port.

The force was divided into four geographical divisions, another for the Motor Vehicles Department and one for the Hackney Carriage and Rickshaw Department. The last was a very necessary administrative measure to control the hundreds of 'gharry-wallahs' (horsedrawn carriage drivers) and thousands of Indian or Chinese rickshaw pullers. Of the four divisions, Western, Central, Eastern and River, only the last ranked as a District Superintendent's appointment, the others, including the two purely administrative divisions, were in charge of Assistant or Deputy Superintendents. The Assistant Commissioner was in direct control of the

Motor Vehicle and Hackney Carriage divisions, all traffic police and internal security measures, including all police protection for the Governor and any other important officials, as the situation required at any one time. The Deputy Commissioner was responsible for all crime investigation work, political intelligence and related matters. Both these officers worked closely together on many overlapping responsibilities and had daily consultations with the Commissioner. The latter had the authority to call out 'the Military in aide of Civil Power' in an emergency; a situation which arose more than once during my time with the force.

I have included this factual section on the organisation of the Rangoon Police because I spent an unexpectedly long time on secondment to the force. I held three divisional appointments in succession, followed by the post of Assistant Commissioner before moving on to completely new work.

*   *   *

Crime was less prevalent in this division than in any of the other three but there were a number of important sites in the areas to watch and to safeguard. Foremost, for a potential trouble centre, was the University campus with its halls of residence. Student unrest had become a favourite gambit for the more militant political agitators. The Shwe Dagon Pagoda's extensive precincts, around the premier religious shrine in the country, were favourite meeting grounds for delivering inflammatory speeches on occasions and were also used as hiding places for absconding criminals. Both these extensive sites required constant surveillance. Government House and the grounds around with numerous ancillary buildings, were another area requiring permanent Police protection.

In addition to these possible vexatious spots, the Military Cantonments and the Civil Lines - the latter housing all the senior Government officials stationed in Rangoon, a hundred or more - were within the divisional boundary. Most of the wealthier business and commercial communities lived in the pleasant residential areas in the jurisdiction. Burmans and Karens lived in the sectors along the Rangoon river bank. Few Indians lived, but many worked, in the western part of the town.

I took some time to settle down in my urban surroundings. I missed my touring days and the variety of district work, much of it outside the scope of normal police duties. In Rangoon, the work was akin to that performed in any large city. The only main difference was the need to learn about, and then deal with, a much greater variety of peoples and customs. At first, I also felt that I had lost some independence, since my superiors were now on my door-step, so to speak. I soon found that I was still expected to use my judgment freely and that interference from above was as limited as it had been in the districts.

I did wonder how my fiancée, who was arriving in a few months, would react to this kind of city life, after I had indoctrinated her to all the delights of rural life, which would take her back to the happy days of her childhood in the country. I had painted enticing pictures of a small civil station with people living in harmony with each other, glossing over the trials and tribulations of possible social in-fighting by certain wives who held decided views on the seniority of their husbands' official position. Above all, I plugged hard the delights of the leisurely and comfortable touring conditions. Instead of all this, she would now have to start her new life in a town, which compared to her Edinburgh, would seem strange, not only in the anticipated changes, in moving from the West to the East, but also in the quaint outdated social customs still imposed on the urban European community, mainly by the wives of superior civil and military officers, revelling in the unexpected social powers, conferred by the hallowed and all-prevailing seniority caste system. On the other hand, she would start her new life with amenities still unavailable in most district headquarters: running water in bathrooms, modern toilet (in some houses, not our first one), electric fans instead of the sluggish hand (or toe) pulled punkhas (air-conditioning was still unknown), refrigerators and some large European stores. All these assets might help her to feel less home-sick in her first months of sojourn. I need not have worried; right from the start she became highly adaptable and took an immediate liking in exploring unusual sights in the city. My Karen police driver was largely instrumental in providing local information and acting as her guide when she discovered his intimate knowledge of the town and its people.

Every official who has served overseas must have dealt with countless written petitions, presented to him in person by members of the public or by subordinates in his office or even at his home. These letters were usually written by professional petition writers. English was the official language of the courts and these scribes congregated in numbers around every law courts' building in the country. The contents were couched in the most flowery language, designed primarily to win over the recipient in the most outrageous terms of flattery, before reaching the hub of the matter. Since most of the population was ignorant of English, the professionals fulfilled an essential need and most of them were kept busy, as the indigenous population, particularly the Indians, rich or poor, resorted freely to litigation, even in minor matters.

A favourite opening gambit in these elaborate compositions was the phrase:- "I pray to God, whom your Honour resembles so much" then followed by an enumeration of the recipient's qualities and qualifications, imaginary more often than real, before approaching the real purpose of the letter. Sometimes, however, the petitions were laudably brief, either because the petitioner could not afford the professional's fee and had to make do with the efforts of a relative or friend, with limited knowledge of English, or he even wrote the letter himself. On one of my earliest regular rounds of Police stations, I received the shortest petition in my whole career. During the period set aside for interviews with subordinates on personal business, an Indian constable marched in, saluted smartly and without a word handed me a sheet of paper, which contained the following succinct message:-

"Honoured Sir,
Police Constable No. ..., is fuking (sic)
my wife and I want your Honour to stop it.

Your Honour's loyal and obedient servant
P.C. No. ..."

Most reported crime was of a petty nature. Sneak thieves were numerous; attracted by the open houses occupied by Europeans who, in contrast to other races, hardly ever bothered to close windows and doors, day or night. From time to time a murder would be notified, more often than not caused by someone who had lost control of his, or even her, temper, an all too common trait amongst the Burmese. An outbreak of communal tension in a locality was an ever present possibility. These sorts of local troubles, usually provoked by some trivial irritation, were kept from spreading by prompt Police intervention to separate the parties and arrest the ring leaders. But after I had moved from the Western Division, I experienced some of the worst communal riots ever witnessed in Rangoon.

I played a great deal of tennis in those days, sometimes at one of the clubs and sometimes on private hard courts at the houses of my more opulent friends. I had one fairly regular fixture at the house of the Medical Superintendent in charge of the large Mental Asylum. The ball boys were always inmates of the place and they seemed to enjoy the opportunity of doing something new. Our host told me that he had to be careful to allocate the tennis court jobs in strict rotation, since there were always more volunteers than places. One young Burmese patient appeared regularly when his turn came round; he had been well educated and spoke quite fluent English. The Superintendent told me that he had seemed set on a promising career in one of the large commercial concerns, when he began to show signs of eccentricity. He gradually became worse and the climax was reached when he seriously assulted another youth in a fit of rage and jealousy. He was declared mentally disturbed and was confined to the Asylum for a period. He was always cheerful and quick-footed on court. I got to know him sufficiently well to have a chat before and after a game. He liked the opportunity to air his knowledge of English.

One day, I received a message from the Police Station near the Asylum that a murder had been reported from there. Before I left my bungalow for the scene of crime, the telephone rang again. The speaker was my tennis friend, to say that the murderer was the nice Burmese ball boy. On arrival, I was told that the fatal assult had taken place in full view of other inmates and warders, in an open yard. The victim was another young Burman; apparently the two had become friends and were often seen together. For no apparent reason the culprit had suddenly stabbed his companion in the chest, as they were walking together. The wounded man had been taken to the infirmary where he had died soon after. The murderer had made no effort to resist apprehension and had refused to say anything. The accused would not speak to me at all, in spite of my repeated endeavours to engage him in small talk unconnected with the crime. He remained largely silent during the whole of the subsequent investigation, making no effort to justify or explain his sudden violent attack on an apparently innocent man. The verdict was predictable, he was found guilty but insane and remanded back to the Asylum. A sad but not uncommon case in Burma. The Superintendent of the Asylum, like his colleagues in charge of Jails, employed inmates as domestic and outdoor staff. One of my acquaintances had been Commissioner of the Andaman Islands, where the Government of Burma maintained a high security prison for dangerous criminals. His large establishment was entirely staffed by occupants of the penitentiary; he told me that the head servant, a Burman who had been convicted of a double murder and had been sentenced to death, later commuted to life imprisonment, was the best servant he had ever employed. He and his wife were quite happy to leave the Nanny and the children in the house alone with the murderer; I found that this attitude of trust was common amongst other employers of prison labour.

Another case, in which I was an involuntary participant, occurred one evening when I was giving a small dinner party. The station officer, from the Police Station in the Burmese quarter near the river foreshore, rang up in the midst of the meal. He reported having difficulty in apprehending a lunatic who had run amuck. He wanted to know if he could use his revolver to wound the man as a last resort. I told him to do nothing serious as long as he could contain the situation and that I was on my way to the scene. I left my guests to fend for themselves and drove off, still in my dinner jacket. Alighting from the car at the edge of a large crowd which had assembled to watch the fun, my appearance caused quite a stir. In those more formal days, dressing for dinner meant a stiff-fronted shirt with stand-up collar, both in immaculate white, patent leather black shoes and, usually, a black silk cummerbund instead of the dinner jacket's waistcoat. I was not quite sure whether the crowd's silent reception was one of awe or suppressed amusement. The Burmese are a naturally polite people and any open expression of mockery or derision towards a stranger is considered bad manners, unless meant as a deliberate insult.

The crowd had formed a rough wide circle around the prancing figure of the madman. I squeezed slowly through the throng, and in my progress, received free advice and information from the excited onlookers. I reached the inside edge of the crowd, where I was joined by the station officer and two constables. Apparently the chief actor was known for his periodical tantrums, in some of which he had tried to attack unwary onlookers. The officer had brought some other men who were keeping the crowd at a distance from the madman. The latter, I now saw, was holding a long hunting 'dah', which looked sharpened as it glinted in the reflections of the street lights. He was shouting unintelligible words at the top of his voice and, at the same time, making mock runs in different directions, scattering those nearest to his onslaughts. He had not noticed my arrival and when I addressed him he had his back to me. He turned round and saw me for the first time in all my glory; probably never having seen a dinner jacket in his life. Abruptly his shouting and prancing stopped, he glared at this wonderful and weird apparition with popping eyes. I seized the opportunity, shouted to the others to close in, shot forward, bumped into the madman, knocked him over with my weight and fell on top of him with the other three piling on my back. The lunatic dropped his dah as he fell over, which I had the sense to grab before he could recover the weapon. The poor chap must have felt badly crushed by the heap of humanity on top of him; I was completely winded for a moment. After some confused seconds, we sorted ourselves out and, to my relief, the collision had sobered up the culprit; he answered me quietly when I told him to keep still and that nothing more was going to happen to him.

My dinner suit was in a sorry state as we had fallen on to a busy part of the river bank. The area was covered in garbage of all kind, dropped during the loading and unloading of the countless small craft which plied busily between the riverine villages and the Rangoon foreshore with local produce. Jacket and trousers were smeared in streaks of dirt and one sleeve of the former had a long gash; probably caused when I was grasping for the dah during the struggle. Next morning, I was recounting the incident in the office and the Deputy Commissioner's dry comment was:- "What a pity you were not wearing your full-dress uniform, you could then have claimed compensation for damages to an obligatory piece of expensive uniform ruined in the course of duty".

As already mentioned, Government House was in my jurisdiction. This responsibility brought me into frequent contact with His Excellency's staff. I would thus pick up some amusing gossip from one or the other of them; mainly about incidents which occurred during some social function. The following three apocryphal stories refer to a Governor, Sir Harcourt Butler, who had departed before my arrival but they are, I think, amongst the best I heard. This particular Governor was one of the outstanding administrators, produced by the defunct Indian Civil Service, to reach the rank of a Provincial Governor in British India. He also, more unusually, did not shed his sense of fun when he reached his exalted position.

The first story refers to his efforts in trying to raise money to establish the University of Rangoon. In his keenness for the project, he conceived the unorthodox idea of suspending the Burma Gambling Act for six months and to levy a 10% contribution towards the University Building Fund, from all winnings! At that time Burma was still a province of India and only the Viceroy had the power to suspend local laws for special reasons. The Governor's enthusiasm for the idea was not dampened by the daunting prospect of persuading a devout High Church Viceroy, Lord Irwin, to encourage wholesale gambling, albeit for a worthy cause. In fact, the Governor decided to press his case in person. In due course, he returned from New Delhi without having achieved his purpose. He related the whole story at his next large dinner party at Government House, more or less in these words:-

After I had explained the reasons for my unusual request, the Viceroy was silent for a moment and then said, "You have asked me to make a very difficult decision, Sir, I shall have to ask you to excuse me for a while so that I can pray for divine guidance." (This particular Viceroy had set up a small private chapel in Viceregal House for his own personal use.) He then withdrew, leaving me to sip his excellent whisky. After a while the Viceroy returned, sat down, looked at me sorrowfully and said, "I am sorry Sir, I prayed to the Lord for guidance and the Lord said 'No'." I stood up, bowed without saying a word and withdrew from the Presence; after all, who was I, a mere Governor, to argue with the Almighty.

In spite of this initial setback, our energetic Governor did eventually collect the necessary funds to carry out his project.

The second and third stories received their inspiration from the Governor's well-known Rabelaisian sense of humour. This time the Bishop of Rangoon was the butt of the story; again alleged to have been related at a Government House dinner party. The Bishop was said to have rung up, requesting an urgent appointment with the Governor. On arrival he appeared ill at ease and hesitant to mention the purpose of his visit. The narrator in his own words said, "Come along Bishop, cough it up". "Well sir", said the latter, "are you aware that a house of ill repute has been opened near the gates of Government House?" "Yes", I replied, "but what has that got to do with me?" "Well", came the embarrassed reply, "it is also said that Your Excellency is the chief customer"!

The third story was related to me by a senior Civil Servant, who had known the Governor quite well, having served on the executive meetings at Government House, in his capacity as head of one of the departments in the Secretariat. A suggestion had been made to recruit female typists. The then Chief Secretary had thought the proposal sufficiently revolutionary to merit the Governor's opinion. In due course, the file containing the suggestion was returned from Government House. The great man's views were contained in one brief sentence:- "I have no objection to the proposal, provided rule 50 (say) of the Secretariat code is strictly observed". With some difficulty a copy of this little used manual was unearthed; rule 50 read, 'Typewriters must not be screwed on office tables'!

The Burmese New Year occurs in April, one of the hottest months of the year. Very sensibly, water plays a great part in the celebrations. After the early morning religious observances at the pagoda, the fun of the day starts. It is a great time for old and young to let down their hair by squirting, even dousing, water indiscriminately on each other with gusto. In Rangoon, where the water supply was pumped around the city in modern style, hose pipes effectively implemented the more traditional methods of splashing water from containers. District officials, including non-Buddhists, would ceremoniously sit in some prominent spot and allow themselves to be thoroughly soaked by well-wishers. During my time, this rather charming acknowledgement of a native custom, by an expatriate official, began to disappear. The throwing of water upon a European began to be abused by people who wished to air their immature political gestures. The throwing of water changed from a gesture of fun and goodwill into an abusive one accompanied by derogatory remarks. But in my earlier days, the old custom was still prevalent and I received many a soaking on the appropriate day in my respective districts but never quite as abundantly as in Rangoon.

The town's non-Buddhist inhabitants were not all inclined to accept being splashed with water and the Police had to be on the look-out for communal tensions developing as a result. I toured around my division in my Ford tourer car with the hood down, watching the fun and receiving the occasional stream of water from a hose or bicycle pump. By the time I reached the last Police Station my driver and I were more than damp. I went inside to have a word with the staff and to wish them a happy New Year. One of my two Inspectors happened to be there, also on his rounds, with his small son standing beside him. The boy smiled at me and ran outside. After a few minutes I followed, stepped into the back of my car and sat down. In the next moment I was deluged from head to the small of my back by a bucket of water, poured over me from behind. Turning round I just saw the small figure of the Inspector's son disappear round the building. I shot out of the car, chased after him and caught him before he could run inside. I brought him back to the car, laughing and struggling half-heartedly, where my driver, with a keen sense of anticipation, was standing alongside the car holding a fair-sized jug of water which I proceeded to pour on my captive's head, at the same time wishing him a happy New Year. My driver later told me that the boy had climbed on the back bumper of the car, waited concealed until I had sat down and then poured the water over my head. The back seat of the car took longer to dry out than I did.

20
Rangoon – Central Division

Quite unexpectedly I was abruptly transferred at the beginning of July 1934 to another division, the central area of the town, after only three months in this pleasant and not too onerous job. My former chief and mentor from Mandalay district had been appointed Deputy Commissioner of Police a month or so after I had taken over the Western division. His main task in this appointment was the supervision of all crime investigation work in the city. Within a short time of his arrival, he unearthed an extensive netwok of bribery and corruption within the force, the core of which was amongst the personnel in the Central Division. At the end of a long and meticulous inquiry, which ended in several criminal prosecutions and more dismissals, a considerable number of transfers took place, chiefly in the Central Division. One of the results was the appointment of a new Superintendent, myself.

The Division was the smallest in area but the densest in population, the richest in wealth and the biggest for crime. All large commercial enterprises, foreign and indigenous, had their main business premises in the area. This concentrated turnover of goods and money attracted all the slick entrepreneurs and outright criminals of the clever and sophisticated sort. A policeman was exposed to more temptations here than in any other police jurisdiction in the whole of Burma. The largest section of its population was Indian, followed closely by the Chinese, living in their own well-defined 'China Town' block. For some years, previous Superintendents of Police had been Indians and I was the first European in the job for some time. My official quarters were a modern brick house, the first abode for me with running water and modern toilets. The house was situated in the midst of a congested Indian quarter, quite unlike the site of my old bungalow near the Cantonments and Civil Lines. The lack of privacy and the increase in neighbourly noises was quite startling to say the least. The house itself was larger than my previous home but the garden was smaller, which was just as well since my predecessor had obviously shown no interest in it. The only limited privacy was a sad looking clump of plantain trees in one corner with a weed-covered lawn as the only other ornament. However, the neglected garden was not the drawback it might have been elsewhere, since the noisy and close neighbourhood precluded any prospect of relaxation out-of-doors. All my Indian neighbours seemed to thrive on noise, the more the better; even indoors, it took me some time to adjust to this constant interference of sound and to the closeness of the other houses. What I missed most was the privacy I had enjoyed in my previous bungalows with their spacious compounds in amongst similar official quarters. Soon after my arrival, I was in my sitting-room reading and sipping my evening drink. The french doors and the windows were wide open to catch whatever slight breeze might spring up at that time of the day. Suddenly an Indian rickshaw puller staggered into the room and fell headlong on to the settee. He was near naked with just a loin cloth round his middle and dead drunk. My scandalised Burmese servant and I had quite a job to revive him sufficiently to set him on his way.

I began to wonder how my future wife, now due within weeks, would take to these new surroundings. I was concerned about the incessant noise enveloping the place, the lack of privacy and of congenial neighbours. I had been transferred after she had sailed from Liverpool and her mental impressions of what to expect were still based on my descriptions of my previous abode. I had painted in words as glowing a picture as I could about the romance of living near a historical military Cantonment within sight of the world famous Shwe Dagon Pagoda. I became sufficiently worried to consider the possibility of asking for a transfer to escape my uncongenial surroundings. All senior Police officers in Rangoon, unlike their district counterparts who paid rent, lived free in the houses specially allocated by Government and there was no way in which I could have wangled another residence in the Civil Lines. Before I had to make my decision, fate took a kindly hand. My successor in the Western Division was an Anglo-Burman with a large family. One day when I was mentioning my dilemma to him in idle conversation, he replied, to my astonishment, that he had been thinking of asking me to swap houses with him since he found the bungalow too small for his requirements. I was delighted with the proposition and we both approached the Commissioner for permission to exchange homes. Although my old place was not strictly within my new division, it was near enough for me to reach the area in minutes by car. The Commissioner kindly agreed to stretch a point and we exchanged to our mutual satisfaction. So all was well in the end; in due course I carried my bride over the threshold of the home which I had so enthusiastically described to her in my letters.

My work load had increased a great deal. In addition there were many new appointees at nearly all the five Police stations in the Division, including two new Circle Inspectors (the next senior in rank). All these officers had to catch up as quickly as they could on the geography and feel of their respective charges, whilst coping with all the day-to-day duties. I for one had never been busier; I was on the move all day between my office and the Police stations and many evenings were interrupted by one incident or another. In no time at all the great day of my bride's arrival dawned. I went downstream in a Police launch to meet the ship and managed to board her even before the Customs officers. Quite a few passengers leant over the rails to see who the important official could be, boarding the ship first; their disappointment at seeing an unknown young man bound up the ship's ladder did not detract from my joy in holding my girl in my arms after so many months of separation. We were married a few days later from the Commissioner's imposing residence and then lived happily ever after.

The Police had to investigate a large number of fraud cases in which considerable sums were involved. In one of the biggest of these a British Bank was the victim. Rice was then exported in huge quantities through the port of Rangoon. The very large European shippers of rice did their own buying in the districts but many smaller exporters bought theirs through brokers, who toured the districts at the end of the harvest to purchase the commodity at the cheapest price. The earlier they managed to be on the spot, the better their chances of an advantageous deal. The Burmese growers were more often than not in debt to their absentee landlords, the ubiquitous Chettyar money-lenders from Madras. Consequently, the former were always in need of ready cash and therefore tempted to accept the first offers that came their way. The brokers stored their purchases to await the expected upturn in price. The better known ones could increase the profitableness of their business by borrowing money to make additional purchases offering the quantities already purchased as guarantee, All the banks in Rangoon had clients of this kind and loans of considerable size were commonplace. The banks employed their own inspectors to verify the stocks offered as securities.

The Bank involved in the case mentioned here, had lent an exceptionally large sum to one of the best known Chinese brokers in town. Their inspector, a Burman, had made his usual visit to the godowns (sheds) where the rice, offered as security, had been stored and had reported favourably; all seemed well. Some time later the Bank's employee failed to turn up for work. The Bank became suspicious and sent another employee to check on the stored rice. When the godowns were opened everything seemed in order at first glance; huge quantities of sacks of rice were piled high in tidy large rectangles. The suspicious investigator was not content with this cursory inspection; he ordered the sacks to be shifted. The labourers moving the rice then discovered that each rectangle was in fact a hollow mound with just one outer layer of bags on each side and on top, held in place by planks of wood. The well-known Chinese broker had in the meantime escaped to another land with the lion's share of the Bank's money, to live comfortably on his ill-gotten gains and perhaps even try to repeat his successful coup elsewhere. The Burmese bank employee was eventually traced and sent for trial and sentenced to imprisonment but not before he had managed to gamble away his share of the loot. The Bank lost many thousands of pounds, the largest loss suffered by them in Burma.

The Burmese like the Chinese are inveterate gamblers. The Burma Gambling Act was introduced to limit, as much as possible, the uncontrolled spreading of gambling dens and the suspect games of chance which only favoured the promoters. China Town boasted the largest concentration of gambling clubs in the country. Under the act, a Superintendent of Police had the powers of a first class magistrate and could issue warrants to raid places where gambling was suspected. In the course of my duties, I issued a number of such warrants and also participated in several raids myself, if they appeared to be more important than the usual run-of-the-mill establishments. On several occasions we caught leading members of the public, much to their embarrassment. Both the Burmese and the Chinese were usually quite reckless in their gambling habits, indulging in high stakes, which most of them could ill afford. In a tense game, the gambler would often be virtually ruined in one sitting. Both races were stoic and resilient when suffering large losses, often bouncing back to material wealth, only to lose it all again. Nevertheless, this widespread love of gambling led to a lot of heartbreak and misery in many families.

A Police raid in China Town always followed a set pattern. All gambling dens were strategically sited, to foil easy access and thus give the promoters time to dispose of the tell-tale material evidence, before the Police broke in. The gambling place would invariably be situated above ground level; the front access would be up a straight flight of stairs, with a stout wooden trap door, often covered with sheet metal, across the top of the steps. The escape route at the back would have a similar lay-out but since the Police invariably covered the rear of any premises to be raided, escape was hardly ever attempted.

Besides, the back of most gambling premises faced what was referred to as the 'Back Drainage Spaces'. These were the narrow areas between tenement houses, whose fronts were on main or side streets. Rangoon did not enjoy a modern underground drainage system and in the congested central parts of the city, all waste, including human, was poured into a wide deep drain at the rear of the buildings. The Corporation had the duty to cleanse regularly these potential sources of epidemics and, on the whole, did a good job with powerful jets of water. Nevertheless, much of the filth did not always fall into the drains and remained lying around for a while until a subsequent cleansing would perhaps remove it. As a result, the Back Drainage areas were infested with large ferocious rats, the size of cats, which did not hesitate to attack when cornered. None of us liked to venture into these unsavoury areas at night, when innumerable angry eyes glared back in the light of our torches. Once or twice, some unfortunate person was savagely bitten by a large rat and had to receive the painful injection against plague.

As soon as the look-outs raised the alarm, down would come the trap doors, front and back; this manoeuvre inevitably held up the Police, who had to break down the doors with axes. On entering the room, the raiding party would be met by a scene of quiet domesticity, men and women (also great gamblers) would be sitting around quietly talking or playing an innocent game of cards, some of the women even doing a bit of needle work. There would be no sign of any money, gambling counters or chips. The long search for evidence would then begin. In earlier raids, the lavatory cistern was a favoured place of concealment until it became too commonplace. Soon more and more sophisticated hiding places were thought up. Hollowed-out spaces in walls and under floors, drainpipes, false bottoms in drawers and many other unusual places were used to hide the implements of gambling. In the end, the Police became expert in overcoming the ingenuity displayed in methods of concealment.

From the Police point of view it was important to find the material evidence to support the information on which the raid had been based. I always admired the unemotional way in which the promoters and the gamblers greeted the successful discovery of the material evidence, after a long and thorough search. Seldom did anyone abandon the look of injured innocence assumed by the crowd when the Police ultimately managed to break in. The self-control of the promoters was really remarkable since they had the most to lose in a successful raid. I never saw one betray his true feelings by so much as a bat of an eyelid. Now that my Police career is long over, I confess to having had a feeling of sympathy for the gamblers caught in raids but not for the promoters; the latter were the real culprits, the former the victims of the misery caused by reckless gambling.

I suppose that the Gambling Act did some good in keeping a check on bad activities but, by and large, it failed to stop widespread gambling and was a ready-made source of bribery for the Police. On a larger scale, a rich promoter would try, sometimes with success, to come to an understanding with a Station officer. The arrangement would consist of an agreement between the promoter and the Police station officer, whereby the latter would only raid selected premises at times stipulated by the promoters. The arranged raids were quite genuine in substance but did the least financial damage to the organisers. So, the local police record, on the prevention of gambling, remained satisfactory. In fact, police officers who did not succumb to this sort of corruption, often had fewer successful raids and prosecutions to their credit. The comparative ease whereby dishonesty could thus be hidden, made it difficult to gather sufficient facts to ensure the eventual punishment of dishonest policemen. Quite often, even when sufficient evidence had been collected to start departmental or even criminal proceedings against a culprit, the case would collapse because witnesses went back on their statements. There was always money available to defeat the ends of justice, particularily in the lucrative gambling trade.

Another widespread offence was the illicit smoking of opium, a practice which had not yet spread worldwide. In this respect China Town again led the way, with more opium dens to the acre than any other part of the town, or of the country for that matter. The number of registered opium smokers was large; they were allowed to purchase stipulated quantities of the drug from licensed opium shops, controlled by the Excise department. These addicts obtained permits of purchase on the production of medical evidence that the consumption of a stipulated quantity was essential for the smoker's unavoidable needs. One idea behind the scheme for registered consumers was the hope that, by gradually reducing the authorised quantities, the addict would be cured or at least reduce his intake to less harmful amounts. The other aim was to facilitate the task of suppressing illicit smoking by unlicensed users, thus eventually stamping out the evil.

In practice, the task was impossible. Cultivation of the poppy, from which seed the opium was derived, was widespread although illegal in the remoter parts of the Shan States and in the neighbouring countries, where the growing of poppy plants was tolerated. Smuggling into and through

Burma was on a vast scale. Neither the Excise nor the Police had the necessary manpower to maintain effective counter measures. The dens in Rangoon were numerous, dingy, small and dirty rooms, dotted all over the place but well concentrated in the Chinese quarter. As soon as one place was raided and shut down, another would spring up more or less next door. Prosecutions had little effect on the hardened consumers, even if they were jailed after repeated offences; as soon as they were set free, they would be back on the pipe. Whenever I entered one of these insalubrious dens, I felt more sorrow than anger for the emaciated and decrepit smokers, lying around on filthy couches or floors, invariably looking years older than their real age. Like gambling, this vice caused a great deal of family distress and poverty. On the whole the Indian addicts of drugs stuck to the less harmful 'Ghany', an Indian hemp which could be smoked or chewed. In those days the practice of opium smoking appeared to be largely confined to the Mongolian races. I could never understand how anyone persevered long enough to enjoy the practice. I once tried to smoke a pipe of opium long enough to induce the feeling of well-being which it was supposed to create, but I had to give up after a few puffs feeling quite sick. I suppose that had I persisted in the attempt I might have achieved some evidence of the claims made, but I just could not contemplate any further nauseating experimenting.

The Central Division also gave me a wider than usual insight into the sleezy and seedy side of a large sea port. Brothels, pornography and other titillating activities thrived in this congested area of the town. Although, in theory, all these activities were liable to Police attention, the manpower problem again precluded much effective action, particularly in the attempts to reduce the dangers from venereal diseases. The substantial presence of a constantly changing sea-faring community was a tempting inducement to the trade in prostitution and pornography; much of the latter imported from Europe, despite the vigilance of the Customs Department. There had been some European prostitutes in Rangoon, who had made substantial sums of money whilst they had managed to keep in business but all had been driven away for one reason or another by the time I was in charge of the area which they all favoured. All the different races were represented in this profession, as they were in other ports. Most of the places of assignation were nearly as dingy and as dirty as the opium dens, sometimes deliberately so chosen in order to avoid undue attention from the authorities. As elsewhere, the more opulent prostitutes operated from their own hired premises and catered for a better clientele. In short the general picture, provided by the multitude of venal divertisements, was no different than in any other busy seaport or large town, it was only the degree of sophistication that varied.

Quite early on after my transfer, my telephone rang one night, not an unusual occurrence but the inspector at the other end had a more than usual incident to report. He said that an English woman had run into the Police Station, clad only in her night dress, shouting that her husband had threatened to kill her and that she had run out of their flat; the husband meanwhile had emerged on their balcony, brandishing a revolver from which he had fired two shots into the air, which had attracted the inevitable curious crowd in the street below. He had locked the front door of the flat and had refused to open up when the Police arrived on the scene.

On my arrival at the Police Station, the woman was still in a highly emotional state; someone had given her a uniform great coat to throw over her flimsy garment, and one of the Police wives was sitting with her. As I was leaving the Station to proceed to the flat, the European Sergeant, attached to this Station, came in so I told him to join me. On our way I remembered that I had seen the woman in the ladies' hairdressing department of one of the large British stores, where I had taken my wife shopping a few days previous. I mentioned the fact to the Sergeant and he confirmed that she worked there and was married to a Burma Railways employee. He added the fact that she was only partly English, her father had married a fair Anglo-Indian girl who had, in turn, produced a fair daughter.

A fair sized crowd had gathered in the street, all looking up at the gesticulating figure on the balcony. After squeezing through the assembled people and joining up with the Inspector and his men, I called to the figure on the balcony to keep still, stop shouting and listen to me; all I got in reply was a torrent of abuse, more gesticulating and waving of the revolver. I made signs to the Inspector to keep the man's attention whilst I motioned the Sergeant to follow me surreptitiously into the building. The Inspector was quick to guess my intentions and cleverly kept the man occupied on the balcony by getting members of the crowd to engage him in back-chat. Meanwhile the Sergeant and I mounted the stairs quietly to the first landing; as expected the front door of the flat was still locked.

The Sergeant had followed me from the Western Division, at my request. I had got to know him quite well; he had come to Burma with a Scottish Regiment, had married a local girl and, when his Army service had ended, joined the Rangoon Police. We had been in one or two tight corners together and I had complete confidence in him. We could hear the man still ranting on the balcony; I now realised that his sentences were disjointed and his speech slurred. He was either drunk or drugged. There was a small landing in front of the door. We stepped back and hurled ourselves at the door, which crashed open with greater ease than I had expected. We both fell to the floor inside. The husband on the balcony had, of course, turned round as soon as he had heard the commotion. He sprang back into the room, as we started to scramble to our feet, pointed the fire-arm at me and pulled the trigger. I heard the click as the hammer was released but there was no explosion. My Sergeant, with great presence of mind and courage, had shot forward and had hit the man hard over the head with his truncheon; he went down as if pole-axed. I do not recollect that any special thoughts raced through my mind as I faced the levelled revolver, but I did have a delayed sense of fright immediately afterwards. The Sergeant brought a jug of water and threw it none too gently over the prone figure's face. He came round slowly and, as soon as he saw the uniformed figure standing over him with an empty jug, he let fly a stream of screaming abuse. By then my sense of fear was changing to anger and, I regret to say, I gave the cursing culprit a hefty kick in his backside, pulled him to his feet and told him that if he did not shut up at once, I would order the Sergeant to repeat the dose with the truncheon. That threat brought silence; meanwhile, the Inspector and two of his men had appeared in the flat; I ordered the prisoner to be handcuffed and removed to the Police Station, whilst I picked up the discarded spent cartridge cases. Presumably, the bullets had been fired into the air when he was entertaining his audience from the balcony.

At the station, our prisoner began another shouting match this time with his unfortunate wife, still sitting at a table with her woman companion. I gave him short shrift, told him that we had all had enough of him for one night and that he would be locked up, still in his handcuffs, if he did not behave himself and do what he was told which was to shut up and remain silent until spoken to. He quietened down after I had enumerated in brief what his offences had been, namely threatening his wife with bodily harm, attempting to cause serious injury, perhaps even murder, to a Police officer, causing a disturbance in public and firing shots in a dangerous and reckless manner. I told him to let the Inspector know if he wished to see a solicitor in the morning. The seriousness of his position sank in at last and he went into a cell without further trouble. The wife returned to the flat with the policeman's wife and I went home, to a rather anxious wife, who despite the late hour was wide awake awaiting my return.

My first experience of serious communal trouble took place without prior warning. I cannot recollect the original cause which sparked off the tension but, in no time false rumours were spread that the Muslims had desecrated one of the Hindu temples by slaughtering a cow in front of it and that the latter had reciprocated by throwing a dead pig into a Muslim mosque. Within an hour several attacks had occurred in the streets, two being fatal.

This rioting was confined to the Indian quarters, in the centre of the city, by prompt preventive action, by both the Military and the Police, who were deployed in force early on. Vigorous patrolling in the disturbed areas and the prompt apprehension of trouble makers restored calm and order within forty eight hours. The Commissioner of Police was the only senior officer present who had experienced extensive street disorders in the past; he was quick to assess the situation and to call in additional help from the Army. His prompt action was a lesson to all us others that it is better to re-act quickly and effectively than to wait for the trouble to spread. It is better to be accused of over-reaction than of no action at all. Unfortunately, later on, we witnessed much more serious unrest which spread rapidly to other parts of the country despite vigorous preventive steps from the start.

I had to deal with one more short period of communal tension before I left the division. This time, the matter was resolved largely thanks to the resolution displayed by one of the communities involved. For some unknown reason, several isolated Chinese were severely assaulted by groups of rowdy Burmans in outlying parts of the town. Encouraged by these easy victories, the Burmese entered China Town in force and began attacking the locals; they received an unpleasant surprise. The Chinese were quick to organise themselves into vigilante groups and, in no time, began to give as good as they got. When the Police had managed to deploy on the scene, most of the attackers had had enough and were retreating out of the area. The Chinese let it be known that if any more of their compatriots were killed or wounded on their dispersed plots of cultivated land, around the outskirts, the community would seek revenge in the Burmese quarters. This warning had its effect and we were able to withdraw the special Police precautions within a few days.

An annual time of anxiety for the authorities all over India or wherever the Shiah sect of Mohammedans had a settlement, was their yearly day of repentance for the deaths of Hassan and Hussein, the descendants of the Prophet Mohammed. This sect rejects portions of Mohammedan law, based on the Prophet's words but not written by him; whereas the larger sect of Sunni Mohammedans accept them. The traditional tension between the two sects reaches its climax on that day of observance by the Shiahs. Invariably, elaborate precautions are made to meet any potential trouble, and Rangoon was no exception, since we had sizeable numbers of both sects in the town, living mainly in the Central Division.

The culmination of the Shiahs' atonements on the day is a procession after dusk. During this march, the participants indulge in severe acts of self-flagellation. They carry short stout staffs ending in several strands of metal chains with sharp half-moon shaped blades fixed at intervals along the chains. The marchers are bare-backed, recite prayers and repeatedly invoke the names of the martyred Hassan and Hussein. Every so often the procession comes to a halt, the chanting reaches a crescendo, the flagellants flog themselves as hard as they can on their bare backs with the chains. At the end of the march most backs are a mass of cuts oozing blood. The excitement and the pain, thus generated, make all the marchers a fanatical and unpredictable crowd. Any incident which under normal circumstances would be dismissed without aggressive reaction, could spark off a violent response from a frenzied mob. For two successive years I had the responsibility for arranging the required security measures along the processional route. We all sighed with relief when the event was well and truly over.

I had been in the Central Division for over one and a half years when I was becoming due for promotion to District Superintendent according to the hallowed seniority list. Promotion was not automatic but one's record had to be bad to be passed over when it was 'Buggin's turn'. It was usual for a newly promoted officer to be put in charge of a light district in the first instance; most of these were in Upper Burma. I was therefore again listing the delights of district life in the better half of the country to my receptive wife; we were both looking forward to a complete change from urban life.

Again the unexpected happened. I was duly promoted to the higher rank but remained in Rangoon. I was posted to the River Division, the only divisional job in the Rangoon Police to carry the rank of District Superintendent.

Rangoon City Police — Central Division, c. 1935
Author with Inspectors (one on each side of him), Sub-Inspectors, and Station-Writers (seated in front)

21
Rangoon – River Division

My third transfer, within the City force, in January 1936 was due to the fact that my predecessor, who had been in the job for several years, was unexpectedly going on long leave prior to early retirement for health reasons. The Commissioner wanted him relieved by an officer with recent experience in Rangoon as disruptive incidents were on the increase, thanks to the more aggressive tactics adopted by the new generation of politicians, impatient for power and what that could imply for their personal benefit. Port labour and student discontent were becoming promising sources for political agitation. Although I was disappointed to miss a congenial posting, which, on the other hand, could have turned out a disappointment if I had drawn a less pleasant district in the Delta, with its hordes of mosquitoes, I did like the other senior officers in the city force and was happy to retain their friendly professional and social association. Their spontaneously expressed pleasure, in the managed retention of my services, compensated a great deal for the loss of an independent district.

I did not have to deal with the same volume or importance of crime in my new job. The seniority of the appointment was due to the various other authorities involved in the administration of the port. Close liaison had to be established and maintained with senior staff in the Customs Department and in the Port Trust Authority, as well as with big shipping agencies and ships' captains of various nationalities. In short, the duties called for a fair amount of public relations work in addition to the usual professional work. Rangoon was a busy and important international sea port. Immense quantities of rice, teak, oil and other natural resources were exported by sea to all parts of the globe. At one time, most of the rice consumed in Western Europe came from Burma and teak was used by nearly all ship-building companies in the world for the deck surfaces of their vessels. The loading and unloading of vessels went on day and night at berths alongside as well as in mid-stream.

The Port Trust Authority was established in 1879 and became a thriving concern, never ceasing to improve passenger and cargo handling facilities until by 1941 transit sheds, wharves and landing places extended along the whole length of the foreshore, within town limits, a distance of more than six miles. Most of these facilities were totally destroyed during the war, in fact, Rangoon became the most heavily damaged port in the whole of South East Asia. Reconstruction work began after the war and major restoration was completed in the 1960's, largely with the help of a loan from the World Bank.

Pre-war, the general pattern was for a ship to unload cargo alongside and then anchor in mid-stream for loading. This continuous traffic in goods and people attracted hordes of petty thieves as well as the more ambitious ones. The Police, Customs Preventive staff and port durwans (watchmen) were constantly on the look-out for pilfering. A more specialised thief was the sampan-wallah criminal; these individuals were skilled in the art of manoeuvering their light craft stealthily alongside the barges, busily engaged in moving goods on or off an anchored ship, stealing whatever they could and getting away before the crew became aware of their presence. At night this type of theft became child's play and the Police launch patrols were kept on their toes throughout the hours of darkness. Even so, many culprits repeatedly escaped capture.

Another more special task for the Port Police was constant checking on the number of barges loading or unloading cargo, on or from a ship, lying in the river. The Rangoon river was tidal and when the tide was running out, the flowing current would run at the rate of knots. Ships were held at their moorings by four heavy long chains, each secured to a massive block of concrete bedded in the bottom of the river bed. Even so, the swift strong out-going tide placed an enormous strain on these chains. Hence the Harbour rules laid down precise regulations about the number of barges which could be attached alongside each hatch of a ship and for an overall total. The rule was not more than five barges to each hatch, limited to three on any one side of the ship; the overall total was as I recollected to a maximum of six hatches i.e. thirty barges at any one time. Stevedores, in their eagerness for business, would always try to ensure a quick turn-about for their barges and Ships' officers were constantly calling for Police assistance, to remove surplus loaded barges, which refused to cast off when told to do so. A special launch, with a European Sergeant on board, was employed solely on this duty, which resulted in several dozen prosecutions each week. In spite of these precautions there were occasions when a chain snapped and a ship started to veer, causing near panic to neighbouring vessels. Luckily, we never experienced more than one chain breakage; two could have spelt real disaster.

For some reason the Government had decreed that the Port Police should handle all applications for British Passports, including the preliminary inquiries to ascertain the applicant's suitability for such a document. As elsewhere, qualifications, in the first instance, rested on place of birth or length of residence to be eligible for naturalisation. These requirements were not always easy to establish in a country where documentation was not as comprehensive and sophisticated as in Europe. Eligibility for a British passport was based on the same rules and regulations as applied all over the Empire. This document was greatly prized by all indigenous races and many would not hesitate to falsify their claims to obtain the precious booklet. The Chinese, in particular, were troublesome cases; time and again, an applicant would declare that he qualified by length of residence in Burma, when it was discovered that he or she had only arrived on a limited visa in a Chinese passport a few months, maybe even only weeks, before. Wealthy applicants were prepared to pay large sums for a favourable police report on their applications, or for an accelerated inquiry. I had to keep a sharp look-out for attempted bribery. Most members of the passport section did their work honestly and the few undesirables were soon weeded out. To keep temptation at bay, I arranged frequent transfers of investigating officers. I cannot now recall many of the frequent minor amusing incidents which took place during such inquiries and one that I do recall clearly was the Indian gentleman who appeared with an application form and photographs of himself and his wife. By chance, I was looking at this particular set of documents before the inquiry and remembered seeing the woman's picture in a previous application. When I taxed the applicant, thinking that I had caught him red-handed in a fraudulent act, he disarmed my suspicions by frankly admitting that she was the same person. "You see Sir", he said, "I am a poor man and I have to share one wife with my cousin brother to save expenses". The term cousin brother was widely used by English speaking natives to describe someone who might, or might not, be very distantly related.

The Port Police also checked and stamped the passports of all incoming and outgoing passengers. Again, the Chinese caused most bother. To enter Burma from China, they had to obtain British entry visas. The great bulk of Chinese immigrants or visitors, coming by sea, embarked in the ports of Swatow, Amoy or Fuchow on the China coast. There were British Consulates in all three ports. One alert passport-checking officer noticed that the British visa on a Chinese passport appeared to be the same as he had seen on an earlier one. We began to mark the visas discreetly and note the passport numbers. Sure enough it was not long before the same numbered and viséd passport re-appeared with a different traveller. From this sleuthing, a gigantic misuse of Chinese passports was uncovered, not only in relation to the port of Rangoon but to many others where Chinese passengers travelled regularly. The drill was for special agents to collect Chinese passports from their holders, once they had safely entered the country. These viséd travel documents would then be returned in bulk to the port of issue. The Chinese officials there would then, presumably for a hefty fee, replace the photographs, stamp thereon the official Chinese Government seal and thus issue, for practical purposes, another valid travel document. The shipping agents became much more careful in scrutinising Chinese passports after a while, since they had to repatriate, at their own expense, any passengers refused entry. At the height of the traffic in ready-to-travel papers, the Chinese officials in those ports must have had a lucrative business. The fraud was taken up by the British Government at the highest diplomatic levels but I never did learn the outcome of our official complaints.

The novelty of becoming involved in all kinds of maritime activity, in a large harbour, gave me an opportunity to renew my colloquial knowledge of French and German, when speaking to captains and crews of foreign ships. The French, Germans, Norwegians, Dutch and Greeks all ran regular sailings to the Far East, and many of their ships called at Rangoon, outward or inward bound. Although most of these ships' officers spoke English, they seemed pleased to meet a British official who could converse in a Continental language. I can still savour many of the national titbits I was pressed to accept whilst on board. One German skipper was so overcome to be addressed in his mother tongue, when I met him on reaching the bridge after boarding his ship in mid-stream, that he abandoned the pilot momentarily to call his steward. The latter was instructed to fetch a bottle of the captain's special Hock and a loaf of special Black Forest bread, which he insisted I should take ashore with me.

Normal police work, the prevention and detection of crime, was rather more humdrum after some of the sophisticated types of crime inflicted on the wealthy businesses in the town. Although the value of goods, pilfered from the ships and transit sheds, was sometimes high, the procedure was usually straightforward and did not call for exceptional investigation skills. The main difference with the other police divisions in the town was geographical. The Port Authority's writ extended beyond the city's limits which ended on the east bank of the Rangoon river. On the west bank their jurisdiction extended for a couple of miles inland to the Twante canal, and downstream for twenty miles to Elephant Point, the mouth of the river on the Bay of Bengal.

The Twante canal, originally one of the many waterways formed by the Irrawaddy on reaching the delta, had been artificially widened and deepened to take all the thriving inland water traffic, particularly the steamers of the Irrawaddy Flotilla Company, one of the largest inland waterways concerns in the world. Their craft penetrated to the remotest areas in the vast delta, up the Irrawaddy to Mandalay and on to Bhamo, up the Irrawaddy's main tributary, the Chindwin, to Kalewa, and beyond whenever navigation by the specially designed sternwheeler steamers became seasonally possible. Besides accommodating the screw-driven, hundred feet long Delta creek vessels, the canal was sufficiently wide and deep to take the huge mail-boats which plied between the capital and Mandalay. These vessels were over 300 feet long and towed two, 250 feet long flats (barges) one on each side; with a combined width of three craft of something in excess of 70 feet. These mobile floating islands could accommodate several thousand deck passengers and up to a couple of thousand tons of cargo.

This highly efficient, Glasgow based, enterprise did a great deal to open up the country for trade and development, more even than the subsequent building of roads and railways. Their expansion over the years built up the largest inland waterways fleet in the world. This whole fleet was destroyed in 1942 so as to deny its use to the Japanese and the Company was expropriated after Independence. The Burma Government now runs a nationalised inland water transport service but I am told that it is only a slim shadow of the former thriving private concern. I was told that the famous Mississippi River Boat Company wished to find out why the Irrawaddy steamers appeared to be more efficient than their own and sent an engineer to find out but without success. The story goes on that, at an early stage of building paddle steamers, the Glasgow engineers discovered that, by not immersing the whole paddle blade into the water, they were able to increase the speed of the boat without increasing power; information which was jealously guarded by the company.

Two small Burmese villages were established near the Twante canal entrance. In the vicinity was a Port Police Station, the only one on that side of the river bank, and the only Rangoon Police Station in a truly rural setting. Whenever I felt like reviving my old district life I would direct my launch towards these small village communities, call on the village elders for a general gossip, with many of the population looking on or participating in the talks. Rangoon city life would then seem to be far away. After a while, I began to sense a certain atmosphere at the Police Station during my visits and concluded that the station staff had formed their own opinions about my periodical visits; more frequent than those of my predecessors. Their discreet assumptions were finally laid to rest when my wife began to accompany me on these trips, to see at first hand how the country Burmans lived in their villages, having had only my verbal descriptions to go on so far. Thus, I hope, died the delectable rumour that I must have had one, if not two, pretty little Burmese mistresses discreetly tucked away in either, or even both, of these outlying places.

Elephant Point was the furthest place in my jurisdiction and, as far as I know, had never been visited by the head of the Port Police. The name intrigued me sufficiently to wish for a look at the place, but I could think of no good excuse to use a launch for the best part of the day for no reason at all. Fate was kind to me; a dacoity, of all crimes, was reported at the light-house situated near the mouth of the river. Such an event had not taken place in the Port's jurisdiction for a very long time and caused some excitement. The Port Surveyor offered to take a police party in his own fast, comfortable launch to the scene of the crime. We arrived at the river's mouth around midday; the light-house was in fact on the opposite bank to Elephant Point. Unfortunately, the tide was still well out and we had to wade through thick, oozy mud, sometimes above knee level, for what seemed a long time, before we reached the steps leading up to the lighthouse. The heat was overbearing and we felt completely exhausted and breathless on arrival and remained speechless for several minutes.

The reported facts were that five Burmans, armed with two shot-guns and 'dahs' had silently approached the place in darkness on the previous night, using a small country boat. The four lighthouse keepers, all Indians, had been caught unawares, tied up and threatened to disclose their valuables. According to the occupants, the dacoits were diappointed at the smallness of their haul and had vented their displeasure by wrecking some fittings but had, luckily, failed to damage the mechanism serving the big light, which had continued to function. We were shown the broken-down door at the rear of the building, where entrance had occurred and some broken chairs and crockery. My Burmese sub-inspector suggested that he and two constables should visit the surrounding villages to seek further information as it looked as if the crime had been committed by local bad hats. The rest of us then returned to Rangoon. Within a few days, I received the investigation report, which gave a very different story. The dacoity had never taken place; both the information and evidence from the complainants had been false; they had all signed confessions to that effect. Apparently, the lighthouse keepers had concocted the story to lend force to an application they had made for a special allowance, on the grounds that they were serving in an isolated, potentially dangerous place. So ended what could have been one of the few important crimes, as dacoity was defined, in the annals of the Port Police.

I never did discover how Elephant Point received its name. Someone suggested that an early British visitor to Burma, venturing up the river, had seen an elephant grazing on the bank. This is an unlikely story as it is not very probable that a heavy animal like an elephant would venture to graze so close to the marshy banks. As for me, I never dreamt then that one day I would re-visit the area several years later, in the guise of an Army officer, sent to liaise with a Gurkha parachute battalion, deputed to capture a network of underground bunkers built by the Japanese to defend the sea approach to Rangoon; but that is another story.

I had a break in my tour of duty in the River Division. My wife had gone home, on medical advice, for the birth of our first child. After the event, I applied for short leave on urgent private affairs. The Port Trust Authorities flatteringly pressed for an assurance that I would be re-posted to my job and the Commissioner of Police kindly recommended my leave application on those terms. In spite of the short period, my leave coincided with some world-absorbing events.

I flew home (the first time I had ever been in the air) in the then incredibly short time of four days. The Dutch ran a regular service between Holland and Java, via Rangoon. In those days aeroplanes had to come down frequently for re-fuelling. Nights were spent on the ground. The first stop after Rangoon was Calcutta; someone bought an American magazine and I read, for the first time, all about Mrs. Simpson and the new King. We flew across India and the Arabian desert. At Baghdad we had to doss down at the airport because a revolution had broken out in the country. We took off before dawn; after half an hour's flight I discovered that I had left my pocket-book, with all my money and my passport, under the pillow of the camp bed in which I had slept for a few hours. We had been warned to beware of nimble thieves roaming around the place and I had chosen the pillow as my best safe-deposit. The captain of the aircraft was most helpful, short of turning round; he radioed to their agent and, to my intense relief, received a message back within the hour, that my belongings had been recovered intact and would be sent on by the next flight.

The next stop was at Lydda in Palestine (now Israel) then a British mandate under the League of Nations. Jews and Arabs were already then engaged in fighting each other; the British troops in the middle, received unwelcome attention from both sides. We were hustled through a meal while R.A.F. planes were landing and taking off continuously, on their way to Iraq to protect the large British air base at Habbaniya, which was being attacked by revolutionary local troops. Refuelling in Rhodes, we had the pleasure, during our meal, to listen to a ranting speech from Mussolini who had just invaded Abyssinia. In Rome I was not allowed out of the aircraft as I had no passport; that was the official reason, but a more probable cause was an intensified anti-British feeling due to our official disapproval of Italy's aggression in the horn of Africa. The final stage of my air journey from Amsterdam to Croydon was by courtesy of a German Junker plane. The Lufthansa pilot was the only one prepared to fly his aeroplane over the Channel in thick fog on that day. I was in a hurry to see my wife and first-born, so decided to take the risk.

The two most memorable sights on this journey were, firstly, the amazing variations in deep colours of purple and crimson shades, thrown across the sand dunes of the immense desert, as the sun began to rise over the horizon below us, when we flew from Baghdad to Palestine. Secondly, the wonderful blue of the Aegean sea contrasting with the stark green and white of the numerous islands between Rhodes and Athens. Unfortunately, we did not fly over the Greek capital and missed a view of the famous classical ruins there.

I arrived home six weeks after my son's birth, just in time to hear Edward the VIIIth's abdication speech on the wireless that evening. During a visit to my mother in Geneva, I found officials of the League of Nations in turmoil over Germany's recent decision to withdraw its membership of that International body. Many of these functionaries were friends I had known since childhood, and at social gatherings to which I was invited during my stay, the talk was no longer lighthearted banter but mostly of gloomy forecasts which I then thought unnecessarily defeatist. Before I returned to Britain, the Spanish Socialist Government was forced to abandon Madrid to Franco's forces; this development cast more despondency amongst the International community in Geneva.

We returned to Burma in May 1937, all the way by sea, from Liverpool to Rangoon, a journey of thirty-one days. As it turned out, this was the only occasion on which I travelled with the family. The ship was half empty at this time, the end of the so-called travelling season. We had plenty of space, spreading ourselves in two adjacent cabins at no extra cost and had a very pleasant voyage. Both the captain and the purser were old acquaintances and made us welcome. We called in briefly at Gibraltar but anchored in the bay, passengers could not go ashore as the duration of our stay was so uncertain. The Spanish Civil war was at its height and there was an ineffective international naval blockade to prevent outside assistance to either side. We were anchored next to a Dutch cruiser stopped briefly on its patrolling duties. Despite these precautions, German and Italian 'volunteers' were helping one side and the International Brigade the other.

A few hours after our departure from Gibraltar, the German airship, the famous Graf Zeppelin, flew over our vessel on its return voyage from Brazil to Germany. Two huge Swastika black crosses on circular red backgrounds had been painted on both sides of the frame as an advertisement for the coming to power of Hitler and his Nazi party. The airship had gained world notoriety through its historic long flights over the two Atlantic oceans and the two American continents and was now engaged on a much publicised air postal and passenger service between Germany and South America.

In Rangoon, we found that the Port Trust Authority had rented a delightful house for us from a Chinese landlord. This building was quite different in shape and style from any of the usual run of official accommodation. The owner was wealthy and had built two similar houses, well apart, in a sizeable plot of land on a small hill near the swimming club, a favoured recreation spot for the Foreign communities. The two dwelling houses were similar in their irregular two storeys shapes, giving a more oriental than western impression; in some respects reminiscent of those historical buildings illustrated in pictures of the old imperial city in Pekin. The result was spacious, comfortable, picturesque and cool. The good-sized garden, planted with high shady trees and containing a grass tennis court, an unusual feature in that part of the world, gave us more than adequate privacy. The greatest asset was a huge ground floor covered verandah, with deep eaves to keep off the sun running around the whole of the front and one irregular side of the house. An unusual feature of this facility was the distinctly unique mosaic stone floor; altogether the most comfortable and coolest place in the house and we spent most of our time there.

An unusual feature in the house was that every window and every door, even those inside doors leading from rooms into the downstairs hall or the upstairs landing, had massive expanding metal shutters inserted into the frames. There were extra strong expanding shutters on the main front and back doors and at the top of the staircase. These solid, heavy precautions must have taken servants some time, each night, to draw and lock into position, and would have taken a gang of accomplished house breakers hours of hard cutting, to gain access. Our Chinese landlord must have possessed a great many valuables to safeguard them in this elaborate manner. We had nothing like that sort of wealth to justify these extraordinary precautions. The shutters on all doors and on all the windows remained undrawn, day and night, during our stay in the house. At no other time have we enjoyed so much space and privacy. Our friends would refer to visiting our country estate, such was the impression of peace and withdrawness.

I had been back from leave for nearly a year, when the Chairman of the Port Trust Commissioners asked me confidentially if I would be prepared to consider an extended contract of service to run the Port Police. I told him that I did not think that the Government would be ready to consider such a novel idea, even if the Commissioner of Police were prepared to accept the proposition. He asked me to think over the matter before giving a final decision as the Commissioners of the Port were ready to pursue the proposal officially. From an immediate personal point of view, the suggestion had attractive aspects and financial awards. I had no illusions however, that my long term prospects in the Service would not be benefitted by absence in what would be regarded a specialised appointment, partly under foreign management, so to speak. Before the matter went beyond this preliminary probing stage, the

Commissioner of Police solved the problem for me. He summoned me to his office and announced that he had asked the Government to sanction my appointment as Assistant Commissioner from May 1938. Once again, my secondment to the City Police was extended.

Discussing security measures with Todd, Assistant Traffic Manager, during first racial riots (Indians v Burmans)

22

Assistant Commissioner of Police

In theory, the Deputy and the Assistant Commissioners of Police ranked as equal seconds-in-command to the Commissioner of the City force. In a nutshell, the Deputy Commissioner was responsible for the supervision of all crime work and the Assistant Commissioner for the supervision of all general duties. In practice, the former appointment was always held by one of the senior District Superintendents whereas the status of the latter fluctuated, from the top to the bottom of the senority list of District Superintendent, according to the appointee (very much to the bottom in my case!).

The Assistant Commissioner was in charge of Administration and Finance and of the sections dealing with the control and Licensing of public vehicles (taxis, gharries, i.e. horse drawn vehicles, and rickshaws, then all pulled by human beings), firearms' licensing, traffic control and special police arrangements at public gatherings and other special occasions, such as sporting events, racecourse meetings, political meetings and processions; in fact, ensuring that any kind of gathering, which might lead to trouble, was adequately policed. Last but not least, the Assistant Commissioner of Police was the ex-officio Secretary of the Burma Film Censorship Board!

General administration and finance took up a great deal of my time and kept me tied to my desk at headquarters for long hours each day. Only when serious disturbances made us all abandon our offices for hours, sometimes days, on end was I relieved, temporarily, from the substantial volume of daily paper work. Although I had some familiarity with Government methods of financial control and budgets, when in charge of a District Police force, those applying in the office of a large city force were more complex and onerous. In fact, our annual budget was so large that, under the then prevailing regulations, we had to employ an accountant trained by the Accountant-General's department and then certified fit to deal with the accounts of a large spending department. My mentor, in this respect, proved to be invaluable and indispensable; not only was he faultless in all his work and a competent controller of his staff, but he also thoroughly understood all the ins and outs of the Accountant-General's office; like most of his professional colleagues, he was a Bengali.

We had to submit periodical statements, listing all receipts and disbursements of money, to the Accountant-General's office. If the latter wished to raise any query on any item, he would issue what was euphemistically known as a half margin. This was a form divided down the middle; the Accountant-General, or rather one of his countless minions, would write the question in the left half and the recipient would record his answer in the right half. After my first week in the office, my accountant appeared with a batch of these wretched forms. I expressed consternation at the large number put before me but was assured that this was by no means an unusual batch, and he withdrew. I started to read through the forms, the more I read the more I became confused, the phrases just did not make sense. I rang the bell, told the chaprassi (office messenger) to ask the accountant to return. He appeared so promptly that I surmised he had been waiting outside my door for just such a summons. I explained my dilemma; he just smiled understandingly and asked me whether I would allow him to write the replies, adding charmingly "as I used to do for your predecessors". I thankfully accepted the offer and, in due course, he brought back the forms ready for my signature. I started to read what he had written but his replies made no more sense to me than the questions. I had to summon him again to confess that these sentences, although written in correctly spelt English, were just words strung together meaninglessly and that I really could not sign something which I did not understand. Again he gave me his shy half-smile and said, "Sir, please just sign, all will be well and you will hear nothing more about the audit objections". So I signed, still in doubt about the incomprehensible replies to the incomprehensible questions. Lo and behold, that was the end of the matter. Throughout the rest of my time, my accountant corresponded with his colleagues in the Accountant-General's office, both exchanging meaningless (to me) English sentences to their mutual satisfaction over my pro-forma signature!

The City Police contained a small force of European Sergeants. Some of them were Anglo-Indian or Anglo-Burman. In normal times they and a number of selected Head Constables and Constables were employed on traffic control duties. The combined force was housed in special quarters, known as the 'Mogul Guard' which also housed a mounted section of Sergeants and Indian constables. The 'Town Lock-up' was in practice a transit jail for prisoners under trial in the law courts; there were always a substantial number of them since, besides the lower local courts, all the High Court Judges had their courts in Rangoon, which meant that all appeals were heard in the capital. The building was a substantial one and also housed the stores department of the City force. Here, we employed several tailors and cobblers full-time on making, altering and repairing uniforms and boots (the latter were fabricated in jails but needed frequent repairing owing to poor workmanship). These artisans worked rapidly and efficiently. I once gave a bolt of Shan silk to one of the tailors, asking him to make me as many pairs of Shan pants as he could; these were wide loose pyjama-type trousers with a broad linen band arround the top, which the wearer tucked over. These garments were worn instead of the tighter fitting pyjamas by nearly all Europeans in Burma. The day after I had handed the cloth to the tailor, I had to visit the Lock-up after office hours for some purpose and I was astonished to be presented with eight pairs of well-made Shan pants. The tailor was overcome by my generosity when I insisted that he should accept a five rupee tip (seven shillings and six pence!). Both the Mogul Guard and the Town Lock-up were under the direct control of the Assistant Commissioner, each had an Inspector in charge.

My wife, like all her European sisters, never ceased to marvel at the dexterity and speed of the Indian and Chinese tailors and cobblers. She was a highly competent dress-maker herself and made most of her own evening dresses, once the bought ones had worn out. She would take some of the material of a new evening dress to the Chinese shoemaker in the bazaar and he would make her a new pair of elegant evening shoes, covered with the dress material, in twenty-four hours, less if the need be. I would go to an Indian tailor in the same bazaar for my tropical suits; he never once took up a tape measure, just gave me a good look, up and down, and then produced a good-fitting suit within a day or two, according to my requirement, at a cost of a few pounds (but then even genuine Scotch whisky was priced at around five shillings a bottle!).

In normal times, the Mogul Guard and the Town Lock-up were inspected formally each week; the Commissioner would occasionally turn up at these formal functions, in which case a bit more ceremonial would be applied by all concerned. The Mogul Guard was a substantial modern block of flats and communal rooms, with stabling for a dozen or so horses at the rear for the mounted section. The building occupied nearly the whole length of one side of the street from which it derived its name. The flats and single rooms were occupied by the European Sergeant, the Indian Head and Ordinary Constables, all employed on traffic control duties in the city in normal times. Unofficially, they were also considered as a sort of strategic reserve in troublesome times, but their numbers were insufficient to form an effective trouble-shooting contingent.

One of my unofficial, nevertheless compulsory duties was to act as Father Christmas at the children's party at the Mogul Guard. Many of the children belonging to the Indian policemen were, of course, not Christians but that was no bar to attending the festivities. Residence was the only valid qualification for participating in the jollifications which they all, irrespective of race or religion, looked forward to and enjoyed. A less welcome official duty was the revision of punishments, meted out by subordinate officers, if the culprit chose to appeal. Dealing with minor disciplinary cases was usually simple and quickly disposed of. Formal departmental enquiries were a different matter; elaborate rules of procedure were laid down for the conduct of such cases, not far removed from those observed in the law courts. Very often, I had to order the findings to be quashed because of procedural errors and for the whole weary process to be re-commenced or, worse still, have to take over the case myself. I only did this as a very last resort. The time wasted on having to listen to an endless stream of witnesses, most of whom knowing little or nothing of the relevant facts, was time and patience consuming. In the great majority of cases, the defendant was a firm believer in the maxim 'safety in numbers'. He would, therefore make every effort to drum up an impressive number of defence witnesses. The rules were drawn up in such a way as to make it as difficult as possible for the officer, holding the inquiry, to debar a witness from appearing until it was clear, beyond doubt, that he was not in a position to offer any relevant evidence. In practice, this meant that the unnecessary witness had to be examined for some time before it could be established that he was wasting everyone's time.

Each year, the Governor of Burma reviewed the Military and the Civil Police, including the Rangoon City force, at a large ceremonial parade. The ceremony was held in the capacious grounds of the Burma Athletic Club stadium, in front of a large invited and still larger uninvited audience. As Assistant Commissioner it was my duty to command the city contingent, on that occasion on horseback in full-dress uniform, which was dark-blue for us. I did not possess a pair of dark-blue riding breeches (in the district forces, we wore khaki service dress). I borrowed a pair from a brother officer for the occasion; they were a tight fit when I put them on just before going on parade. As I mounted my horse, to my horror the breeches split right down the middle of my back from the waistband, much to the amusement of the men drawn up in two ranks behind me. I had no time to do anything else except sit firmly on my steed and hope for the best. The parade went off without further hitches but there was a problem ahead.

After the parade, it was customary for all officers to dismount, when the rank and file were moving off, to line up for presentation to His and Her Excellencies. I managed to convey my dilemma to the senior officer commanding the parade just before the crucial dismounting order. With a wink in his eye, he ordered me to lead the troops off the parade ground. I had fondly hoped that my absence from the presentation would go undetected but it was a vain hope, the Governor asked the parade commander why I had ridden off with the men instead of dismounting like all the others. The officer then had to confess the reason for giving the unorthodox order. A few days later I received a mock-serious letter from the Military Secretary conveying His Excellency's condolences for my accident and good wishes for a speedy recovery of the wounded breeches!

Any large function at Government House, or elsewhere where either the Governor or his wife were to be present, required special police arrangements for which the Assistant Commissioner was responsible. In important functions his personal presence was expected. The Military Secretary and I would usually have a preliminary meeting to discuss details, if the arrangements were to be more elaborate than usual. On these occasions he would refer to the special car park for V.I.P.s as the 'Accouti' corner. The local papers, English and vernacular, always carried large regular advertisements proclaiming the miraculous propensities of the 'Royal Accouti' medicine 'for rich men only' suffering from sexual debility. The drug guaranteed instant success even in the most stubborn cases. On one occasion, I witnessed the out-wagging of my friend the M.S.; a senior official, stepping out of his chauffeur-driven car under the porch at Government House overheard one of the ADC's being instructed to direct the car to the 'Accouti' corner; the V.I.P. turned to the M.S. and said with a straight face: "I am afraid I do not qualify, I have not yet had

The annual Governor's Parade for Rangoon City Police. Author on horseback with contingents of European Sergeants, Sikhs, Punjabi Mussulmans & Hindus, Gurkhas, Karens and Burmans; also a contingent of Military Police.

The Governor, Sir Hugh Stevenson (seated centre) on the occasion of the annual parade, 1936.
U Ba Yi, Superintendent Eastern Division, the first Burmese Superintendent of the Rangoon Police
is standing second from right; the author second from left. Note mourning arm-bands for George V.

121

the need to sample the product!"

I am not a racing man but, in my official capacity, I was occasionally invited by the Rangoon Turf Club to one of their celebrated 'Champagne' luncheons, which they gave on important Saturday meetings. Regardless of my lack of interest in horse racing, I always accepted with alacrity these invitations to lavish entertainment. The police always had to make elaborate arrangements to control the vast crowds attending all the race meetings. Besides payment to the Government for these special police precautions, the Turf Club sent five complimentary tickets to my office each week, admitting the holder and a companion to the members' enclosure. I would distribute these on a strict rota basis to all senior ranks who were known to be racegoers. As on most race-courses in the world, but rather more so here, the stewards had a busy time keeping a sharp eye on shady goings-on. Rigged races and doped horses were not unknown. A great deal of money changed hands before and after every race; the Burmese and the Chinese being, as expected, the most enthusiastic supporters of the Tote and of bookmakers. The whole of Rangoon seemed to stream to the race-course at week-ends in their best bib and tucker. I doubt whether a crowd anywhere else in the world could then rival the kaleidoscope made by the cosmopolitan assembly, particularly the Burmese in their never clashing bright clothes and hair decorated with real flowers. The other side of the coin were the swarms of pick-pockets drawn to the course like bees to the honey-pot.

I remember two amusing incidents from my race-course days. On one occasion, two respectable members of the Turf club, who shared the ownership of a much favoured racehorse, decided to make a killing with the bookies. The horse was piebald and also had some black spots. The owners decided to add some more spots and optimistically hoped to run the horse under an assumed name. The plot was of course detected without much difficulty and the two dejected owners were warned off for a period.

Another owner had a hyphenated name, both names beginning with the letter H. He called all his racing horses by hyphenated names also beginning with the letters H-H, e.g. "Happy-Heaven". He applied to the Turf Club to register a new racehorse with the name "Hoof-Hearted" and he nearly got away with the attempt!

The Rangoon race-course was then accepted as one of the best in that part of the world. The buildings were modern with the latest amenities for riders, horses and the public. When I returned with the Army in 1945, the race course and the swimming club were the first amenities to function again after a lapse of four years.

When war in Europe appeared imminent in 1939, I was suddenly thrust into a role I disliked. My desire to keep up my knowledge of French and German led me to make a point of mixing with these two national communities in Rangoon. Both were small and friendly. The Germans, whether out of tact or indifference, seemed uninterested in the Nazi ideology. The only mild supporter of that regime was a member of the American community of German extraction, who also joined in their social activities. When my wife and my small son went home early in

1939 to escape the hot weather which had been affecting my wife's health, this American whose wife had also departed at about the same time, came to share my house. He made no secret of his limited partiality to the Nazi doctrine and we had many friendly altercations on the subject but, in the end, his presence in my house caused eyebrows to rise.

I was summoned one day by the Director of Intelligence C.G. Stewart, a senior officer of the Indian Police. My knowledge of French and German was of course known to the authorities and I had on occasions been asked to translate some intercepted or copied documents and had even been invited to express an opinion on the importance or reliability of a specific communication. On this occasion, he asked me rather diffidently to keep an eye on my German friends and to report anything I considered of value. In short, I was asked to spy on them. I did not relish the prospect and said so, adding that I would be surprised if any of them, except perhaps the honorary Consul, had any connection, or any desire of involvement, in the German spy ring known to exist in India and further East. Whether I was incompetent in this new role or whether my surmise was right, I never did discover any suspicious activities.

On one occasion, my American paying guest asked me if he could arrange a bachelors' dinner party at the house for some of his German friends to celebrate someone's engagement. He invited me to participate but I had already accepted another invitation. I returned from my social engagement after midnight to find the party in my house in full swing. They had got to the stage of singing ribald German student songs and they were all well primed. I was pressed to join in and we carried on for another hour, ending the evening with a rousing rendering of "Deutschland uber alles in der Welt", the German National Anthem. My official residence was within earshot of several other Government houses, including that of the Deputy Commissioner of Police. The next morning, in the office he said to me: "I know all about your special assignment with the Intelligence Bureau but I did not realise that you had to go so far as to lead them in their National Anthem"! I had my leg pulled for some considerable time after this, especially as war broke out soon after. Some of my friends started to address me as Herr Tydd for a while, until more serious matters gave them better things to think about.

On the day that war was declared in Europe, we had to arrest all the Germans for internment. I never hated a task more. I saw the Honorary Consul first and he arranged for the community to assemble at his house at a given time. I arrived with my formal escort at the rendezvous, feeling and no doubt looking self-concious to arrest people who a few hours ago had been on friendly social terms with me. They made the official action easier by displaying good manners and understanding; quite unlike the popular image of the hectoring arrogant German. Later on we had to round up the few Italians in the town; amongst them was the universally known and popular head waiter of the leading hotel, known affectionally as Mussolini by all his numerous patrons. Incidentally, both Italians and Germans had been established in Burma for a long time. The former could boast the first western visitor to the country, Marco Polo, in the thirteenth century, and later compatriots were brought in by the King to cast the huge canons which graced the Fort in Mandalay. The Germans had established a flourishing rice export trade at the same time as British firms were entering that market.

The Indian National Congress had stepped up the struggle for Independence throughout the decade following the first world war. The Indian Communities in Burma, Hindu and Muslim, were not immune from the incessant propaganda, despite their own differences. I still remember distinctly standing under a large banner, spanning one of the main thoroughfares of the town, trying to keep an excited mob of Muslims and another of Hindus from attacking each other during one of the periodical local flare-ups. The irony of the situation was in the wording on the banner which read:- "British go home, Independence is India's birthright". I called the ring-leaders of both factions to join me in the middle of the road. Pointing to the legend on the banner I told them that I was thinking of following the advice now. The inappropriate timing of the message, under the circumstances, seemed to sink in; both groups began to melt away in different directions, just in case I did decide to withdraw the thin blue line.

Political agitation amongst certain classes of Burmese followed the Indian lead throughout the nineteen thirties but, in a minor key compared to the terrorist campaigns waged in Bengal, the Province closest to Burma. The agrarian population in the districts remained largely indifferent and took little notice of the machinations occurring in some of the larger towns. Rangoon inevitably bore the brunt of demonstrations and agitations, organised by the more militant political agitators of the day. The campaign of attempted disruptions was usually aimed at the Burman's ingrained dislike of foreigners. This prejudice is never far away in the Burmese mind and is deep rooted in the country's history. For instance, the Burmese word for man 'lu' is never used by a Burman in reply to the question "how many men," when referring to a foreigner. He will reply, "there were four Kalas", meaning Indians, or four Tayok, meaning Chinamen, or four Kabia, meaning half-castes; if he said there were four Lu he meant Burmans. The huge influx of Indians after the British annexation, when the country became an additional province of the Indian Empire, was a ready-made and popular motive for stirring up trouble.

Like anyone else who takes an interest in what is happening around him, I had my own views on the wisdom or otherwise in the timing of the steps taken in stages towards the implementation of inevitable independence, officially proclaimed as the ultimate goal. My role was one of minor executive importance and I do not propose to pontificate on these issues in these recollections. However, I shall allow myself one personal observation. I had a degree of sympathy for the Burman's resentment about the peaceful invasion of their country by the peoples of India, largely encouraged by the British administration and the commercial interests of foreign concerns.

My two years as Assistant Commissioner were eventful and coincided with a period in which the Rangoon Police had to learn to live under mental and physical strains never experienced before and which persisted until the Civil Government ceased to function, with the advent of the Japanese Army. We spent more and more time on the streets, dealing with one disturbance after another, instead of being occupied with our other, more orthodox, Police duties. We were often physically exhausted but my youth (I was under thirty years of age at the time) made me resilient to the trying circumstances and I recovered quickly during the period of respite.

In some respects the worst time for me was waiting for the findings of the Riot Inquiry Committee, set up by the Government to inquire into the causes, events and handling by the Police of the wide-spread serious disturbances, which occurred in the middle of 1938. The riots broke out spontaneously in Rangoon, spread like wild-fire to many parts of the country, causing great loss of life and property. I was sucked into the events right at the start; indeed, in a manner of speaking, I could claim to have initiated the violence! I had therefore more than a passing interest in the Committee's conclusions. I was one of the main Rangoon Police witnesses, summoned to account for my actions. The inquiry was presided over by a European High Court Judge, Sir Harold Braund, and an equal number of Burmese and Indian Assessors, all men of repute and prominence within their respective communities. They spent several weeks travelling around taking evidence in great detail. The inevitable charges of Police brutalities and excesses were vehemently and stridently voiced in the Burmese vernacular press, in contrast to those printed in the Indian papers. The Indians had been the victims and the Burmese the aggressors in this instance, so the Police had by and large support from the former with occasional accusations of partiality and lack of firmness in dealing with the attackers.

The Committee was painstaking in recording and assessing all the facts and it took them a further number of weeks to draw their conclusions and produce a comprehensive report. Those of us who were professionally concerned about the outcome could not feel relaxed until we were officially exonerated by the findings of the Committee. I was relieved to read that my actions met with no criticisms and even drew some approving remarks. I have set down the Rangoon incidents more specifically in the next chapter.

23
The Riots in Rangoon

To quote the words recorded in the Final Report of the Riot Inquiry Committee:- "The riots were deliberately caused by a piece of unscrupulous political opportunism".

The brief facts leading to the trouble were some contentious writings in a book, published several years previously, deliberately revived to foment unrest between Burmans and Muslims. The writer of the book, a Burma Muslim, had made some disparaging remarks about the Buddhist religion. A meeting was organised at the Shwe Dagon Pagoda by an association of young Buddhist monks. Inflammatory speeches were made to a large gathering of priests and laymen. At the end of the meeting, the audience was worked up into religious fervour and willingly adopted a proposal to march into the Muslim quarter of the town "to protest and show disapproval", to quote the wording of the resolution. The real object of the organisers was to encourage the use of violence and thus to spread alarm and despondency and embarrass the Government.

The Shwe Dagon Pagoda meeting was by no means the first step in this campaign of unrest. Leaflets, containing extracts of the more objectionable phrases on the book, had been previously widely circulated in and outside the capital. The driving force behind the propagandists was a collection of less reputable politicians who wished to harm the reputation and popularity of the Burmese Ministers in the Government. These opposition politicians had taken steps to broadcast the distorted propaganda on the book as far afield as possible.

Burma had been given a new Constitution on its separation from India in 1937 (the date was the ominous first of April). The Act, in line with the concessions made in India, provided greater powers for the elected Legislative Council, which became the House of Representatives. The Burmese Ministers, in charge of "Transferred" Departments, created under the earlier constitutional changes, were also given greater powers in fulfilling their responsibilities; the Governor was now required to act on their advice in matters transferred to Ministerial control. This considerable step forward in self-government awakened naturally more political ambitions; some well-motivated by a genuine urge to help the people reach full democratic liberty; others, more selfishly inclined, were envious of the new political spoils available to those politicians forming the elected majority and redoubled their efforts to discredit the record and standing of the ruling party or parties. Whilst these riots were not primarily a genuine outburst of nationalism, they indicated the willingness of interested parties to foment dangerous racial prejudices and an increasing challenge to law and order.

My responsibilities did not include the assessment of Intelligence reports on Internal Security threats, that duty fell upon the Deputy Commissioner. He, of course, kept the rest of us informed on information received and on his assessments thereon. On this occasion, the intimation about imminent serious trouble came very swiftly. I was in my office, just about to call for my afternoon tea, when the Deputy Commissioner burst in. He told me that a large crowd, of pongyis (priests) and laymen, was just leaving the precincts of the Pagoda, intent on marching into the Muslim quarter and the Soortee Bara Bazaar to demonstrate. He then left in his car to meet the procession in its early stages to assess the mood of the people, whilst I headed for the Mogul Guard, to intercept the European Sergeants and Indian Constables just about due to relieve their colleagues on traffic control duties in various parts of the city. I scribbled a hasty note for the Commissioner, who was attending the weekly meeting of the Municipal Corporation at the Town Hall, in his capacity as a nominated member.

The Soortee Bara Bazaar was one of the two main markets in Rangoon, owned by a private company, formed by leading members of the Muslim commercial community in the capital. The very large building contained many individual stalls, rented to small businesses and was bordered by three main thoroughfares on three sides; one of these led straight from the Shwe Dagon Pagoda to the Rangoon river foreshore. In many respects it was the focal point of the Muslim Indian business and residential community, which surrounded the place on all sides. Incidentally, it was a favourite spot with my wife; she loved the oriental atmosphere, the variety of goods on display and the good-natured back-chat with vendors, never failing in their natural courtesy to a foreign customer.

I arrived at the Mogul Guard just in time to stop the relief men dispersing to their various traffic points. I managed to gather together twelve European Sergeants, fifteen Indian Constables and the Inspector of the Mogul Guard, an ex-warrant officer from the British Army. All had their regulation batons but no fire-arms. This small force reached the part of the bazaar building situated at the intersection of roads, one of which led straight to the Pagoda. The crowd was emerging at the other end of this road as the Police took up position. I had divided my force into two sections, one on each side of the wide road. When the procession drew nearer they did not seem to be excessively noisy or disorderly and I decided to let them pass and follow up in the rear. My decision was influenced by the fact that I was doubtful whether we could have stopped them peacefully by throwing a thin cordon of policemen across their path. I had not detected any weapons amongst the crowd but some were carrying sticks (later on we found out that some of the pongyis had concealed dahs in the folds of their robes). By adopting the alternative choice, we had time to regroup as one body of men for an effective baton charge should that become necessary. I explained to all of them that, if and when I gave the order to charge, they should act swiftly, decisively and forcefully as one compact group. I did not add that I was at a loss as to what I would do if we failed to disperse the mob at the first attempt; I kept that thought to myself.

I judged the crowd to be in excess of a thousand, of whom nearly half were wearing yellow robes (anyone could shave his head and put on the priest's robe without questions being asked as to the wearer's true intentions). The subsequent official inquiry confirmed my estimate. The marchers were chanting anti-Indian slogans and did not take much notice of us as they passed. Before long, however, as the head of the procession began to file past the side of the long building, people peeled off to loot the open stalls placed against the outside wall of the bazaar. Stones flew through the air and the marchers turned into a shouting mob; it was clear that any peaceful protests, if ever there were any, had gone by the board. I ordered the charge and was amazed how effective our determined action proved to be. Within minutes the road in front of us was clear of people; the mob had run away, melting into the side-streets. A quick assessment revealed one or two minor injuries amongst ourselves and two pongyis crouching on the road holding their heads. One had a cut on his forehead and I despatched him to the General Hospital nearby. Damage to stalls and to the building was minimal and wholesale looting had been prevented.

By this time, the Commissioner and his Deputy had arrived at the scene with some reinforcements and some fire-arms. I had already been told that the anger of the Burmese was now also directed against the Police for their brutal assault on compatriots. Whilst we three were conferring on the next measures, reports reached us of attacks on Indians in various parts of the town. Alarmist rumours were spreading that armed gangs were massing to penetrate into Indian quarters. The Commissioner swiftly concluded to call in the Military; "in aide of Civil Power" was the euphemistic term. The British battalion, earmarked for such duties, was stationed at Mingaladon, eleven miles from Rangoon but kept a detached Company in barracks near the Pagoda. A Military Police battalion, housed in the old Cantonments, was also available but, with detachments stationed in half a dozen surrounding districts, it was always well below full strength.

Within the hour of the baton charge, confirmed reports arrived of assaults on Indians and the burning of houses, always a first hazard in a disturbance, built mainly of wood and other easily flammable materials. Before leaving the Mogul Guard with my small force, I had taken the precaution to leave instructions for the special Control Room there to be activated as quickly as possible. Contingent plans had been made some time ago to provide a central Riot Headquarters. The Commissioner had gone there as soon as he was satisfied that I had the situation in hand at the bazaar. Arrangements were made to guard the area as best we could for the time being with the reinforcements from the nearest police stations; the Superintendent of the Central Division was left in charge and I followed my superior to the Mogul Guard.

When I arrived in the Control Room, all the emergency telephones had been manned and were ringing continuously. Calls about fighting, looting, arson and injured victims requiring medical attention, were coming in thick and fast not only from nearly every police station in town but also from terrified citizens, reporting gangs of armed Burmans roaming the streets, chasing any Indian, Hindu or Moslem on sight and looting wherever the opportunity arose. In all instances the local Police were inadequate in numbers to contain, let alone suppress, the violence; several unfortunately isolated policemen had been savagely attacked by mobs and at least two were reported killed. For the time being law and order had ceased to exist on the streets in large parts of the capital.

The very first priority now was to obtain reinforcements properly armed as quickly as possible and to place them in all police stations of the city, so that adequate mobile patrols could be sent out to deal with the armed gangs and restore some measure of security. The first to arrive were men from the Military Police barracks, under three British officers; these were despatched at once to the worst areas. The Divisional Superintendents had by then toured around their respective divisions, at no little personal risk, and were told to dispose the armed patrols to best advantage. Numbers were still inadequate, night was approaching and the outlook was grim.

The Commanding Officer of the British battalion, the Gloucestershire Regiment, and his Adjutant arrived at Riot Headquarters at dusk, shortly followed by the Company stationed in Rangoon. He told the Commissioner that the bulk of his force would be available for patrol work during the night; this was welcome news indeed. A hurried conference between the Military and the Police, attended by the Home Secretary and the Governor's Secretary, set down priorities for preventive action. In those days, neither the Army or the Civil forces were motorised; the few vehicles available were quite inadequate for the work in hand. A large fleet of buses, operated by the Rangoon Electric Supply and Bus Company, a British concern, was requisitioned. These were then manned partly by troops and partly by police; the mobility and rapid deployment capabilities of these improvised motorised patrols proved invaluable and very effective during that first night. In my judgement, Rangoon town, or at least a very large part of it, was saved from catastrophic damage by this then unusual combined patrolling on wheels.

Meanwhile, the Indian communities had made some efforts to organise themselves, for self-protection in the first instance, but also for revenge. Reports of killings and woundings by both sides were now being received. The use of fire-arms was also reported in some instances. The serious phase of the disturbances, as far as Rangoon was concerned, lasted for two days and nights before a measure of control was regained in the streets by the authorities. During these forty-eight hours, murdering, looting and arson went hand in hand in most quarters of the town. Both the Military and the Police had to open fire on several occasions when violent mobs refused to disperse. Incidents dragged on for another fortnight before it was judged possible to dispense altogether with further help from the Military. The anti-Indian and anti-Police attitudes spread swiftly beyond the confines of Rangoon and soon the more populated parts of the country, containing Indian settlements, were affected. I do not recollect now precise detailed figures of all casualties. The total number of victims from these communal clashes was around 1,500 killed or seriously wounded, of whom about 170 resulted from encounters with the law-enforcing authorities. The Police and the Military suffered a few minor casualties, mainly from stones and other missiles thrown at them during road clearing operations; three unfortunate policemen were lynched by mobs, who caught them unawares and isolated.

I spent days and nights away from home and family. When I was not doing my spell of duty at Riot Headquarters, I was on the move, either with a bus patrol or with an armed guard in my car. The British soldiers seemed partial to a conducted motoring tour round the town by the Assistant Commissioner. I have forgotten many of the incidents in which I participated or was a close spectator; for some reason, a few incidents have remained more vividly in my mind.

Rangoon boasted another famous Pagoda, not so well known to the outside world as the Shwe Dagon, but greatly venerated by the Buddhist population. Built in the twelfth or thirteenth century, the Sule Pagoda stands in the centre of the main quarters of the City, at the intersection of its two principal thoroughfares. The strategically important site must have been the reason for the Burmese Government to erect an Independence monument next to the Pagoda, in recent years.

On the first day of the riots, soon after I had arrived at the Mogul Guard and was watching the first British troops arriving from their Rangoon barracks in two trucks, a very agitated Burman, whom I knew slightly as an employee of the Municipal Corporation, ran up to me shouting that a mob of Indians was approaching the Pagoda, chanting that they were going to burn it down. This proposed act of folly would have set the whole country ablaze with fanatical hatred from the Burmese. I realised the importance of swift action. The Colonel had just stepped out of the Control Room to welcome his men; I told him that I required them at once for this task of the utmost importance. He was splendid in his reaction to my request which really amounted to more like a directive, under the instructions in the booklet issued to troops "in aide of civil power"; after all I was not a great deal more than half his age. He ordered the subaltern in charge of the platoon to remain in the vehicles and to carry out my instructions.

We lost no time in racing to the scene of trouble, which was not far away. The officer in charge got his men in open order across the broad road (the widest in Rangoon) leading straight to the Pagoda. We then doubled down the road, bayonets fixed and rifles at high port, arriving just before the Indian mob debouched from the road, which intersected ours at the Pagoda's precincts. The unexpected sight of British soldiers advancing in a menacing line, fully armed, was too much for the crowd who turned tail and fled back from where they had come. So far so good, but the bolder elements, back in the Indian quarter, re-grouped and successfully incited more men to join them. Leaving a section around the Pagoda, I told the officer that I intended to break up the gatherings forming at street corners. Again, the men formed a line across the road, I stepped forward and ordered the crowd to disperse. A few stones were thrown at us without effect and the crowd stood fast, being harangued passionately by an obvious trouble-shooter standing on a chair at the back of the mob. I then issued a warning that force would be used to disperse them. This further message had no effect so I told the officer to move in. Again I was surprised at the ease with which a show of force achieved its object. The troops charged, the crowd turned tail and fled, some less quickly than others. I recollect the picture of one rather fat man, who had presumably stumbled or had been knocked over in the rush, lying on the ground with a rather small Private standing over him with the bayonet of his rifle just touching his quivering rotund stomach; the poor man thought his last moment had come. He shouted for mercy in broken English only to be told in a few choice words beyond his comprehension, that the owner had no intention of soiling his clean steel on fatty's blood and guts. Further on, at another street corner, we had to clear more mobs intent on mischief; one persistent agitator, who refused to stop inciting the people to further violence, was wounded by a single deliberate shot during the operations. We got back to the Mogul Guard after dark, weary but on the whole satisfied that a potentially disastrous piece of sacrilegious vandalism had been prevented.

The day after the baton charge by the Police at the Soortee Bara Bazaar, the Burmese Press launched a bitter attack on the Police. To quote again the words in the Riot Inquiry Report:

> The attitude of the Burmese press in relation to this incident was, we think, one of the worst examples of irresponsible journalism inspired by a deliberate desire to create trouble.

So what had started as a series of protest meetings against some old criticisms about Buddhism, turned quickly into a violent countrywide two-pronged attack on the Indian minority and on the Police, with side kicks against the Burmese Ministers in power. Although matters gradually returned to normal, relations between the indigenous peoples and the alien minorities never really reverted to the pre-riot days. Prejudice and grudge were kept alive by the growing number of professional politicians with no experience of power or responsibility. In the midst of all this upheaval, there were cases where people of different races who had rescued and hid an unfortunate individual of the other side were chased by a blood-thirsty gang. There were also instances of comic relief in the all-prevailing gloom which occurred when least expected. Here are some recollections.

When the feelings of the Burmans turned also against the forces of law and order, several attacks were made on the houses of Police officers and other Government servants, living outside the town. I became anxious about the safety of my own family; my house was near the Shwe Dagon Pagoda, within a stone's throw of the road on which the procession had walked to the Soortee Bara Bazaar. My household staff were splendid in this emergency. During my more or less continuous absence, Maung

Pyaung, my old butler, moved from his quarters into the house and slept at night across the threshold of our bedroom with a sharpened dah cradled in his arms. The other servants all took it in turn to mount sentry duty around the compound organised by my orderly and driver, both members of the Rangoon Police. This tiny 'Home Guard' was widely representative of communities in the city. The butler and his assistant were Burmese, the orderly was a Gurkha, the driver a Karen, the cook and his mate Mughs (Muslims from Chittagong now in Bangladesh), the sweeper was an Untouchable from Madras, the mali, and his part-time mate, were high caste Hindus, last but not least our Karen Nanny remained her calm reliable self during the whole crisis. They all rallied round the 'thakinma' (the wife of the 'thakin'; both terms used in the same way as 'sahib' and 'memsahib' in India).

I decided to arm my wife with a fire-arm and brought home a revolver with some ammunition. With much reluctant participation on her part, I showed her how to load, release the safety catch and fire the weapon. She continued to raise objections to having this dangerous instrument in the house; even paraded her household guards, armed with an assortment of cold steel, to convince me that there was no call for the added precaution. I insisted, however, and impressed on her the need to keep the revolver handy and loaded at all times. When the situation improved, I thought it possible to withdraw the weapon she disliked so much. When I asked her to hand it back, she went out of the room and was away for some time. On her return, with the fire-arm, she explained that she had forgotten on which 'almirah' (large wardrobe) top she had put the weapon. I was handed the revolver together with a neatly tied parcel containing the cartridges. She had unloaded the fire-arm as soon as I had left it with her; much more terrified by this loaded menace than by the prospect of any potential attack on the house. So much for my effort to protect my nearest and dearest.

Another, less creditable tale, concerns my excellent driver. He took the opportunity, due to his frequent absences with me, to offer his room in the servants' quarters as a discreet place of assignations for love making, on a sliding scale of fees, by a loving couple. The Assistant Commissioner's compound must have been regarded as a relatively safe place in these troublesome times and what a loving couple needed for their privacy, judging by the number of comings and goings which came to light. Ironically, it was my wife who inadvertently gave the game away; she liked my driver a great deal and he in turn was devoted to her, delighted to be her guide around Rangoon, of which more anon.

When conditions had reverted to quieter times and I was able to return to a more normal routine, she said to me one evening when we were discussing recent happenings, "a lot of people seemed to be using our compound as a short cut during the riots". I pressed her further and it transpired that, when she could not sleep at night, she would sit on the verandah, outside her bedroom, and see people hurrying silently towards the rear of the house. Even the best of servants had a curious sense of loyalty towards each other and I had to exercise unfamiliar pressure on Maung Pyaung before he came clean and disclosed the business. Saw Pan

Daik, the driver, did not attempt to deny his part in the matter when he realised that I knew all. I was able to satisfy myself that he, himself, had not acted as a pimp but more like a benevolent but rapacious landlord. This saved him from dismissal which I would have had to impose. Instead, I demoted him from Head Constable (he received promotion when I became Assistant Commissioner because I was entitled to a police driver of that rank) for six months, but kept him on as my chauffeur, much to my wife's relief. I suppose that his demotion must have hurt him but he never showed any resentment and continued to serve us both, cheerfully and efficiently, to the end of my time in the Rangoon Police, six years since he had first joined me in the Western Division.

An amusing episode took place when we first used tear gas to disperse crowds. This weapon was then fairly new and had only been tried a few times in street riots in India. An urgent request was sent to the Government of India for the loan of an Instructor. He arrived by air a few days later with a supply of the gas. A special squad was set up under my direct command to go through a crash course of instruction; the instructor then departed within a few days. The Army Ordnance supplied us with the rather cumbersome service gas mask as there were no others. The tear gas grenades could be either fired from a special short gun or thrown by hand. We had to apply our newly learnt skills within twenty-four hours of being declared competent in the use of this equipment. A large crowd had refused to disperse when so ordered and it was decided to use tear gas instead of the usual tactics. We, in the special squad, donned our masks, which in themselves intrigued the crowd and caused some consternation; we fired several grenades and lobbed a few more into the mob and – 'Hey Presto' –the people fled headlong down the street, pursued by the smoke of the gas. Well satisfied, we removed our masks and I was just telling the officer in charge of the armed patrol to take over, when a strong gust of wind veered round and drove the gas clouds, still hanging around in the street, straight back at us. So, while the mob was running one way, we fled as fast as we could the other; the whole length of road was then well and truly empty.

Shortly after that incident there was another comic interlude to relieve tensions. One of the Police stations reported that they had arrested a prominent 'pongyi' agitator and that a large mob had surrounded the station, demanding the release of the prisoner. The Police had, so far, managed to keep the crowd outside the building but needed urgent assistance. I happened to be at the Mogul Guard when the report was received and decided to join the stand-by platoon of Gurkha Military Police, embussing for the trouble spot. On arrival we had difficulty in gaining access and had to exert considerable force, and again to clear a way for the arrested man to be placed in the bus. As soon as the prisoner and his escort were ready to depart, a crowd of yelling teenage girls surrounded the vehicle and clung to the sides. As they were pulled off, they or others immediately climbed back. It was clear that these new tactics were paying off; we were reluctant to use the sort of strong arm measures employed on the men. The Gurkha Subadar sensed my dilemma, came up and asked for permission to use his own method, assuring me with a large grin, that it would be quite painless but effective; I told him to carry on. Within seconds there was not a girl to be seen near the bus which then moved off to the Town Lock-up with the agitator inside.

The Subadar's method had indeed been effective and rewarding, in more ways than one. He had placed some of his small, wiry men around the bus and at a given signal they had each pulled down a girl's longyi (skirt). Burmese women did not wear pants in those days and the resulting display of nudity was too much for the victims who with shrieks, jumped down from the side of the bus, hurriedly pulled on the discarded garment and ran off shame-faced into the crowd. Even the angry mob, after a moment of stunned silence, burst into loud laughter at the sight of all the rounded young bottoms. This incident again illustrated the inborn sense of fun in the Burmese and how quickly both men and women could revert from anger to laughter and vice-versa. Even the Burmese vernacular press, who were still printing vituperative articles about imaginary Military and Police savagery, reported on this particular incident more in humour than in anger.

Six months after the troubles had started, we decided that my wife and child should go home before the onset of the hottest weather preceding the rains; I was hoping to get my next leave before the end of the year. One of my last acts, which could be related to the abnormal times we were still living in, was to send a reassuring cable to her on board ship in Colombo harbour. The local papers there had picked up a Rangoon report, in which it had been stated that the Assistant Commissioner of Police had been injured and taken to hospital. Someone had shown the article to my wife who had, understandably, sent off an anxious message of inquiry. The truth was that a brick had hit me in the back and the jagged side had torn my shirt and broken the skin. As a precaution against infection, I had dropped in at the General Hospital on my way home, to have the wound cleaned and dressed. Some enterprising journalist must have seen me going in or coming out.

Tension between the communities diminished but never really reverted to normal during 1939. The oubreak of war had renewed tensions, both communal and political, but more importantly from my point of view had meant the cancellation of all home leave. Members of the Indian Police were informed that they would not be called up, by virtue of their Commissions in the Indian Army Reserve of Officers, which some of us still possessed, nor would any of us be allowed to retire prematurely or resign as long as the war emergency lasted. My wife then decided to return to Burma, the day war was declared, against my and her family's reservations. She eventually reached Rangoon safely, after a long and adventurous sea journey, subjected to delays and diversions. Our nevertheless very happy and welcome reunion happened within a few weeks of my release from the Rangoon Police.

My long attachment to the City Police force had been a congenial one, despite all the trials and tribulations during the abnormally long periods of tension. Many of the rank and file were now known to me by name and by sight. The Inspectors of Circles and the Station Officers together with many of the attached Sub-Inspectors, had at one time or another participated in matters and incidents in which I had been directly involved. I would be sorry to leave them, when the time came, but I now realised that physical exertions and mental strain, for days on end, had taken more out of me than I had realised. I think the same applied to the other senior officers who had borne most of the heavy responsibilities. When the opportunity arose for a complete change of work, I thought it sensible to accept. So, in February 1940, I was seconded to the Customs Department.

24
Assistant Collector of Customs

Customs and Excise were separate Departments in India and Burma. Excise duty was levied by the Provincial Governments and Customs duty by the Central Government of India. The senior ranks were recruited into the Imperial Customs Service, one of the All India Services. When Burma became separated from India, the officers serving there remained seconded for a while whilst 'Burma' men could be trained. The posts of Collectors were soon filled by members of the Burma Civil Service (the Indian Civil Service was now the Burma Civil Service, Class I). A third Assistant Collector was in charge of the Preventive Service, the Outports and the Land Customs Stations. This post was still filled by a senior Assistant Collector of the Imperial Service and he remained on secondment in this post for more than two years.

The seconded officer was eventually due for promotion to Collector of Customs in India. His recall became a matter of urgency and the Burma Government was in a quandary, since nobody had been selected to train for this more specialised work. The new Collector, Harold Oxbury, was an old friend of mine; he had started his official career as a Subdivisional Officer in Mandalay district when I was undergoing my training there. He pressed me to consider transfer to Customs work since I was familiar with the Port and its workings; particularly the Preventive Branch of the Customs. When I was in the Port Police, I had worked closely with the departing Assistant Collector on several smuggling cases and knew something of the set-up.

The political situation had changed a great deal in the last few years. Both India and Burma were promised full independence after the war. We younger members in the various civilian services could no longer expect to serve for the normal period before retiring on a full pension. In short, our prospects for a full career in our chosen professions were now non-existent. I had therefore no second thoughts in accepting the proposed change of work when the Government gave its blessing to the request for my services.

I was allowed to work for two months under the guidance of the outgoing Assistant Collector before assuming the appointment of 'Assistant Collector of Customs, Outports, Land Customs Stations and Superintendent of the Preventive Service', the full cumbersome title of the post. I had still a lot to learn when I was thrust into the saddle, but words like: Ship's Manifest, Bill of Lading, Bill of Entry, Clearance

Certificate, F.O.B. (Free on board) had acquired some meaning. The most important of my diverse responsibilities was that of being in charge of the Preventive staff. This service was, in effect, the 'Police force' of the Customs department and consisted of a Chief Inspector, several Inspectors, Preventive Officer and Customs 'Peons'. The latter were collectively known as the 'Rummaging Staff', searching ships and transit sheds for contraband, acting as watchmen on dock gates and in sheds, under the direction of Preventive Officers. When I joined, most of the officers were Anglo-Indians or Anglo-Burmans, since the educational requirements for entry were higher than those achieved by most Burmese lads in the vernacular schools of the country. This policy of recruitment was not meant to be deliberately slanted in favour of the mixed races, but a good knowledge of English, spoken and written, was desirable, indeed necessary to deal efficiently with the work. Burmanisation began soon after I took over and, by the time the Eastern war began, over a third of the staff were Burmans, thanks to a rapid expansion of the force to deal with the Burma Road transit trade to China; the Peons were nearly all Indians.

Although sea-going trade visited the half-dozen outports, ninety-five per cent of customs duty was collected in Rangoon; consequently the bulk of the Preventive staff worked there. My official quarters could not have been more strategically placed for close and constant contact with the staff and their work. This accessability was essential but had its disadvantages; being new to the game, I started by allowing thrusting importers to ring my front door bell at all times after office hours. The usual plea was that the goods were either highly perishable or urgently required for one reason or another. I soon learnt to harden my heart and let it be known that if callers, on urgent business, turned out to have given false facts, they would be penalised by applying all the available red tape (and there was plenty of it) to delay the clearance of their future imports. This warning was widely broadcast by my staff and had a most salutary effect on my peace in leisure hours or in sleep.

I was provided with a large, spaciously roomed flat at the top of the Custom House, running more than half the length of the whole long building. Another flat on the other side of the staircase was occupied by one of the Burmese Assistant Collectors. The flat itself was not unlike a very big railway carriage, all the rooms were in line with a corridor running the whole length of the three bedrooms, bathrooms, dining room and sitting room. The kitchen and servants quarters were at one end, separated by an archway and door, which nobody ever shut. This long rectangular design for the living quarters left a considerable open space on the flat roof of the main building. My predecessor had built an impromptu garden, consisting of large wooden tubs full of flowers and small bushes. In the middle of this display he had set a large metal frame, covering it with flowery creepers which were also trained across the horizontal struts on top. The general effect of this structure was that of an open-sided garden house where he and his wife had most of their meals and drinks in the evenings. This 'garden' delighted my wife who soon set about improving the flora. She was a keen gardener (and still is) and never ceased to be surprised by the abundance of colour and variety of tropical flowers and plants. The great advantage of this 'garden' was its accessability to an abundance of water, so that when her friends' gardens withered away in the dry season, she could still display a riot of colour and greenery. We even had the benefit of this display when sitting indoors because the corridor was open-ended on the garden side and every room had French windows, which were permanently open. Needless to say, the 'garden house' was our favourite spot after sundown, all evening meals were eaten al fresco, unless we had more than four people at a sitting. Penthouses were not common then in Burma and our roof-top abode was considered unique by visitors who envied us not a little for this unusual home. Another asset was ready-made divertisement for us and anyone else present. We never lost interest in sitting around watching the unceasing activities in the river and alongside wharves. At night, the scene was even more entrancing with countless fairylike lights displayed on large ships, alongside or at anchor in mid-stream, or on all the small craft darting busily to and fro. We had a happy life in this elevated home of ours until the Japanese ruined it for us, as they did for countless others.

Unfortunately, I was unable to make any trips to the outports because of the rapid increase in the transit trade to China which took up more and more of my time. In the end, the Government recognised the impossibility of the situation and appointed an additional Assistant Collector, to relieve me of responsibility for the outports, much to my personal regret at having to forego the prospect of some pleasant sea trips to the furthest ends of the long Burma coast line. In fact, overseas trading to and from the outports had been increasing steadily for some years and the Government were considering a proposal to provide the Customs Department with a sea-going yacht, so that senior officers of the Department could inspect and supervise staff at outports without being at the mercy of scheduled voyages by coastal steamers, thus nullifying any prospect of surprise checking, an essential element for effective supervision. The war put an end to this enticing project.

My arrival in the Custom House coincided with the beginning of a rapidly expanding transit trade overland to China. The Japanese stranglehold on the Chinese mainland had virtually closed the sea ports to imports and exports, to and from those parts of the country still in the hands of the Chiang Kai-shek Government. The Americans were supporting the Chinese in their struggle against the invader and were sending strategic war materials through Burma into Yunnan Province where the Chinese Government had taken refuge from the advancing onslaught. Anglo-American assistance was provided to undertake the costly and large-scale improvements to transform a poorly surfaced and narrow road into a highway, to carry a constant stream of heavy traffic. The road ran from Lashio in the Northern Shan States, through the border to the Chinese town of Kuning, with little more than a track beyond to the new capital of Chungking. Intensive work had been going on for over a year and the highway was now capable of taking a fair amount of heavy-goods vehicles without too many hold-ups for landslides and other mishaps, caused by the difficult terrain. As communications improved so did the amount of traffic and the number of commercial goods seeking the isolated markets in Western China. I shall comment in more detail on this particular aspect of my new work in a separate part because it took up more and more of my time and was a new experience for the Customs Department.

The importing of salt from India to Burma in bulk was a paying trade which had led to a scandal in the Custom House before my time. The procedure was for a salt ship to be rigged with special scales, belonging to the Customs Department, and for Preventive Officers to tally the number of off-loadings into the special containers provided with the scales, before the load was tipped into the waiting barges alongside. The cheating procedure had been simple: the importer offered a bribe for missing a container's unloading every so often. He only paid import duty on the actual quantity unloaded; a certain amount of wastage was accepted as inevitable in transit due to contamination mainly because the loose salt was loaded straight into ships' holds. The deception could only operate successfully if everyone concerned in the operation was squared; which meant from the humble Customs Peons doing all the manual work, through the tallying Preventive Officers to the Inspector in charge of the unloading procedure. The result of the departmental inquiry ended with the dismissal of a number of the Preventive staff and a revision of the checking procedures.

Ever since the unsavoury incident, special additional precautions were imposed whenever a salt ship arrived in port. The Chief Inspector, or his Deputy, was placed in direct charge of the unloading operation and the Superintendent of the Preventive service made more than the usual number of surprise visits to the ship, to impose random recounts against tally sheets, which meant unloading the salt from the barge into the ship's hold. These extra precautions cost time and were of course unpopular with the importers and the stevedores' employers. I must admit that, like my whole staff, I disliked the arrival of this cargo. The sticky salt tended to cling to clothes, hair and skin; the heat soon set up intense skin irritation where the salt clung to the exposed skin. Most of us tried to minimise the discomfort of irritated skin by wearing long trousers, long sleeves and buttoned-up shirts. This partial protection was achieved at the cost of intense sweating, which could become as great a bane as inflamed skin. Bad as conditions were on deck, they were far worse in the holds of the ship where the near-naked coolies were shovelling the loose salt into large buckets which were then hoisted to the salt scales above. Amongst the variety of tasks which the Preventive staff had to perform, some more popular than others, working on a salt ship was easily the last in the popularity stakes. I had a duty roster, in the form of a chart hung on the wall of my office, which was written up daily so that I could check that everyone received the same share in the various duties which had to be performed.

As in any other big port, smuggling attempts were constant; from the universally practised petty smuggling by otherwise respectable passengers, to the more serious deceptions attempted by unscrupulous importers. People were caught daily either in the transit sheds or at the wharf gates, attempting to remove packages before they had been cleared by Customs. Another method was to practise deception when declaring the contents of packages, either in regard to quantity or to quality. Since it was manifestly impossible for the appraising staff to open and examine in detail every piece of crated cargo, some importers could achieve occasional successes at the cost of the Department. However, those who were caught at this game ran the risk of heavy on the spot fines and confiscation of the goods under the Sea Customs Act; the Collector and his Assistant Collectors had wide powers to inflict heavy fines, many times the value of the intercepted goods. More specialised smuggling operations were organised by experienced operators dealing in high-priced contraband such as drugs, precious metals and stones. Some of the ingenuity displayed in such smuggling attempts was truly remarkable. Methods of concealment were varied and clever; the more valuable the goods, and thus the ill-gotten gains, the more devious and costly the methods adopted. Out of the many cases, big and small, which came to my notice in the two years I spent in Customs work, the following show the sort of unusual ingenuity we came across in our Preventive work.

*   *   *

At the outbreak of the war in Europe, the export of gold from India was prohibited. The price soared in the markets of the Far East and a large illicit trade developed. Some of this traffic from India came by sea to Rangoon where an active underground gold market flourished for some time. We knew that a number of smugglers were engaged in taking 'Queen Victoria' golden sovereigns out of the country. They had been hoarded for decades, ever since the rapid advancement of trading between Britain and India after the Great Mutiny. The spectacular rise in the price of gold, due to the war, had now released this hoarded wealth for enticing profits. Soon, the small coins were joined by bars and even large pieces melted down into various shapes to fit inventive places of concealment. In order to put an effective brake on this increasingly ambitious illicit traffic, substantially increased rewards were authorised for information leading to successful interceptions.

One evening, as my wife and I were having our usual pre-dinner drink in our roof garden, the front door bell rang. The caller was one of my 'regular' informers; by this I mean that he had brought me reliable information on several occasions which had led to successful circumventions of smuggling operations. He was in an excited state and told me that he had just received news that a large quantity of gold had been concealed on board a ship which was now arriving. He could not tell me more for the moment but had arranged to meet his source of information again to obtain more details as soon as possible. He was adamant that the amount of gold was worth "many lakhs of rupees" (about £7,500). If the ship could be delayed from berthing whilst he obtained more precise knowledge about the place of concealment, we would stand a much better chance to intercept the contraband. I ascertained from the

Port Authority that the incoming vessel, now due within an hour, was one of the steamers on a regular run from Calcutta; she was well-known to me and so was her Captain. I asked the Conservator of the Port, also a long-standing friend from my Port Police days, to instruct the pilot to make fast at one of the mid-stream anchorages, instead of bringing the vessel as usual alongside, explaining the reason for the emergency request. My friend agreed at once to make the necessary arrangements but added that he hoped my information would turn out to be true. Failure to justify delaying a ship's berthing was a serious matter, particularly one on a regular run; the shipping agents were bound to raise a lot of trouble all round if we failed to find the gold.

Bidding my wife a hasty farewell, I left to board my speed-boat with three Preventive Officers on duty in the Custom House, having left instructions for the Chief Inspector to bring along a follow-up party with an adequate rummaging crew, as soon as my informer had contacted him with the hoped-for additional information. By the time we had cast off, the ship in question was coming up river slowly, making for one of the vacant mid-stream anchorages. I did not wish to raise the alarm before it was necessary, so waited until she had made fast. Meanwhile, two additional customs launches, on routine patrolling, had been instructed to join me and so did one of the Port Police craft, coming to see what it was all about. Again my previous association with law and order in the Port came in useful and I asked that boat to join my two launches in keeping all small craft well away from the sides of the anchored ship until I gave the all clear. Once on board, I had a meeting with the Captain who was understandably mystified and upset at the sudden changes in the routine berthing procedure. I quickly told him the facts as I knew them so far and he reacted, as I had expected, offering any help he could give. My news about hidden gold on board his ship was the first he had heard. He made several useful suggestions about likely hiding places but I told him I preferred to wait until I had more precise news. Time went on, more Customs Officers came on board, bringing a rummaging crew of twenty. By now passengers and ship's crew were agog about the goings-on but still no Chief Inspector with the vital additional information. The ship's agents' representative, also known to me, now appeared on board in a pretty bad temper. He wanted to know why all the delay and fuss. It took me some time to calm him down, but he knew all along that my head could fall first, if the ship's hold-up proved futile.

I had realised from the start that, unless we could obtain more precise facts about the location of the hoard, the chances of recovering the gold were greatly diminished. A ship has hundreds of nooks and crannies difficult of access in which, with a little ingenuity, objects could be safely concealed for a long time. It was more than likely that the smugglers would now leave the gold to lie where it was for one or more voyages, until the hue and cry had died down. Time was passing; the agent and even the Captain were getting impatient again, although I explained that if the ship was allowed to berth alongside, I would have to submit the passengers and anyone else leaving the ship to the possibility of tedious and embarrassing personal searches if we had reason to suspect anyone as a carrier. This possibility deterred the agent for a while longer. Meanwhile, without much hope, I had ordered a general search of the ship to begin, to give some justification for the delay.

Just as I was thinking of allowing the ship to be brought alongside so that the passengers at least could be disembarked and put through Customs clearance, my Chief Inspector arrived out of breath but looking pleased; he drew me aside and disclosed that the gold was definitely concealed somewhere in the first class saloon. I called off the general search, asked the few passengers, still drinking duty-free alcohol, to leave the saloon, brought in the rummaging crew and told the Captain that the ship could now berth. We proceeded to search the area minutely, from one end to the other, without success. Dejectedly, I sat down on a padded bench, which ran right round three sides of the saloon, under the windows opening on to the deck. Each window had the usual let-down framed pane of glass as well as a frame of wooden slats, for protection against the sun or the waves in rough weather. All the windows and slats were let down for coolness. Looking idly round I suddenly observed that in a number of windows the glass and the slats were above the sills, whereas in the majority of windows they were flush, as one would expect, when let down to the full extent. Normally, the odd ill-fitting window would not have raised suspicion since in this climate the wood did lend itself to warping, but under the circumstances anything was worth trying. The panels below the suspect windows were removed and in the process several gold coins fell to the floor. In every ill-fitting window, the hollow space to accommodate the lowered frames for window slats, was crammed tightly with small ingots and sovereigns. Just to make certain, we also dismantled all the other panels to satisfy ourselves that we had recovered all the gold.

By the time the search was concluded it was well past midnight. I decided to have the gold removed to my flat in the Custom House, where I had a safe to store temporarily valuable articles seized by the staff, pending proper storage. My wife had, of course, long since gone to bed. I crept into our bedroom with two of the six stout canvas bags in which we had placed the seized gold, and emptied the contents of small gold bars and sovereigns all around her sleeping form. She woke with a start to find herself surrounded by pieces of gold. As she said later, rather pragmatically, it was better than in the fairy tale, where the princess only woke up to a kiss. Next day, the gold was removed to the Reserve Bank for weighing and valuation. The value was in excess of 50,000 rupees (I cannot remember the full amount) but on the black market it would have fetched a great deal more and at today's price of gold, many times the amount.

The second substantial haul of gold was equally well concealed. On this occasion, the same informer reported that a carrier was bringing in the gold concealed amongst his belongings. He said that his source of information would let him know the identity of the carrier as the passengers disembarked. On the due date, my informer discreetly positioned himself strategically to receive the tip and to pass it on to me. The practice in Rangoon was for the Customs to set up a mobile enclosure in a transit shed where passengers were shepherded from the ship's gangway for the examination of luggage. As it was the end of season for migratory influx of labour, the number of passengers was not unduly large.

The informer gave me the pre-arranged signal, identifying the carrier. To my astonishment, he had singled out an insignificant emaciated coolie, who must have travelled as a deck passenger. He was wearing little more than an old none-too-clean dhoti, carrying a metal pail with each hand, which seemed to be filled with dirty rags. I looked back questioningly at my informer who nodded vigorously in reply. The man was apprehended at the exit from the Customs enclosure and taken to the room set aside for personal examinations. The traveller did not, or pretended not to, understand any other language than his native Telugu. This was the language of the seasonal workers, coming from South India to provide cheap labour in the fields on the roads and elsewhere during the dry season. We searched all the belongings crammed in the two pails and then the man himself without result. The Telugu interpreter confirmed that the suspect was a genuine illiterate coolie; he was convinced that the man knew nothing about any gold.

I stepped outside to have a word with my informer; he was pretending to be looking for a friend amongst the passengers. I drew him aside and told him that he must have made a mistake, or that his source had let him down since the man we apprehended just did not have the wit to carry out the smuggling. My man said that he was sure no mistake had been made but that he would re-check with his source who was still around. He was back in a short time and re-affirmed that no mistake had occurred and that we had caught the right person. So, back I went to the room and we went through the whole searching process again; still no gold. In sheer exasperation, I kicked one of the buckets which had been emptied out. Instead of rolling over as one would expect from a hefty kick, the bucket only wobbled and remained upright. The fact took a moment to sink in, then I picked it up and realised our interception had not been in vain. The two buckets, although empty, were very heavy. After removing the outer and inner metal coverings at the bottom of the pails, we found sandwiched between them solid round ingots of gold, two inches deep, shaped to fit the circumference of the base of the pails. We had overlooked the curious fact that the base of the buckets had been flush with the bottom of the sides whereas normally a bucket's base is inset from the bottom by an inch or two. This seizure was valued at over 30,000 rupees, a great deal of money in those days. The carrier protested his innocence to the end and denied all knowledge about the ingots. His story was that a stranger on board had approached him before the ship was due to berth, had offered him a sum of money to take the buckets ashore and through Customs. He gave us a vague description of the person which could have fitted many of the other native passengers from Madras. In any case, if there had been another, the real smuggler, he would have made himself scarce as soon as he saw that the buckets had been intercepted and long before we had extracted this story. Despite the inordinate weight of each empty bucket, which must have aroused curiosity, if not suspicion, I was inclined to believe the yarn. My interpreter was convinced that our man was a simple-minded illiterate coolie, incapable of putting on such an act and such disguise. This supposition would also tend to explain why the informer had been unable to describe the suspect to me in advance and had to wait to the last minute for the disclosure. The informer may well have been in league with the plotters, become dissatisfied with the promised share of the eventual profit or have decided that the reward money could turn out the better deal.

Informers were a necessary evil both for Police and for Customs Preventive Officers. None of us, employing such types, had any illusions about their integrity or honesty. Their predominant motive was a money reward; sometimes revenge, blackmail or to curry favour were secondary motives. The only few times when an informer disclosed information to me for higher motives than personal gain, was when I served in Military Intelligence during the war. The general rule was that the recipient of information never probed into how or why it had been obtained. I seldom dealt directly with informers, the intelligence would be collected by subordinate officers from their own sources. Sometimes, when the news was unusual or valuable, the informer would be brought before a senior officer, either at his own request or because the officer thought it prudent or necessary. Occasionally, an intelligent informer would seek to approach higher authority directly, thinking that the reward would thus be greater or that he would not have to share it with the recipent of the news – a bit of truth in both reasons! Some few times, because the matter was exceptional, I would take over an informer or employ my own man, giving him direct instructions; pulling rank on an informer made him less liable to consider the temptation of double-crossing the officer.

We had one strange happening whilst I was in the Customs. In fact the broad outline of the event could serve as suitable material for expansion into a mystery novel by a writer better gifted with imagination that I am!

One morning, the Port authorities notified all departments concerned that a Russian ship had arrived without proper ship's papers. The Captain had declared that he was carrying arms and ammunition "for urgent delivery to China". Pending further instructions from the Government, the ship had been detained below the bar. A large sandbank stretched across the Rangoon River above the main anchorage of the port which was reached through a dredged channel; hence the expression 'below the bar' to indicate that the vessel had been isolated from the harbour proper. This information caused quite a stir in Government circles and a flurry of cables to various places. The Port Police were ordered to keep a watch and deny general access to the ship until further orders. As nobody had as yet given any special instructions to Customs, I decided to satisfy my aroused curiosity by boarding this maritime conundrum in the course of a routine inspection of staff working on ships.

The speed-boat, in which I normally moved around the harbour, reached the isolated ship at the end of my rounds around mid-morning. She turned out to be a small, ugly, dilapidated coaster, painted a sort of battle-ship grey all over, with numerous rust spots on the hull and superstructure. She looked as if she had spent many days at sea in all kinds of weather. I did not spot any name at the bows, before reaching the rather tattered gangway. A short stout figure, dressed in badly creased dark blue trousers and an old reefer jacket, wearing an equally old nautical cap, met me on deck and introduced himself as the Captain, in broken English. I pointed to the blue Ensign with the Crown in the fly, fluttering from the stern of my craft and said "Customs". That settled, he invited me on to the bridge where he introduced me to the second officer - a woman! Recovering from this surprise, I noticed a number of potted plants placed on both sides of the bridge and in the wheelhouse, presumably evidence of the feminine touch on board, but her general appearance did not invite badinage on this supposition. She was dressed in the same fashion as the Captain, bowed but did not offer to shake hands. Neither her figure nor her looks fitted the proverbial spy.

I explained to the Captain as best I could in a mixture of three languages (he seemed to know a smattering of each, English, French and German) that my visit was only a preliminary look around. He readily admitted that he was carrying military hardware and produced a bundle of papers, worn at the edges, containing lists of words and numbers which turned out to be an apology for a ship's manifest. I asked to have a closer look at this document and he led me to the main saloon, a long rather narrow room with a table running down its length and chairs on either side, all fixed to the deck. Rather to my surprise, the second officer had followed us; this time she removed her cap and I was again disappointed to find that even her hair was not the proverbial long blonde kind, but black, parted in the middle and severely brushed back into a tight bun at the back of her neck. The Captain explained her presence by stating that "my second officer, she speaks French" adding that, as I might have difficulty with the cargo list, she might be more help than he. Difficulty was quite an understatement. I could not make head or tail of the lists, and she certainly knew more than his dozen or so words of French. She sat down beside me, silent and unsmiling, until the Captain walked out, then in an unexpectedly pleasant voice and a smile said that she was also Russian.

Whilst we were going through the lists in a slow hesitating way, a Chinese steward in dirty white shorts and a singlet appeared and proceeded to lay a knife and fork on the table at the other end from us. Shortly after, a giant of a man, he must have been over six and half feet in height, walked in. He was wearing dirty long trousers and a singlet. His hair was close-cropped and he came up to me, clicked his heels, bowed and said "Chief Engineer" in a deep voice. I stood up, shook hands and said something commonplace, whereupon he shook his head vigorously and said "No speak" and marched off to the end of the table, picked up the knife in one hand and the fork in the other. He sat down, planted his elbows on the table with the eating implements upright at the ready in his ham-fisted palms and roared one strange word. The Chinaman appeared instantly with an enormous plate, on which was a whole large roasted chicken, a mound of boiled whole potatoes and another of uncut French beans (I can still recollect this huge amount of food distinctly). The silent giant proceeded to eat his way through this mountain of edibles, the only sound was the steady mastication of his jaws. I pretended to be looking through the lists whilst surreptitiously trying to count the potatoes, as they disappeared into his mouth but it was difficult and I gave up after the first half dozen. When the plate was quite empty, the man stood up, just missing the ceiling with the top of his head, turned towards me, clicked his heels again, bowed and departed without another word. My lady companion had not taken the slightest notice of this remarkable achievement and in reply to my question said briefly that he was a "Check". It was obvious that she did not wish to enlarge on the crew or their idiosyncrasies. It was anyhow no longer my official business to probe into details about the crews on ships. During my hour or so on board, I only saw about half a dozen people, including those mentioned; the rest seemed to have retired out of sight.

The Captain re-appeared in the saloon, asked if we had got through the list and would I like to see some of the cargo? I still had made little progress in trying to identify details of arms and ammunition by the manifest entries. I got out of this difficulty by stating that a detailed examination of all the records would have to be made at the appropriate time, I would just like to glance into a hold. We all three went on deck where a couple of men were already taking the heavy tarpaulin and planks off one hold. The Captain and I went down the short fixed iron ladder. Besides the sort of stout reinforced crates in which small arms and ammunition are packed, there were also bundles of rifles. It seemed apparent from the markings on crates and boxes that this weaponry had been manufactured in Eastern Europe. I asked the Captain who his agent was ashore and he replied that he was waiting to be contacted by a Chinese official; again he was reluctant to pursue the matter. At this stage, I really had no official reasons to visit the vessel, let alone make detailed inquiries, so I did not press for more explicit information. In any case, any investigations into the puzzling presence of the vessel would be a matter for the Police, acting on higher instructions. Nobody would have thanked me for risking a diplomatic incident by my probing before such a risk became an unavoidable possibility. The Captain had been friendly and had met my requests within limits whether out of ignorance of my weak official status pro tem or for the desire to avoid antagonism at all times. Before I left, he insisted on taking me to his cabin for a drink; the expected full glass of vodka was handed to me. I never did like vodka, even diluted or mixed, and was quite unable to drink it down in one long swallow like the Captain; he was disappointed that I would not have another fill-up to keep him company. We parted on even better terms than at the start.

I sent in a report on my visit and suggested that an expert in weaponry should perhaps take a look around the cargo to identify more precisely the various firearms, ammunition and their places of origin. I explained why I had not pressed for better answers to my controversial questions, expecting to receive a rocket, either for not being pressing enough or for asking any questions at all. Some days later, the Director of Intelligence, a senior officer of the Indian Police, who had occasionally sought my services previously, summoned me. To my surprise he seemed to approve of my uncalled-for visit to the ship and thanked me for a 'useful' report. He then asked me for my views on this puzzling and apparently unexpected arrival. He told me that the official Chinese Agency, monitoring the transit of war materials overland to China, professed to know nothing about the matter nor did any of the shipping agents in Rangoon. I then told him my theory in view of what he had disclosed.

The Independent Chinese Government, now pushed into Western China by the Japanese, claimed to have effective administrative control over those remaining Provinces. In fact, there were still a number of semi-, even wholly, independent warlords in some of the remoter regions, particularly in those adjacent to the border with Northern Burma and Laos. They were the old-fashioned remnants of a regime which flourished for a long time, when the far-off Authority in Peking was but a name. The modern warlords were always on the lookout to improve their armoury with modern weaponry. There had been, long before the Burma Road, an intermittent illicit arms trade overland into China. It was my belief that the mystery ship was carrying contraband arms and that some of them had already been sold elsewhere on the black market and that the Captain (or his employers) was seeking buyers in Rangoon. This is what I told the Intelligence Bureau; whether my theory was near to or far from the truth, I never knew. The mystery ship and its crew disappeared soon after, without unloading cargo in the port. I was never told anything more officially but surmised that the Burma Government, perhaps acting on pressure from London and/or Chungking, had ordered the vessel to leave.

More often than not, the Preventive staff did not receive precise information on where contraband had been hidden in a ship. Even if a general location was indicated, the search could be long and tedious. In a 'general rummage' the ship had to be searched from stem to stern; this required a large staff of searchers on a protracted, dirty and tiresome routine, disliked both by the Customs and the ship's agents, since time was money. The mostly Indian Customs 'Peons' were divided into gangs each under one or more Preventive Officers; each gang would be given a defined section of the vessel to rummage. The operation always consumed hours of searching, unless someone had a lucky break. Sometimes in a large steamer the search would drag on into the next day and even longer, as there were hundreds of places where contraband could be hidden. Sometimes clever operators would deliberately leak information so that Customs could discover some of the illicit goods and then depart, leaving the bulk intact for collection when the coast was clear.

In the relatively short time of my two years in the Customs, the ingenuity and the trouble taken to conceal contraband on ships amazed me on many occasions. Behind bulkheads, inside ventilators, lifeboats, lavatory cisterns, bath and washbasin drainage S bends, in remote spaces in cargo holds, the list is endless and they all had to be looked into. On one occasion, a huge quantity of lighter flints (of which there seemed to be a chronic shortage in the Far East) were concealed at the extreme end of the propeller shaft tunnel in a small coaster. On another, a substantial amount of opium was found under a great heap of coal in a fuel bunker on an old ship engaged in the coastal trade between China and India; the laborious task of having to remove tons of coal before recovering the cakes of opium in their protective bags appeared to be no deterrent to that determined gang.

The amount of wealth involved in the maritime trade through Rangoon had grown steadily, ever since the advent of the British in 1824. By 1942 Customs duty revenue had overtaken Land Tax revenue, until then by far the largest source of income for the Government. The single main contributory factor for this shift in Government income was the enormous increase in the overland transit trade to China, made possible by the great improvements and innovations on the famous 'Burma Road'. The Government had always appreciated the importance of a well paid Customs service. The Appraisers and the Preventive Officers were the I.C.S. of the Provincial services (old All-India Services' hands will appreciate the comparative simile!). The Department, in turn, demanded a high educational standard and, in the beginning, the posts were filled mainly by domiciled Europeans or Anglo-Indians who had been educated in English language schools. By the time the Japanese put a stop to Customs work, Burmanisation had progressed rapidly and nearly half the appointments were held by Burmans or Karens. My own time in the Custom House came to a sudden and abrupt end, as I shall recount. I had found the work absorbing and full of new interests and would have been happy to complete the five years, stipulated as the minimum period of my secondment from the Police.

25
The Burma Road

A motorable road had existed for some time from Lashio in the Northern Shan States to the border and then into China, following an old trade route. The road was subject to landslides and flooding in the higher regions and was infrequently used by motor cars and lorries. Conditions were said to be worse on the Chinese side, little more than a cart track in places. When the Japanese effectively closed all the ports on the China coast for strategic supplies to the hard-pressed Chinese Government now established in Chungking, Yunnan Province, Western China, such supplies had to come overland through Burma. The American Government were giving increasing aid and advice to the Chinese and were pressing the British Government to improve access into China through Burma. Considerable road works were then undertaken and, by the end of 1939, the old trade route had been transformed into a busy highway for continuous heavy road traffic. Conditions were still inadequate on sections of the road but improving all the time. During 1940, the volume of goods moved had increased ten-fold on the previous twelve month period. The main purpose of the new road was strategic but the traffic, which had now grown from a trickle to a torrent, included also a considerable commercial trade, in addition to war materials. The Japanese forced the British Government to deny the movement of strategic materials on the road for some months, when our fortunes of war were at a low ebb. Pearl Harbour put an end to this duress and an optimum flow of traffic was resumed and maintained until the Japanese invasion of Burma effectively cut off all traffic in 1942.

The Customs Department had to expand rapidly to deal with the increased business. New rules and regulations were promulgated, new staff had to be recruited and trained as quickly as possible; in particular, the Preventive staff which had to be increased by a third to ensure that the procedure for this large volume of transit traffic was adequately supervised. For practical reasons, it was not possible to use the bonded warehouse system or to arrange for the repayment of import duty, when the goods had reached the frontier. Furthermore, income had to be created to pay for the large additional administrative and maintenance costs directly related to this trading. A new 1% ad valorem transit duty was imposed on all goods passing through which were not classified as strategic war materials, on which no charge was made. Consignments for China, landed in Rangoon, were examined by Customs in the usual way and then assessed for the 1% transit duty; the goods were then strapped and sealed by the examining officers and handed over to the consignees on payment of the duty for onward despatch by rail, road or river. Before the goods left Burma, the packages were subject to a further Customs check to ensure that straps and seals were still intact.

At the beginning of this Burma Road traffic, the outward Customs check was made in Lashio, over a hundred miles from the Chinese border, because there were no facilities of any kind at the frontier, not even a village. Besides the undesirable loophole created by this hundred mile gap, it soon became evident that, not only was it necessary to expand the Lashio resources considerably, but additional effective spot-checking at the border was imperative. Therefore, one of my earliest assignments was to visit Lashio and the border to assess requirements for expanding Customs activities. The head of the civil administration in the Northern Shan States, G. F. Porter the superintendent, with whom I would have to consult on all matters, was an old Frontier Service friend, whom I had last seen in my far-off Myitkyina days. I received a cordial invitation to stay with him at the imposing Residency in Lashio. Great changes had occurred in Lashio, but these were confined to the railway yards and to the adjacent parts of the expanding town. The Civil Lines were still very much as they had always been, giving that indefinable air of the lingering pioneer spirit, so common still in many Upper Burma district headquarters; after all, British administration had only existed during the past fifty years in these parts of the country. I revelled in the feeling of being once again back in the wide open spaces, if only for a short time.

We had a congenial reunion, he took me to the delightful little club where I met most of the other senior officials of the area. After dinner, we got down to the matter which had brought me there. My friend told me that he was keen to introduce a proper convoy system on the Road, to speed up traffic in both directions because there were still stretches of road where large vehicles found it difficult to pass each other; several fatal accidents and many hold-ups were taking place. The Governor had approved the idea and my friend was now waiting for the arrival of an outside expert to organise and then supervise the convoy arrangements on the Burma section of the Road. I was pleased to hear of this innovation which would make our work much easier too. The next day was spent on surveying sites around the railway station and beyond for space to park vehicles and build temporary transit sheds where packages could be inspected in all weather prior to their onward despatch. Thanks to the considerable help and co-operation from all concerned, the business was completed much sooner than I expected.

We next arranged to travel to the border. My friend had to attend periodical frontier meetings with Chinese officials to settle matters which had arisen since the previous conference. When he had heard of my arrival, he made arrangements for the meeting to coincide with my visit to the border. I was delighted to hear this news, not only because it would give me the opportunity to meet the officials from the other side but I had also heard of these get-togethers and the inevitable hospitality involved. The scenery between Lashio and the border was delightful; only to be expected in a country composed of a three thousand foot plateau with intermittent hills. As I was with the head of the Administration we travelled in style and found a comfortable camp ready at the end of the journey. The following morning we quickly settled on the site for the new customs Post and the ancillary buildings to house the staff, near a natural flat area which could be easily converted into a parking plot for vehicles awaiting the examination of goods carried. The following day was to be the big one, our meeting with the Chinese officials.

The demarcation of the frontier between Burma and China had been the cause of trouble and disagreements for a very long time; I believe that the subject has even been raised again since Independence. The British Administration, to improve matters, erected boundary stones, heavy square blocks, in places where natural features did not readily define the frontier. In my time it was these artificial demarcations which were the subject of periodical complaints from the Chinese. These heavy markers had a mysterious habit of wandering to a new site, increasing the area of Burma. This sabotage was the work of local inhabitants, seeking to escape from the rapacious demands of some greedy, petty, local dictator in the neighbourhood levying local taxes. The enterprising frontier adjusters would thus enjoy a respite until, at the next border conference, the status quo would be restored. Myitkyina district officers had most of the trouble over frontier incidents and the regular meetings, between both sides, were lengthy and important affairs, for transacting business as well as for social niceties. I had heard several apocryphal stories about the lavish hospitality offered by the Chinese hosts when the meeting took place on their side of the border. It was a fact that a Chinese banquet was always a prolonged and splendid meal, lasting several hours and usually in excess of ten courses: the beverage was a glass of champagne, alternating with a glass of brandy, throughout the meal. It was also generally believed that the wily British selected their negotiating team carefully by including hard drinkers, who had to keep pace with Chinese capacities and the limited or non-drinkers who had to deal with the discussions which followed the entertainment.

Our meeting in the Shan States was a smaller affair, by no means bacchanalian, although we did receive generous hospitality from our Chinese hosts. They had insisted on this prerogative, without much resistance on our part, because they claimed with reason to have the better facilities. Our side of the border was barely inhabited, whereas they had a large village immediately across the frontier and a sizeable town not far away. The Superintendent, his assistants and myself were received ceremonially on the dividing line and conducted to a barn-like building, which turned out to be the Custom House, for the meeting. After prolonged complimentary introductions on both sides, the Chinese ones conducted by a smiling man with an American accent, the conference started. The agenda looked impressive but consisted largely of minor administrative problems. The only really contentious item was a Chinese complaint about the recent setting up of demarcation stones without their consent. This particular subject was taken up as the last item, after two hours, the other matters having been dealt with quickly and harmoniously.

The Superintendent was most conciliatory in replying to the complaint, wrapped up in the usual diplomatic phraseology. He disclosed that a letter of explanation had been sent direct to the capital Chungking, because of the importance and urgency of the subject. This statement only partially satisfied the locals; they grumbled about the exact location of each stone. A large map of the area was produced and pored over; in the end it was agreed to adjourn the discussion until after lunch when the members of the conference would visit the sites nearby. We all adjourned to another large house nearby which could have been the residence of the presiding official. Here a long table, covered by a spotless tablecloth, was overspread with what seemed dozens of small and big dishes containing varieties of delicious Chinese food. This was the second richest looking Chinese meal I have ever had; the other was an even grander affair in Lashio, when the official Chinese Burma Road Agency entertained the British Ambassador to China. I soon lost count of the varieties offered for our palates; my neighbour was the American-speaking Chinese. He told me that he had spent some years in America but did not divulge the nature of his activities there. He had learnt some English from American missionaries before going abroad. He maintained a steady flow of small talk whilst partaking liberally of the food and drink, until suddenly he fell silent, excused himself hurriedly and left the room. Back in a few minutes, he turned smilingly to me and said he had now more room for further solid and liquid sustenance! We were drinking some rather sweet white wine during the meal, followed by some brandy at the end. I think we spent a good three hours at the table.

When we broke up, to resume deliberations, there was no more talk of visiting out-of-door places. The rest of the conference passed off in an agreeable smell of cigar smoke and general bonhomie, generated by our hosts' hospitality. My presence had been very much complimentary since Customs arrangements, on both sides, were still at the primary stage. When we returned to our side, my friend took me to see one of the contentious boundary stones. There were four, two on each side of the road about a mile distant from each other. He disclosed that some more, at greater intervals, had been placed along the frontier westwards, towards the site where the Americans had built an aeroplane factory, just over the line on Chinese territory. The large square stone, which I was shown, had a freshly painted white cross right across the surface. My puzzled look drew forth the answer that confidential news had been received recently. The Japanese were contemplating bombing the factory, as soon as they could get within flying distance. The British Government had therefore urgently advised that the frontier should be clearly marked around the danger area. The Superintendent could not, of course, disclose this confidential information to local officials without causing unnecessary alarm and despondency at this stage.

After this pleasant interlude, I was back in Rangoon hard at work, setting out our requirements in greater detail. In a relatively short time, considering the usual leisurely red-tape procedure, effective Customs checks were being carried out both at the border and in the greatly enlarged customs compound in Lashio. Bribery and corruption were still very much part of the Chinese bureaucracy and widely practised by the officials in charge of the transit trade arrangements on behalf of the Chinese Government. I made it a rule to change the Preventive staff, both in Lashio and on the border, frequently to minimise the temptations of succumbing to repeated offers of substantial bribes. Dishonesty was limited to the few; most were honest and did their work conscientiously. Some culprits were caught red-handed but we never did uncover a case of real importance although rumours of heavy bribery reached us in Rangoon from time to time. Whilst large illegal remunerations must have been made at one time or another, I thought that many stories were false or exaggerated, reported through malice or jealousy. I also believed that the policy of frequent transfers, away from temptation, helped those who resisted repeated attempts to corrupt them. Even I, as I shall relate, did not escape the lure. Having been offered only one bribe of one rupee during my eleven years in the Police, I received, within weeks, some succulent offers of presents from the Chinese.

The increase in the Preventive staff, enabling us to improve the physical checking facilities at both ends of the overland transit trade, soon showed its effect. The number of packages with defective straps and seals, or those which had just got lost, falling off a lorry, decreased quickly. Even these improvements did not deter repeated attempts to circumvent the regulations for a quick profit. As it was physically impossible to open and examine every single package landed in Rangoon, for transit into China, false declarations of contents remained a favourite ploy. A case boldly marked "Machine gun parts", thus exempt from transit duty, would reveal when opened cosmetics packed to the brim; commodities in scarce supply and great demand in China. Rumours were prevalent and constant that this sort of cheating, within the Chinese Agency for the transit trade, was widespread and that top officials were making fortunes out of the war situation.

The Americans had decided to build an aeroplane factory, or rather a huge assembly plant, for the Chinese Government, just on the other side of the Burma border, at a place called Loiwing. This was a big project, requiring much imported material for the construction and subsequent operations. A secondary transit trade of some volume was built up as a result, by river from Rangoon to Bhamo and then by an improved existing road along the border. A Customs checking point had to be set up in Bhamo, leaving a gap of fifty miles along the road, still inside Burma, before cargo crossed into China. This loophole was unimportant whilst the factory was building, but when it was occupied by a large work force and supervisory staff of Americans and Chinese, much of the transit traffic contained non-strategic material, in short, goods with a high commercial value in Burma proper; we were losing appreciable revenue on things like liquor, cigarettes and other goods with high import duty liabilities. The problem was raised with the Americans and Chinese; arrangements were made for me to visit the factory and discuss the matter on the spot.

The factory had been built in one of the remotest parts on the border between Burma and China, in a jungle-cleared area, populated sparsely by a few primitive hill tribes. I was staggered by the zeal with which the Americans had tamed the wild region with their civilisation. In one hundred years of British occupation, running water in houses was still very much the exception, outside Rangoon and some of the larger towns. The Americans had built not only a substantial modern factory but also a well-planned motel-type building consisting of a large club house and a connected row of self-contained living quarters. Each room had a fitted washbasin with running hot and cold water and a separate water-closet. In the larger rooms for V.I.P. residents or visitors, each had a separate well-appointed bathroom, air-conditioning (still unknown in Burma) and refrigerator. The main kitchens were as well equipped and as modern as any in a good hotel; the meals, largely American cuisine, were everything one would expect in a well-run catering establishment. American hospitality was at its best and I had a most pleasant interlude in this oasis of civilisation. The official side of my visit also reached a satisfactory solution. We received permission to send Customs officers with road convoys at our discretion, who would then carry out a spot-check on selected loads, before vehicles crossed the border. This arrangement did not stop all abuse but the effect was good under the circumstances. This major project never really got off the ground. After the fall of Singapore, whilst we were about to receive our share of the Japanese onslaught, their air force got within range of the factory. The whole place was destroyed in air raids. I believe that not a single aircraft was completed before the destruction. The jungle being what it is, I suppose that there is now no vestige of this enterprise. The same fate has probably overtaken large stretches of the Burma Road, but there must be many ghosts around that once important and busy link between two countries.

26
Bribes

Bribery and corruption exist everywhere but nowhere more than in the East. The British, in the days of the old East India Company, openly acknowledged the practice. Every young cadet joining John Company had one object in mind: 'to shake the pagoda tree'. With the advent of British rule and the setting up of well-paid Government services, a new standard was expected. Officers who were caught accepting bribes were dismissed. Gradually the doctrine of incorruptibility was accepted and observed. In my time it was acknowledged, not least by the indigenous people, that a British official could not be bribed. Like all generalisations there were, of course, exceptions to the rule, but these were few and far between. I never heard of a definite case of bribery by an expatriate member of one of the Senior Services, only the odd rumour which was never substantiated. The Government had laid down very precise rules on the acceptance of presents from subordinates and the general public. In brief, inexpensive gifts of fruit, sweets, cakes and even the odd bottle were acceptable on festive occasions.

The giving of allowable inexpensive gifts to officials was a widespread practice. Comparatively unknown citizens would appear on one's doorstep on festive occasions with a hamper of fruit and cakes. When I was a young district official of minor importance in Nyaunglebin, I always had a dozen or more visitors around Christmas bearing gifts. I always remember a dear old Chinese man with a scraggy goatee beard, presenting me with a bottle of whisky at each of the two Christmases I spent in that subdivision. He was unknown to me and I never saw or heard of him during the intervening days in the two years. He was the absentee owner of a small business in the town, which, amongst other things, had the franchise for the sale of petrol in the area; so he may have included me in his circle of customers, although we were and remained total strangers to each other.

I have already recounted the solitary temptation which came my way in the Police Department. My introduction to greater enticements came with my advent into the Customs Department. As usual, the season bringing 'tidings of comfort and joy' was the excuse to probe an official's reaction to costlier gifts. The door bell to the front door of my flat in the Custom House would begin to sound more and more frequently in the evenings. My servant would bring in a series of large ornate visiting cards, each bearing the name of one of the many Indian shippers. In would come the particular caller, followed by a coolie carrying a load on his head. After the usual preliminary compliments of the season, the package would be unwrapped by the visitor, begging me to accept 'these few humble gifts'. Some of the gifts were not so 'humble', half concealed under fruit and cakes were, say, several bottles of best liqueur brandy and perhaps the odd silver bracelet for 'the memsahib'. The range of unacceptable gifts went from the less to the most expensive jewellery, cases of liquor, oriental carpets and so on. Generally, the probing first visit was sufficient to stop further attempts at seduction. Those who were more difficult to persuade would eventually get the message when the 'sahib' became unnecessarily officious, invoking as much red-tape as he could when dealing with the clearance through Customs of imports for the persistent presenter of expensive gifts. However, I always made a point of accepting the permissible gifts of fruit, sweets and cakes (mostly unappealing to a European palate but beloved by the servants and their children). I did not extend this courtesy for the second time if the gifts again concealed forbidden fruit. To my surprise a European importer also tried to get me under some obligation by sending me two cases of 'Dimpled Scotch' whisky, one of the more expensive brands.

Surprising as these more ambitious bribery attempts by the commercial community might be, they were nothing to what happened when I came up against the Chinese Transportation Agency, set up to administer that Government's transit trade through Burma. I was, of course, already well aware of the general attitude of their officials towards bribery and corruption and of the persistent attempts to subvert my staff, but I was astonished when they decided to 'have a go' at buying me. I suppose I was slow to appreciate that my extensive executive powers, in relation to Customs control over their transit trade, made me a very desirable compliant target for their top officials. As usual, Christmas time offered the best opportunity to start the process of my moral deterioration.

One day, returning from the office, I was greeted at the front door by an excited wife, "Someone has sent us a lovely big Christmas present, I cannot wait for you to open it", she said, pointing to a large packing case lying in the passage. A decorous Christmas card was tied to the package, the words "with the seasonable compliments of the . . . . . . .Company", the name under which the official Chinese Agency worked in Burma, neatly printed on the inside of the card. On the case itself were stencilled the words "very fragile, handle with care, 48 pieces Chinese hand-painted china service". To make matters more difficult for us, I opened the case and took out an exquisite cup and saucer with a delicate flower and leaf motif painted on an off-white background. Watched by my disconsolate wife, I scribbled a polite note explaining that I could not accept this kind of valuable present and sent the package back in my car.

Three days later my wife was again at the front door when I got back. "See what has arrived now", she said. This time they had sent a complete silver tea set. My driver's grin was broader than on the first occasion, when he was summoned to take back the second offering with a curt note of refusal. Nothing more happened for a week; then the tea set was replaced by three very fine Persian rugs! Back they went, this time without a note. The next morning, when I was in the office, my 'peon' (personal office messenger) came in with a conventional small visiting card, bearing the name of a senior member of the Agency. He was quite well known to me, we had met a number of times socially and officially. He spoke English well and was efficient in his business dealings. We had got on well together in our mutual spheres of official contacts.

He came in smiling politely and sat down. We talked for a while about some hold-up of Customs documents on a consignment, over which there had been some correspondence. When he had finished his explanation, which seemed to clear up the matter, I stood up as usual, thinking he had finished, to see him to the door. He remained seated and said that there was just one more small matter for discussion. What he then said, in the politest round-about way, was in effect, "You are really being very difficult, we are anxious to please you and it would now be helpful if you told us what you would really like to receive"! The degree of diplomacy displayed by him, in putting across the message as inoffensively as it was possible, made it impossible for me to give the sort of curt, rude reply I would have given in a crude attempt at bribery. Besides, I had to go on dealing with this important member of the Agency and I wished to retain the good rapport between us. I tried to explain at length our rules about the acceptance of presents, but I could see that my explanations were incomprehensible and sounded unconvincing to him. He was really a nice cultured person with whom I had found it agreeable to work and was sorry that this meeting should end on an awkward note which could jeopardise our future business relations.

As my visitor was about to leave the room, without his usual farewell smile, I had a brainwave. The Agency had managed to include motor cars under the designation of strategic materials. Large numbers of new American cars were thus imported to China through Rangoon. I told him that I was soon to undertake one of my periodical inspection trips to the new border posts and that this time the trip would include a long rough ride along the border to Bhamo. I explained that my car, an English one, was not really suitable for that kind of a journey and that an American car, with a high back axle, would be a better proposition; could he perhaps arrange for their Lashio office to lend me one for that part of my tour? Like the sun suddenly appearing after a cloud burst, his face lit up with pleasure. We parted, the best of friends again, with his assurance that a car would be ready and waiting at the railway station in Lashio on the day I arrived.

Some days later, I departed on my extended tour. My wife had gone ahead to stay with friends in the Shan States; we had arranged to meet up at our friends' house after my trip and then return together to Rangoon. When I stepped from the train in Lashio, after a long and rather tedious journey, I saw a brand new large American saloon car parked prominently at the station entrance. I looked around to see who the V.I.P. was, to be met so imposingly; there had been few first class passengers on the train and none of them seem to be expecting this reception. The Chinese driver saw me look around, came up and wordlessly thrust a card before my face;

on it was written my name in block letters. I was nonplussed, a brand new car would have pounds written off its value, after the sort of journey I had to undertake. I told the driver to take me to the Agency's office.

The local manager of the Agency knew me from previous visits; he assured me that no mistake had been made about the car. I tried to point out the silliness of letting me have a new car for travelling on rough roads and, sometimes, on mere tracks. Nothing I could say would persuade him to let me exchange the vehicle for an old one. He more or less implied that it would be more than his job was worth to countermand the specific instructions he had received from his chief in Rangoon. Time was short and I had to adhere to my tight schedule, so I had no alternative but to accept the use of the new car and its driver.

I did not keep an account of mileage we covered on roads, cart tracks and even paths, but the car received the expected battering. By the time I reached our friends' house for a few days respite the engine was still as sound as at the start of the journey but the bodywork had developed a few squeaks and the paintwork was no longer pristine. Our friends' home was in fact a P.W.D. inspection bungalow, placed at his disposal whilst he was doing an extensive survey of soil erosion in the Shan States. As usual in such buildings, the living accommodation was upstairs, stores and an office downstairs. Our host and my wife were sitting on the large covered verandah when I arrived. My servant unloaded the car whilst I made the driver understand that the trip was over and that he could return to Lashio, about forty miles away; he refused to accept the tip I tried to give him. I then went up the stairs to join the others.

After a while, my host noticed that the driver was still sitting in the car under the porch. I called my servant and we went down to see what was wrong. My 'boy' seemed to converse with the man better than I did and he repeated what I had already said about returning to Lashio; I thought that he was perhaps regretting the impulse which made him refuse the tip and proffered the money again. He shook his head, said something which my servant translated to mean,"Who is going to take me to the railway station?" I tried to find out why he could not drive back in the car. After a few more puzzled misunderstandings, I finally grasped the fact that he had orders to hand the car over to me after the tour. I had to sit down and write a letter to the Lashio office, thanking them for the use of the car, explaining that I could not keep it and that I would clear up the matter when I got back to Rangoon. Even so, it was with the greatest difficulty and a final show of anger by me, that the driver took the letter and reluctantly drove off. I had to suffer some humorous leg-pulling from our hosts for turning down such a gift horse.

Back in Rangoon I wrote another polite letter of explanation to my over-striving seducer at the Agency. As half-expected, he arrived in my office a day or so later. This time he seemed to have accepted my incomprehensible attitude and cheered up when I told him how grateful I was for the loan of the big car which had made my travelling on bad roads so much easier. As he was leaving he said,"Nobody would have minded the giving of a car from the many we are importing through your port". I was glad that the whole series of episodes had ended without souring our relations. I do not think that they admired my resistance to bribery; on the contrary, they must have dismissed it as an act of stupidity. The lesson for me was that it brought home forcefully the great temptations to which our subordinates, on much lower salaries, were exposed; the only effective way to relieve pressure on the honest and curtail the scope of the dishonest, was through frequent changes of staff. The Chinese were not slow to appreciate the policy and did not waste expensive bribes on officials who did not remain long enough to be of growing value to them.

27

The Retainers

My dictionary defines the word Retainer as "used to describe a dependant or follower of person of rank". I had at first written the word servant for the title, but struck it out as unsuitable for individuals who meant much more than that to us. As a side issue, the dictionary definition is perhaps more appropriate than my status implies. When I was home on leave, after the birth of my first son, my wife asked me to call at the fishmonger when I was out with the baby in his pram. The shop owner had been providing fish to her family for a long time and had known them all for years. He was interested to know how one of the daughters was now faring in her new married life out East. So on my visit to the shop I gave him a broad picture of our way of life and of my work. After the chat, as I was about to leave, pushing the pram, he said quite seriously, standing in the doorway, "Yes, I can see that you count for a bit more out there".

If I were asked to mention something I miss greatly from my overseas days, the household staff would be high on the list. The choice is not as blatantly materialistic and selfish as it appears. A great number of us grew very fond of our servants and kept them for years, paying a retainer whilst we were away on long leave. Many of them reciprocated our feelings and became devoted to the whole family. Accounts about the Indian Mutiny of 1857 mention time and again the loyalty of staff, trying to save their employers and families at the risk of their own lives, during the holocaust which swept through the land. My reminiscences would be incomplete without a tribute to our own retainers who remained steadfast until they were no longer required and released from their duties when we had to abandon our home at very short notice.

I did not employ a complete household staff until I came to Rangoon. I started off in the Mandalay Mess with one personal Burmese servant, called a 'lugalay' (literally 'small man'); he did not remain with me after I left the district. His successor, Maung Shwe, stayed longer until after my marriage; he was a good servant but a 'bachelor's man', as the saying went. Before Rangoon, I shared other servants with the joint occupier of a bungalow. When I returned from leave and had my first unshared accommodation, I took over from my bachelor predecessor his household staff, apart from the personal lugalay. I was aware that they had only worked in bachelor households and were unlikely to stay on when I married in a few months time. This was no reflection on a prospective wife; it was common for single men to lose their servants on marriage. The custom was not without merit since it usually sorted out the good from the lazy. Many bachelors, however, had excellent servants and many of these would continue to serve happily when the wife appeared. I was, thus, not surprised when my lot gradually left after my marriage.

About a week after returning from our brief honeymoon, my wife said that my lugalay seemed willing but not very bright; "Whenever I call him, there is a long delay and then he appears with a pot of tea". Mystified by this inexplicable behaviour, I questioned him. His answer was explicit: the Burmese word for tea is Lapay-yay (tea leaf water); my wife would hear me shout this word every morning when we woke up and were ready for our early morning cup of tea. She concluded, understandably, that this was my servant's name! Perhaps this experience helped him to decide that life in a married houshold was too difficult; shortly afterwards he asked me to release him as soon as it was convenient. He was too polite to give the real reason for wanting a change, but said that he wished to return to his native Upper Burma, for which I did not blame him as I shared his preference. I was sorry to see him go and I think he was too; we had shared the discomforts and some danger during the rebellion and he had looked after me devotedly when I was ill and had to travel from Thayetmyo to Rangoon by steamer and rail.

I had a stroke of luck when Maung Shwe gave me notice. One of my acquaintances was going on permanent transfer to one of the High Courts in India. His Burmese butler, Maung Pyaung, came to see me, having heard that we were looking for a new head servant. He had been with his employer throughout the latter's time in Burma, some twenty years. I had seen him several times during social happenings at the house. He bore a letter from his master which simply said "Maung Pyaung has been with me for twenty years, whoever engages him now will be employing a faultless servant". Needless to say, we clinched a deal then and there and neither of us, I hope, ever regretted the decision. He was relatively old for a Burman (or seemed old to me in my twenties!), wore his hair long in the old-fashioned style, tied into a bun on top of his head, always covered by a 'gaung-baung' (silk head scarf) when on duty. After we had settled details and fixed the date for his arrival, he took me aback by honouring me with the old-fashioned sign of respect, 'the shikoe'. This form of obeisance, now seldom used, consists of kneeling down in front of the recipient, putting the hands together as in prayer, raising them to the forehead and then bowing forward until the head touches the floor. Sensing my embarrassment at this gesture, Maung Pyaung, on getting to his feet said, with great dignity, "Thakin, I am an old Burman and I show my respect in the old way". I was thankful my wife had not witnessed the scene; she would have been horrified by a custom which looks so abject in our eyes. She was upset soon after our marriage when, as usual, I allowed my previous lugalay to bring my slippers, untie and take off my shoes and slip on the former when I returned at the end of the day. I stopped him doing this daily chore, much to his puzzlement, and he asked me whether he should hand the slippers to my wife for her to perform the task? Luckily, my better half had not yet learnt any Burmese!

161

Maung Pyaung was well qualified to deal with all the problems of social niceties, still dominated by the rigid observance of the seniority list, so much cherished by people who had been ignorant that such a thing existed. His former mistress, as the wife of a senior member of the Judiciary, had done a lot of entertaining and had trained him well. The time had come for us to repay all the hospitality we had received so lavishly as newly-weds. We had consulted with Maung Pyaung on whether it was better to have one or two large parties or several smaller ones; he favoured the former method which coincided with our preference. But we did wonder how our still restricted table requirements would look, so thinly spread out. Maung Pyaung said that this handicap was no problem and to leave matters in his hands, except the flower arrangements which, he already knew, my wife could do to perfection.

On the day of the dinner party, I was rather late in getting back. My wife met me looking pleased and worried at the same time; without a word, she led me straight into the dining-room. The table looked perfect with all the condiment sets and flower vases gleaming on a well-polished surface. I expressed approval, my wife asked had I not noticed anything unusual? I looked again and replied that the servants had done a good job. Her reply was, "Don't you see that most of the silver on the table is not ours?" As bachelors our servants borrowed freely from others whenever the need arose, but such mutual lending did not usually include valuable silverware, even if one of us possessed such riches. Maung Pyaung calmed our fears by telling us that, even in the previous august household, he had borrowed when the need arose; this practice of involuntary sharing was apparently just as prevalent in married establishments. The expert display of the flowers was certainly all the better, in the setting of the silver sets and candle sticks, the majority of which were not ours. This lending practice extended to the servants. When we went in to dinner, my two lugalays were flanked by two more Burmese servants, also dressed in their best clothes, providing a display of colour which equalled that of the ladies dresses. In Rangoon, with its large transient European business community from India, many households were staffed only by Indian servants. We, with our mixed staffs of Burmese and Indians, had the edge on them for decorative colours, however smart theirs looked; the Burmese national costume certainly added to the general decor in our homes.

My wife was still very new to her surroundings after Maung Pyaung's arrival. This seemed to make him extra helpful and protective towards her. He certainly did all he could to make her place in running the household smooth and easy. I was astonished to find how quickly she had learnt about the detailed duties of each servant, since her knowledge of either Burmese or Hindustani was still to come. When I mentioned this handicap and asked her how she had managed, she said: "Why Maung Pyaung of course; he understands everything I say to him in English and speaks quite well himself". I had taken it for granted that his knowledge of English would be restricted to a few words, generally picked up by Burmese servants over the years. Such vocabulary was usually acquired in bachelor households and was mostly unusable in front of mixed company!

In all our years together, I cannot recall any occasion in which we had to rebuke him seriously. My wife did catch him out, to his shame, ironing out one of my unwashed sweaty evening shirts for further use on the next day. He not only served us well but had the ability to get the best out of the other servants without dragooning them. He must have had a good reputation as a task master because he never had difficulty in replacing young men after he had trained them. The only time when he lost his temper badly, with another servant, was one evening. He was pouring out a mixed drink for both of us, sitting in our roof garden on top of the Custom House. The Vermouth bottle was nearly empty and, as he held it near-vertical to pour out the last drops, a dead cockroach fell out into my glass! He muttered something in Burmese which I took to be a swear word and rushed off with the empty bottle. There was the noise of a terrific quarrel in the servants' quarters, at the far end of the flat. The next moment our second boy was running down the passage to the front door chased by Maung Pyaung. The boy got out of the flat before his pursuer could catch up. That was the last we saw of him. Maung Pyaung returned breathless to the garden full of apologies to us and threats for the departed servant. Apparently as part of his progress in training, the hapless youth had been entrusted with the task of looking after the drink cupboard. He had obviously forgotten to cork the Vermouth bottle after use, either through forgetfulness or through haste in being nearly caught sampling the contents. Luckily my wife had not been given her drink and did not seem too upset. I could not help wondering how long the bottle had been left uncorked. However, I did not share this thought with her, but I temporarily lost my taste for Vermouth.

In our flat, the servants' quarters were much nearer than those at the back of a house with a compound. I could thus sometimes see Maung Pyaung squatting at ease on his heels, as do most natives (and small European children with native nannies; our little boy did this regularly until he went home). He would usually be puffing at a large Burma cheroot, with his made-up 'gaung-baung' off his head beside him, having a well-earned breather. He would have been upset had he known that I could see him thus off duty. No Burman ever appeared before his employer with head uncovered; such a lapse would have been considered a gross discourtesy. He had been the head servant in a large household for many years and during that time had acquired an unusually large number of 'pasoes' (the Burmese dress longyi) in a variety of silks, as well as the other fine accoutrements of a well-dressed Burman. When he was thus clad for a special occasion or when we entertained, he would look as well-dressed and as distinguished as the most important of his compatriots. There is no dress distinction between well-dressed Burmans of all classes. Men or women, rich and poor, wear the same basic silk garments, skirts, head scarfs (men) and fine linen jackets for both sexes; these are the basic requirements for the fashionable Burmese man or women to look as good as his or her neighbour.

Maung Pyaung stayed with me to the very end in Rangoon. I had moved in with another 'last ditcher' in the last days; we used his house at odd times for rest and peace from the bustle at the Mogul Guard. When the time came for us to embark for our final journey down the river, my faithful servant and my friend's left in the latter's car to join their families, already tucked away somewhere up-country. After the war, when I was summoned unwillingly back to Burma, he returned to serve me again. But this time we both realised that conditions had changed beyond recall; gone were the happy old pre-war years. He was just as sad as I was to witness my last final months so full of worries and tribulations. He insisted on travelling to Rangoon with me, although his home town was Mandalay, twice as near. We had a final emotional good-bye on the quay-side, both near to tears. Dear old Maung Pyaung, we often talk of him and of those far-off happy days when he was always at our side, ready to look to our comforts. May he attain (if he has not already done so) his Buddhist nirvana, which he so richly deserves.

Our cook arrived in our household soon after Maung Pyaung, who was instrumental in his engagement, when my inherited cook decided to give his expected notice. The new cook had worked for neighbours of Maung Pyaung's employer and they had known each other for some years. On these facts and recommendations, I had no hesitation in taking on the man. We never regretted the spontaneous choice. The cook belonged to the Mugh tribe, Muslims from the Arakan-Chittagong area, partly in Burma and partly in Bengal (now part of Bangladesh). These men were reputed to be excellent cooks and were in great demand in European households in Rangoon. Some time after he had been installed with us, we were told from several sources that his reputation in the culinary arts was of the highest. I was never able to pronounce his real long name; he himself at the interview indicated that he had always been known just as 'cook', so that he remained in his time with us.

Cooks shopped in the local bazaar for our fresh food supplies, keeping a record of details and prices in a note book. The book was brought to the employer for checking, usually daily after the evening meal if there were no visitors. Most of us bachelors were pretty slack about this checking process. As long as the daily outlay by the cook was around a rupee (7½ new pence!) per person, the scrutiny of the list was perfunctory. There was a time-honoured item called 'soupmeat' included each day in the list of purchased items; this was generally regarded as the commission charged for the daily trek to the bazaar. Most employers tolerated this small deception of a couple of annas (½ a new pence). Dishonest cooks were, of course, prepared to increase their profit by also fudging the prices paid, but most did not last long at this game.

When I shared house with my brother-in-law in Nyaunglebin, we hardly ever checked the cook's accounts thoroughly. Matters did come to a head once, when we noticed rather frequent purchases of sugar. I totalled up the quantity alleged to have been bought over a month and the amount came to 21 'viss' (a viss was about two pounds). We had not noticed the gradual increase since the price of sugar then was only a few annas for a viss. When we tackled him to explain the use of more than forty pounds of sugar a month, he said we had overlooked the free monthly issue to each servant's household. We told him to collect all the people who received a ration of sugar; so thirty nine men, women and children lined up for our inspection! The cook may or may not have cheated us over sugar purchases but we certainly appeared to be doing our share in supporting the indigenous population in kind!

I was sorry to notice an early degree of coolness between my wife and the new cook; this surprised me as she got on so well with all the other members of the household. I mentioned this tension between them and her answer cleared up the puzzle for me. My wife took all her household responsibilities seriously, including the checking of the cook's book. She had drawn his attention to the ubiquitous 'soupmeat', pointing out that we seldom had soup and suggested that the purchase of this daily item seemed unnecessary. I told her about the custom and she told him to resume buying the soupmeat. So, honour was satisfied on both sides and he soon became as attached to her as the other servants. Matters improved further when my wife offered to show him how to prepare some new dishes. She had trained at a well-known College of Domestic Science in Edinburgh and her culinary expertise aroused his professional admiration and gratitude, for widening his repertoire of meals. As he put it himself, none too tactfully, "Memsahib is a good cook, not many Memsahibs can teach cook new cooking".

He was rightly proud of his own prowess and we were always amazed to see him conjure up an excellent four or five course meal for a dinner party of eight to ten people under primitive cooking conditions. The kitchen was usually a poky plain room, perhaps a few shelves on a wall, a small window, a sink usually without running water and a square brick oven, with open round holes on top, over which were placed the 'degshies' (handleless cooking pan). The oven was another hole in the front side of the brick wall; heat for top and bottom tiers was provided by a charcoal fire, continuously fanned to maintain an even temperature. Until we moved in to the Custom House flat, there was no running cold water for a kitchen sink. Even when we were on our own, the cook always kept up his high standard and produced most succulent dishes. One innovation, introduced by my wife, was soon copied by other friends. She used to receive some large glossy American magazines in which appeared wonderful coloured photographs of elaborately composed dishes of delicious looking food. She would ask the cook to reproduce similar dishes and he invariably rose to the occasion; not only did his finished work of art look as good as the picture but surely tasted as good. We always made a point on these occasions to have the whole dish brought untouched into the dining room for the evident admiration of our guests, with 'cook' smirking modestly in the background, savouring the complimentary remarks.

Every cook had a matey. In theory this individual was meant to be learning the trade from his master. In practice, he spent most of his time doing all the dirty work in the kitchen and keeping the burning charcoal at an even heat by constant fanning. Our cook did, occasionally, condescend to teach him but this tuition never included his own masterpieces. He was particularly good at producing excellent thick sauces, appropriate to the dishes concerned. Even my wife had difficulty in learning about the relevant ingredients, until she teased him about his reluctance, comparing it with her own generosity in showing him what she knew. The kitchen boy did not do so well. My wife found him several times perched precariously on a small stool outside the kitchen peeping through the small window to spy on the cook's activities, the latter having turned him out of the kitchen before proceeding to produce one of his specialities. There are many widespread stories about Indian cooks and their peculiar kitchen habits. The best one, in my view, is about the master of the house going into the kitchen and finding the cook draining the coffee through one of his best black silk evening socks; before he could give vent to his anger, the cook hastily tried to dampen the wrath by saying; "Please master do not be angry, it is not a clean sock". Even our paragon of a cook had his weaknesses; my wife once went into the kitchen hurriedly to find him squatting over the sink cutting his toe nails! A friend of her's went into her kitchen before a dinner party, to find the matey sitting in front of the oven making toast with the slices of bread wedged between his toes!

When we had to evacuate our flat, at the start of the air raids, to shelter with kind friends living out of town, our cook went with us to replace their's who had fled after the first raid. He remained calm and workmanlike to the end, leaving only after the joint families were split up, wives and children to India and husbands doubling up in 'chummeries' organised to over-come shortage of domestic staff and other needs. He left a few days after the split up, also by sea to India, helped to board a vessel by one of my Customs staff, luckier than many of his kind. We often wondered, nostalgically, for years which lucky household somewhere was enjoying his expertise.

Our Karen Nanny, Ma Khaing, joined us when we returned from leave with our first-born, aged five months, and stayed until near the end of our family life in Rangoon. We were again lucky in our acquisition, she had been Nanny to the child of my wife's close friend, from the time of the baby's birth until the child was taken home for good (European children usually left Burma at the age of six years for health reasons). Quite soon she became much more than just Nanny. She added not only friendly competence but also beauty to our expanding household staff. All Nannies, unlike the rest of the staff, lived with the family and slept in the same room as their small charges. Karen girls seem outstandingly suitable to deal with very small European children; they are gentle, persevering, firm yet kind in their patient training. Our's possessed all these qualities, added to her good looks and decorative appearance. She proved her practical competence by having our son out of nappies before he was a year old, which I am told is a good record. Later on, however dirty and untidy he made himself at play with other children, and he was always allowed to join in all the fun, she had him looking neat and clean again at the right times. Her daily laundering of his garments must have taken longer than necessary because of the high standards she had set. She herself was always perfectly groomed, often with a decorative flower set in her black hair, harmonising with the colour of her silk skirt.

My wife's hair was long and fair; she was finding it more and more tiring and irritating to set in the hot weather and several times in exasperation threatened to cut it short. Ma Khaing came to the rescue before my promised divorce over the issue had to be tested. She offered to wash and dress the hair whenever the need arose; she spent long periods brushing and combing the tresses, much to my wife's relief. I think that she quite liked the self-imposed task; the very fair hair seemed to fascinate her, just as much as my wife admired the long, strong jet-black hair of the Burmese and Karen women. She used to assert that most fair-haired women would have preferred dark hair, I would counter this unlikely contention by stating that I could not have married a dark-haired woman!

When Ma Khaing shyly announced her engagement to one of my Karen Preventive Officers, I could not help wondering how the courtship had been carried on. For four years, she had sat in the front of our car next to my Karen driver, several times a week when we were all out for a drive or on a visit to the swimming club. She would talk to her little charge on her knee but never once in all that time did she or the driver exchange a word with each other. My wife has missed her as much as she has Maung Pyaung; even now she sighs at times and says "Oh for Ma Khaing's lovely long combing and brushing and all the other kind things she did so willingly". We were very distressed to hear about the murdering of Karens, in the upheavals which followed the British withdrawal from post-war rule, before the country recovered from the ravages of war. Ma Khaing came from one of two large Karen settlements on the outskirts of Rangoon, where fighting had been particularly fierce. We never did manage to find out what had happened to her and her husband. Dear gentle Ma Khaing, we hope against hope that she was spared the horrors, but the dice were loaded against our loyal Karens much as they had been in the times of the Kings of Burma.

For length of service with us, seniority goes to the humblest member of the household, 'Sammy' the sweeper. He was the only servant amongst those I had inherited from my bachelor predecessor who did not depart after my marriage. Again the hand of Maung Pyaung may have had its part in the matter of Sammy's request to stay on. Soon after his arrival the former told me that he had never met a better cleaner and polisher of floors than Sammy; an opinion which was very much upheld by my wife. This appreciation must have been made apparent to the recipient of the eulogy, it was unusual for one servant to express approval of another, particularly if he was the least significant. Anyhow, he stayed on happily appreciated by us all. Sammy's only vice, as far as I was aware, was alcohol. Every fortnight or so, after receiving his wages, he would disappear for twenty four hours, once or twice for two days, on a blinding drinking spree. Each time he would return rather shamefaced and vigorously get back to work; everything shone twice as bright as before; this was his way to show appreciation for the absence of a scolding which we had abandoned early on when his only known vice appeared incurable. For the sake of a day's inconvenience, we were quite ready to compromise in return for a spotless home during the rest of the time.

Not until I became Assistant Collector of Customs did we live with modern conveniences. When Sammy was relieved of these less pleasant duties with chamber pots and commodes, he seemed to transfer the energy for that kind of work into his floors and passages. Many of our visitors to the flat would spontaneously comment on the well polished floors in our rooms and passages. He also remained with us to the end. He went reluctantly when I was left on my own. This forced departure was a blessing in disguise; he managed to board a ship going to Madras, with a little help from one of my staff, whereas many other humble Indians of the Untouchable caste had to leave Burma the hard way, overland and many lost their lives in endeavouring to do so. He, of all the many Indians I had known in Burma, was the most unlikely one I should meet again.

I had been in the Army for about two years and was on my way from Bombay to the Combined Operations Training Centre, via Madras. I had just come off the train and was looking round for transport outside the main Madras station entrance, when a voice said, "Salaam Sahib", and there stood Sammy looking his usual cheerful self. I was so pleased to see him thus unexpectedly that I threw an arm round his shoulder and patted him on the back much to the scandalised consternation of Indian passers-by, seeing an English Major embracing an Untouchable sweeper. He told me that he was now working in one of the many military establishments which had sprung up in the area; adding with a smile, "No floor polishing now, Sahib". He asked after the rest of the family and wanted to know if my small boy still had the toy motor-car which he used to ride around Sammy doing his household chores! I insisted on giving him the few rupees I happened to have in my pocket, which overwhelmed him; he departed salaaming deeply with tears in his eyes.

During my six years in the Rangoon City Police, I retained the same Karen Police driver for my car; he rose from Constable to Head Constable in step with my eventual promotion to Assistant Commissioner; 'Saw' (the Karen equivalent of 'Maung') Pan Daik had driven my predecessor in the Western division for several years, was a good mechanic and one of the best drivers in the force. As I have already shown he was not a great talker and was not above a blameless record. I never really knew what he thought about me; he was always willing, always available and on several occasions exposed himself unnecessarily to danger by remaining near me, whenever I became involved in some turbulent incident. When the need arose, he spent long hours uncomplainingly on duty, ever ready to drive me anywhere at a moment's notice.

He showed quite an unexpected side to his personality after I married. When he found that my wife displayed a lively interest in everything around her, he turned into the perfect guide for her explorations. Like Maung Pyaung, I found that he could carry on a perfectly adequate conversation in English with her. Most European women in Rangoon had little or no interest in anything beyond their restricted social life; they knew nothing about the congested native quarters of the town or of the people who lived there. With a few notable exceptions, European men and women did not wish to probe below the surface into the deeper facets of life, presented by an unusually diverse conglomeration of races, religions and customs. Like Kipling's Elephant Child, my wife had an insatiable curiosity to know about the strange new life around her. Saw Pan Daik was just the man for the job; his long years of service in the City Police had given him an intimate knowledge of the Town and its people; he had many contacts in all sections of the population, some probably less savoury than others.

In normal circumstances, I did not require my car after my morning rounds and having reached the office, until after five in the afternoon. I wondered how Pan Daik would accept the changed circumstances when, instead of gossiping and gambling with the other drivers in the garage basement of the large office block, he was required to return home to await the 'Thakinma's' pleasure. He never showed any outward sign of resentment in this encroachment on his unofficial free hours, albeit liable to instant interruptions at all times. My wife only told me much later the details of her strange wanderings around Rangoon and the neighbourhood under Pan Daik's guidance. At first he was reluctant to take her into unusual surroundings, explaining that 'Thakin' would probably dislike the idea of her walking about in none too clean streets and shops, surrounded by strange people, whose curiosity would be greatly aroused by the unusual sight of a fair-haired woman (she never wore a topee but carried a small Burmese umbrella instead) in their midst. She soon set his mind at rest. I also suspect that he, like the rest of the staff, had soon realised that our marriage was not in the least in the oriental style, where master's word was law with all and sundry!

So, whilst I was fondly thinking that the car was taking my wife sedately to a friend's house, or on some other social calls, perhaps fitting in some mundane shopping in the few anglicised stores, she and Pan Daik were out on quite different car trips. They visited all the different congested native quarters tucked away behind the main streets, places unknown and unseen by the European community. They looked at Hindu temples, Muslim mosques, Sikh gurdwaras, Buddhist pagodas, Chinese joss houses and other unusual places, some of which were even unknown to me – in spite of all the years moving around the City in the course of my Police duties.

Besides the purely sight-seeing expeditions, my wife became well-known in the conglomerations of small native shops, not least those in the Soortee Bara Bazaar, scene of the 1938 riots. In these places she also met the artisans and learnt about their various crafts, much as I had done in my early days in Mandalay. Amongst her discoveries was a small Burmese pottery on the outskirts where the potter was only too willing to throw earthenwares to her own design, skilfully glazed to her own colours. His skills brought him unexpected customers in the shape of her friends, having seen the finished products in our home. Her fair hair and tall appearance soon became known to individual shopkeepers and craftsmen, always with the equally familiar figure of policeman Saw Pan Daik at her elbow. She told me later on how friendly and pleased these people were to find a white woman showing real interest in their native wares and crafts.

As a by-product of these excursions, we used to receive periodical visits from one of the better known Muslim carpet and rug merchants in the city; his charming manner and salesmanship would have taken him far in any large business enterprise. He would arrive accompanied by one, sometimes two, coolies, carrying on his head a huge tied-up bundle of oriental carpets and rugs. The goods would be unrolled whilst the seller embarked on a long and interesting account of his recent travels in search of merchandise. He regularly visited all the famous carpet weaving centres in Persia and Turkestan, names like Bokhara, Samarkand, Shiraz, Tabriz, Ispahan and so on would casually drop from his lips, always linked with some unusual feature or happening in each place. This well delivered travelogue alone was worth his visit, but to him that was just the foreplay for the real business of persuading a reluctant client to spend money. His method was unusual and successful; when he noticed that a particular carpet or rug took our fancy, he would pack up the rest and say: "I go now Sahib, Memsahib, I leave the rug/carpet for you to decide. When I come back I will take away if you do not buy." He would then depart cheerfully for a few months, leaving us to enjoy the use of unpaid goods. Usually we succumbed to the ploy but, even when we remained firm, he never betrayed any displeasure at having to take back something we had used for so long. Alas, having acquired over the years a collection of good rugs and carpets, we were forced to leave them behind with all our other worldly goods.

Looking back, I must have been pretty dense not to have become aware of my wife's exploring habit earlier than I did. At some dinner party or cocktail gathering someone would say or ask something unusual about the town or its people, and quite often my wife would be the one to answer the question or to amplify the statement. Once, she told a questioner where the little known Chinese cemetery was situated and then explained the peculiar shaped tombstones, which were meant to represent the female womb. (The Chinese say, as you come from the womb, so you must return to the womb.) The old established tradition, for a deceased respectable Chinaman's body to be returned to his ancestral home in China was still widely observed. It was quite common on visiting a Chinese home to see an elaborately carved open coffin displayed prominently in the main living room, ready to receive the head of the house's remains when the time came.

My wife asked me one day whether I had noticed that the erotic statuettes on the Hindu temple near the Mogul Guard had been recently refurbished in flesh-coloured paint and now looked very realistic. I had not even noticed the existence of these figurines, although I had passed the temple on countless occasions! On my next visit to the Police building, I had a good look at the carvings on the temple and was rewarded with some very peculiar life-like poses of intertwined male and female forms, in plain view for all to see; much more artistic and erotic than the pornographic displays in today's Soho.

We both now regret conforming with the unwritten law that Europeans should not visit Buddhist shrines any more, since it now meant the removal of shoes and going bare-foot. With the growth of nationalism, the Burmese insisted that all visitors of whatever creed should observe the national religious custom. The Government duly acknowledged the need to prevent this understandable affront. Most

Europeans, therefore, ceased to visit Burmese pagodas and monastries. My wife told me later that she very nearly did remove her shoes in order to enter the Shwe Dagon pagoda and that only Saw Pan Daik's earnest pleadings stopped her; he was apparently afraid that I would put all the blame on him for allowing my wife to break a stupid convention. I did myself enter that famous shrine with my Army boots on when I had to lead a party of British soldiers to search the precincts for fugitive Japanese troops, alleged to be hiding there, soon after we had re-occupied the town in 1945. Unfortunately, none of us had time to indulge in sight-seeing on that occasion.

After this diversion from Saw Pan Daik, it only remains to record our temporary severance when I left the Rangoon Police to join the Customs. At the end of December 1941, when enemy bombing disrupted normal life in Rangoon and I returned to the Police, he re-joined me as my driver and remained with me to the final hours. His last personal service was to set fire to my car so as to deny its use to the enemy, as we prepared to embark on the launches taking us down river. He joined the other remaining Karen policemen, about to disperse to their native villages. I never saw him again nor could I get any news when I returned briefly after the war. Like so many of his race, he appeared to have vanished without trace.

28

The Last Ditchers

After the bombing of Pearl Harbour and America's declaration of war on Japan, the British Government followed with similar action within hours. The long and meticulously prepared Japanese plans of aggression were spectacularly successful; their forces advanced rapidly in South East Asia. Hong Kong was captured on Christmas Day 1941, followed a few weeks later by the conquest of Malaya and Singapore and the surrender of Thailand. Without a pause, Burma was then attacked overland; the important town and port of Moulmein was lost to the enemy on the first of February 1942. Rangoon was the next main objective in the plan of campaign. So much for this brief outline of main events which dominated our lives during the last weeks in Rangoon.

I had departed on a tour of the Land Customs establishments in the Northern Shan States a week before the news about the Pearl Harbour attack burst upon the rest of the world. My wife had arranged to visit friends in Moulmein during my absence from Rangoon. With hindsight, it now looks reckless that we were so far apart and out of touch at that particular time but the Americans and the Japanese were still negotiating round the table and nothing then portended an abrupt and violent end to these talks, let alone an imminent state of war all over the Far East.

I had just come back to Lashio, intending to complete my tour by travelling along the Chinese border to Bhamo to inspect the remaining Customs posts before returning to Rangoon. I was in the house of my friend, the Resident, when we heard over the radio the news of the surprise assault on the American Pacific fleet. I managed to catch the daily train to Mandalay and, some hours later, was travelling on the night mail to Rangoon, reaching my destination on the following morning. My wife had also cut short her Moulmein visit and was awaiting my arrival in the Custom House flat.

There was already considerable turmoil in government and business circles. The port was as usual congested with shipping and the transit sheds were bulging with cargo; much of it strategic war materials for the Chinese Government. Importers and exporters were all clamouring for an early clearance of their goods. It was obvious to most that the port of Rangoon was to become a prime target for Japanese bombers just as soon as they could be brought within flying range.

Our first personal priority was to find alternative accommodation to the now dangerous site of our flat. We received, unasked, a pressing invitation to make our home with some good friends who lived in a pleasant bungalow near a lake on the outskirts of the town. Accommodation was limited but our excellent butler, Maung Pyaung, came to the rescue. With the help of some nearby villagers, he set up as builder, erecting in a day a temporary extension to one of the bedrooms for Nanny and our child. This hut of bamboo and thatch with a wooden floor cost me only ninety rupees (seven pounds) and provided very adequate and comfortable shelter for the two occupants, until our two families departed to India.

The Japanese air attacks began even earlier than expected, because the Thais surrendered immediately without a fight. Within days, Japanese military planes arrived on their airfields and lost no time in raiding over Burmese territory. The air defences were very weak, a few fighter aircraft and no anti-aircraft guns; but the air raid warning system worked remarkably well, until the fall of Moulmein deprived the Rangoon control room of sufficient early warning time.

The first raids on Rangoon were relatively small and did not create a great deal of damage or many casualties. Nevertheless, the adverse effect on morale was considerable; many panicked and fled but most returned when it was realised that destruction had not been as widespread as thought. Even so, these initial reactions gave an indication of what might happen permanently once the raids became severe and sustained.

We did not have long to wait for the first of the big daylight raids of fifty and more bombers. The Japanese had shrewdly judged that the inexperienced civil population would probably react with curiosity rather than fear during the first large daylight raid. They therefore chose to drop anti-personnel fragmentation bombs quite deliberately on the spectators, crowded into the streets to watch the spectacularly numerous aircraft flying in perfect V formations in the clear blue sky above the city. The result was disastrous; few people had chosen relative safety in the hastily built air-raid shelters. Several thousands were killed or seriously wounded in a matter of minutes. The A.R.P., the Police and above all the medical services just could not cope with the resulting panic and chaos. A mass exodus began at once; this time the manual workers in the docks, in the municipal services and in other utilities fled, never to return. In short, practically every enterprise which was labour-intensive came to a virtual standstill.

The enemy's prime intention to make the port inoperable succeeded only too well. By Christmas Eve the town was completely disorganised. Some essential supplies and services such as light, power, water, fire-fighting and medical care were kept going on an emergency basis by skeleton staffs composed of senior personnel. I was sorry for the bewildered special A.R.P. Commissioner who had been purposely recruited in the United Kingdom to advise and set up an A.R.P. organisation. He was left practically powerless to deal with the tragic aftermath of the raid. One day his organisation numbered several thousands, the next only a handful of senior staff were left on duty. The Commissioner had just not visualised the possibility of total collapse within hours; he had assumed as a matter of course the same sort of devotion and sense of duty as he had experienced in his previous appointments in blitzed Britain. Make-shift gangs of Police and other volunteers had to assume the task of removing corpses and badly wounded from streets and damaged houses. Inevitably, many bodies remained undetected or irretrievable from totally collapsed large buildings and wharves, posing a further health hazard to all the others.

The Japanese air force was now making day and night raids on the town, the port and the military installations as well as on the aerodrome at Mingaladon, eleven miles from Rangoon. Burma had been very much at the end of the queue for military aircraft. When the invasion started, the R.A.F. only possessed some outdated slow Buffalo fighters and these were not much of a match against the enemy's Zeros in the outnumbered serial combats over Rangoon. Later, Hurricanes were sent out as reinforcements. One valuable asset in the air war was the American Volunteer Group; they had been formed to protect the Burma-China Road and were based at Kuming in China. The Chinese Government had recognised the importance of keeping the Rangoon back-door to China open. Consequently, part of this group was now stationed at Mingaladon; their Tomahawk planes and experienced fighter pilots were more than a match for the Japanese. The combined British-American fighter force, of less than three squadrons in all, put up a magnificent performance in defence of the skies above Rangoon. In the two months in which they were able to operate, they shot down around one hundred and thirty enemy machines, mostly bombers and damaged another fifty or more most of which probably never returned to base. After the fall of Rangoon, air superiority went decisively to the Japanese through sheer weight of overwhelming numbers and remained with them until sometime after the final evacuation of Burma in May 1942.

By the end of December 1941, normal working in the Customs Department, as elsewhere, had ceased. Only very curtailed essential functions were maintained. I suggested to my friend, the Collector, that I might now be better employed back in my own service and he agreed to release me if I was needed. I went to see the Commissioner of Police, my old chief from Mandalay days. On the same evening, New Year's Eve, I received verbal orders from Government House to report for special duty in the Rangoon Police. I decided then and there that I would function better if my wife and child were removed right away from danger for the duration. The friend, in whose house we had obtained shelter, had come to the same conclusion about his family. So, that same night, the two wives and the two children found themselves on board a ship bound for India. They remained together for the next four months sharing all travelling hardships through India to Ceylon and back again, as well as the uncertainties and worries about the future for themselves and for their husbands left behind in warring Burma.

My wife was splendid in those last hours we had together. She accepted my abrupt decision without demur, packed quietly the few essential belongings they needed for the journey and waited patiently for my arrival to pick them up for the drive to the harbour that night. We arrived alongside the ship in total darkness, stumbled up the gangway and, all six of us, squeezed into the tiny cabin hurriedly allotted to the two wives and their two children. By now the stark adversity of the situation had hit us all and we had rather lost our composure. Even the inscrutable driver, Pan Daik, had been in tears when he bid farewell to his mistress on the quayside. On board, we told our respective spouses, who declared that they would remain together come what may, to formulate whatever plans appeared most suitable on arrival in Calcutta. With these vague instructions, we all bid each other tearful and anguished farewells.

The next morning, soon after I had arrived on duty at the Mogul Guard, a severe and concentrated air attack was made on the harbour area by a large fleet of enemy bombers. After the all-clear I rang up my companion in sorrow in his office, expressing relief that our families had escaped the last bad raid. To my horror he told me that far from being out of danger, they had been in the midst of the destruction. The ship, which had been due to sail at midnight on the high tide, had fouled a propeller on an underwater cable and had been forced to drop anchor. I dashed down to the river front, saw the ship in midstream with a tug fussing around the stern. My friend, whose Company were shipping agents for the line, arrived as I was wondering what I should do next. He told me that all was well now and that he had been on board. Whilst he was talking to me, the ship began to move slowly down river, too far away for me to see anyone on board. I went back thankfully to my interrupted spell of duty made possible by a kind offer from the man I was relieving to stay on whilst I made my rapid trip to the wharf. Months later my wife told me that, terrifying as the raid had been with bombs dropping all round them, far worse had been the stench of rotting corpses, trapped between the pillars of the nearby destroyed wharf, where the ship had been forced to anchor after the mishap. These victims had been dock workers killed some time earlier in the first raids on the port, when labour had still been available.

The military situation continued to deteriorate daily. The enemy was now poised to cross the last major natural barrier, the Sittang River, before breaking out into the plains leading to Rangoon and central Burma. The stream of evacuees from the town became a flood, which was just as well since essential services were deteriorating rapidly. The Governor, after consulting the Army, issued secret instructions for the likely total evacuation of the capital and then the total destruction of all installations and materials likely to be of use to the enemy. The planned operation was divided into three stages. The first, signalled by the single letter 'E', was to evacuate all but essential military and civil personnel required to carry out the denial policy, now designated 'the last ditchers'. The second phase, to be signalled by the letter 'W', would signify the warning to prepare for imminent destructions; and the final signal, the letter 'D', would be the message for immediate and total evacuation within twenty four hours, maybe even less time.

The first signal was received on the 20th February. By then the population had already decreased from the peace-time total of over half a million to some thousands. Most of these were from the indigenous races, who had no intention of leaving the country but now wished to depart 'up-country'. Rail, road and river transport were barely sufficient to cope with even these reduced numbers. All Police, now not required in Rangoon, were allocated as armed escorts on trains and steamers. This had become an essential precaution since more and larger gangs of dacoits were now preying on the unfortunate evacuees. The growing country-wide chaos offered the opportunity for ever bolder looting and violence. Within forty eight hours of the 'E' signal, the town was virtually empty; those who could not find accommodation on trains, vehicles or boats, formed up in groups for self-protection and marched out into the countryside.

After the exodus, a Military Administration was proclaimed in the city which was declared 'the Rangoon Fortress Area'; the 'Fortress' element being conspicuous by its total absence. The remaining senior Police officers were given local military status; I blossomed forth as a Major. The ever ready Mogul Guard became a Military headquarters; in the last stages, most of us also dossed down in the place, to be readily available in an emergency. The Police now numbered about a hundred, out of a peace-time strength of over two thousand; the Army garrison was one company of British Infantry and another of Burma Rifles and Military Police stationed across the river guarding the two oil refineries. About forty European civilian volunteers had been detailed to assist the military in due course in carrying out the denial plan; meanwhile they did yeoman service assisting the Police in daily chores. The Navy was represented by an old Indian Navy sloop. With these meagre dispositions it was difficult to foster a 'fortress mentality' but we all managed, somehow, to remain reasonably cheerful on the surface. As one wag said at the time, there was not much scope for the sale of laxatives during these last days in Rangoon!

The final fortnight was a traumatic experience. Moving around in a well-known city, now devoid of its inhabitants, was eerie to say the least. Familiar houses, shops, offices, all devoid of occupants were still filled with furniture, furnishings, goods and equipment, despite the increasing sporadic looting. The transit sheds on the wharves were packed with undelivered cargo; cases of gin, whisky, wine, tinned goods, hardware, in short anything found on a normal working day, were lying around awaiting transport which would now never come. It was uncanny to walk into a well-remembered house to find personal belongings still largely intact; clothes hanging or stacked in their allotted places, ornaments and knick-knacks lying around on tables, shelves or hanging on walls, food and other household goods in larders and cupboards, even refrigerators still switched on (electricity was not cut off until final demolitions were under way) keeping food cold. In some instances, tables had not been cleared after the last meal, cutlery, plates and glasses still in their usual places, even half-empty dishes had been left on side-boards. Quite a lot of loose silverware was also in evidence. Looting had been kept under relative control by mobile patrols shooting at looters on sight, until it became certain that the town was about to be abandoned to the victor.

The 'W' warning had also been the signal to release the inmates from the Jail and Mental Asylum (dangerous criminals and lunatics had been removed earlier). Harmless animals, birds and reptiles in the Zoo were also set free. Everyone expected the final signal to be issued within a day or two and the civilian 'last ditchers' were now concentrating at the Mogul Guard. We all mucked in, in a quite literal sense, for washing, sleeping and eating. In some instances, heads of the larger European commercial and industrial concerns, such as the Irrawaddy Flotilla Company, the Burmah (sic) Oil Company and some others, had elected to remain with their volunteers, on the laudable analogy that the captain leaves his ship last.

I recall that when the Zoo was cleared, one of the 'last ditchers' shot a 'gee', a small deer common in the forests of Burma, right outside the main gates of the Rangoon General Hospital in the heart of the city. He brought it back to the Mogul Guard, where it made a welcome and succulent change to the everlasting bully beef and spam to which we had been reduced for some time in the absence of fresh food. In this last week, as it finally turned out, fire raisers became active; they chose the congested native quarters where the preponderance of wooden buildings offered ready burning material for their senseless deeds. Nearly all local staff in the Fire Brigade had deserted and the few remaining officers could do little to fight the fires; they concentrated on creating fire lanes to stop the fires spreading into the centre of the town where we were still operating. The anti-looting patrols were partially diverted to assist the Fire officers in their dismal task of wilfully destroying good buildings to save others.

The other light-hearted incident I recall from those sad days happened when I was talking to the master of one of the very few ships still in harbour who had come to the Mogul Guard on some errand. I had met him on several occasions when I had been in the Port Police and in the Customs, and his ship on a regular run between Rangoon and Madras. We were standing on the pavement chatting idly when he referred to the looting on the wharves. I told him that we had been forced to reduce the anti-looting patrols because of the fire raising. He then ruefully remarked that, had he known about the reduced precautions, he would have helped himself to a silver tray and two silver candlesticks which he had seen through the half-broken open door of a well-known jeweller's shop. On the spur of the moment I came to a disgraceful decision for a Policeman, I told him that I was about to visit my flat at the Custom House (still quite intact in spite of all the devastation around it), offered him a lift in my jeep and told him that we would pick up the loot on the way if it was still in the shop. Miraculously the articles were there; before going on board his ship, he asked me if he could do anything in return for my criminal connivance. I thought for a moment and then asked him to take a ready-packed trunk to India for delivery to my wife, if his agents could trace her. The outcome was a happy one; the agents took a great deal of trouble to find my wife's whereabouts and she eventually received a trunk full of belongings which she had never expected to see again. Unfortunately, it was not the container with our most valuable possessions.

I had one pleasant surprise, proving that peace-time staid administration was still functioning. The Governor of Burma, Sir Reginald

Dorman-Smith at one of his periodical visits to our headquarters, drew me aside to tell me he had just heard from the Secretary of State that I had won my long-standing appeal. This was a matter which had been dragging on for the best part of two years. All Indian Civil Service members, appointed to the Customs Department, received a special allowance and, when I was appointed, I applied for the same perquisite. The Burma Government ruled that I was not entitled because I was not a 'Heaven-Born' (popular nickname for members of the I.C.S.). I then invoked my right of appeal to the ultimate authority, the Secretary of State for India and Burma. The final decision gave me quite considerable material benefit just at the right time, since it was ruled that I was entitled to the allowance from the date of my transfer to Customs, some two years earlier! By another stroke of luck, I managed to get the money paid to my wife in India by telegraphic transfer, just before the banks (now operating from Mandalay) had to close down this form of communication.

The Japanese were known to have entered the country accompanied by thirty young dissident Burmans, who had fled the country at the outbreak of war. They had then contacted the Japanese, who had trained them for military intelligence work. Now, they were acting as guides and agents to the advancing forces. Reports had been received that several of them were making their way to Rangoon, accompanied by disguised Japanese officers, to assess the situation. We began to search suspicious vehicles; this task was not as easy as it might seem in a deserted town. There was appreciable military traffic on the roads to and from the wharves, collecting stores, equipment and personnel for dispersal beyond the city limits. The Military were short of transport and many service drivers had helped themselves to abandoned civilian cars and lorries; there was thus still mixed civilian and service transport on the roads.

Within a short time of the information about infiltration, a Japanese officer was caught with some Burmans, as they stepped from a country boat on to the very foreshore where I had my memorable encounter with a lunatic, still dressed in my dinner jacket and trousers. Several mobile patrols stopped suspicious looking vehicles but drew blanks; one interception developed into an exchange of shots before the suspects managed to escape. I believe that I just missed catching a possible spy. My jeep patrol was overtaking a car with four occupants, all wearing khaki shirts and woollen khaki military caps. As we passed the vehicle, I thought that one of the occupants did not look Burmese. Rather belatedly I told the driver to stop. As I stepped from the jeep, I shouted prematurely to the other driver to halt; instead, he accelerated rapidly just missing me. Our pursuit was delayed by me trying to scramble back into our vehicle. The other driver knew his Rangoon well and made full use of all the twists and turns into the narrow side-streets. We chased him in and out of alleys, some quite unknown to me; the driver had the sense to keep well away from the main thoroughfares, where we might have been in a position to get him cornered with the help of other traffic. At a particularly sharp turn, with wheels skidding and locked by the brakes, one of our front tyres blew out and ended the chase. Despite an extensive search, organised as quickly as possible, neither the vehicle nor the occupants were traced. I am still certain that I missed the opportunity of a capture. On the other hand, as we learnt later, Japanese officers did not surrender lightly if at all. The encounter might therefore have ended in a shooting match in which either side could have emerged victorious.

To complete the historical facts, the thirty young Burmans with the invading forces became known as the 'Thirty Heroes' after the war. Several of them rose to political leadership and participated in negotiations with the British Government for the independence of their country.

The expected 'D' signal, for demolitions to begin, did not materialise within a few days as expected. Instead, we had a series of important visitors at the Mogul Guard. The Governor came to bid us good luck, before proceeding to Maymyo, of blessed memory, where the various depleted Government departments had now been established. Several high ranking staff officers arrived, delivered contradictory statements about the war situation and departed. The general belief was that Rangoon could not be held much longer. Some lunatics, released from the Asylum, appeared on the streets, sitting around forlornly or pretending to direct traffic at road intersections, until relatives or kind samaritans removed them. We received one false alarm for the 'D' signal on the 5th March, which was immediately cancelled.

The next morning, the new Army Commander, General Alexander, arrived at our Headquarters, more or less straight from England, exuding energy and confidence; he ended a pep talk with a categorical statement that Rangoon would be held and that nothing was to be destroyed. Two days later, the 'D' signal was issued at noon and demolitions began at once; these were completed by evening and the 'last ditchers', civilians and garrison, evacuated the town, which was occupied by Japanese troops on the following day, the 8th March 1942. The Army Commander's statement on holding Rangoon at all costs had not been just wishful thinking but had been based on some solid assumptions which did not materialise through no fault of his. The importance of the place, both for the British and the Chinese forces now locked in battle with the Japanese in Burma, was recognised at the highest levels in London and Washington. Both Governments were anxious to keep the port open and joint efforts were being made to persuade the Australian Government to permit the diversion of substantial forces, now on their way back from the Middle East to Australia. These troops had been in Egypt as part of the Eighth Army and were seasoned, battle-hardened soldiers. The Government in Australia had decided to recall them when Japanese forces landed on their doorstep in New Guinea.

The issue remained in the balance for some days; the convoy was even diverted from the direct route, before the Australians definitely turned down the joint request. The troops, now within only a day or so of steaming distance from Rangoon, sailed on to their homeland. These considerable reinforcements could perhaps have made all the difference in the military situation in Burma. On the other hand, the Australians had already suffered large losses in the Desert and in Malaya and must have felt that their need now was greater than ours. Hence, the abrupt change in Burma, from optimism one day to pessimism the next.

The demolition order was followed by a further signal stating that we only had six hours to complete the work of destruction. This unexpectedly short period was due to another crisis. The original plan had envisaged evacuation of 'last ditchers' by road together with Army Tactical headquarters. The Japanese, however, had managed to cut off all road traffic out of Rangoon by establishing a strong road block just north of the town, effectively trapping Army Headquarters already on the move northwards. The revised plan was for the Rangoon garrison to organise a sea evacuation for that evening, which Army Headquarters would join, if they failed to break through the road block. By a stroke of luck, two old tramp steamers, the last sea-going vessels to clear the port, were still steaming out of the Rangoon river into the Bay of Bengal. They were contacted and the ships' masters unhesitatingly agreed to anchor their crafts until midnight at Elephant Point, to await the pick-up from launches.

The mixed teams of civilian and army 'wreckers' went about their work of destruction with efficiency and speed. Explosions were heard in all directions; by five o'clock, the whole town seemed to be engulfed in a cloud of smoke and flames. The greatest havoc was wrought on the wharves and jetties; cranes, sheds, bollards and anything else of the slightest use, were blown up or otherwise made useless. The destruction of the two refineries across the river was on an equally vast scale. Just before we were due to embark in the waiting launches, news arrived that Army Headquarters had managed to resume their journey northwards to Maymyo. The local enemy commander had suddenly and inexplicably lifted the road block, unaware that the new British Army Commander and his whole staff could have been captured. It transpired later on, that our 'top brass' was saved by the Japanese rigid adherence to orders. The road block had been set up temporarily to cover the move of the main force across the road westward. The foe's higher command had decided to assault Rangoon from the west instead of straight down the main road from the north.

We wasted no more time and embarked into the waiting launches at six o'clock, again from the same foreshore where my dinner jacket had been ruined some time ago in what now seemed the distant past. Cruising down river, past the whole frontage of the wrecked jetties and wharves, the whole town was engulfed in flames and smoke which formed an unbroken curtain above the buildings. Subsequently, the R.A.F. reported that their reconnaisance planes had been unable to overfly the stricken city because the clouds of smoke had risen so high. On our way downstream to our rendezvous, we stopped twice to pick up the troops and demolition experts from the two oil refineries; the smaller installation was some way down the river.

The rest of the river journey was accomplished without incident in the rapidly gathering darkness. We met the anchored vessels before midnight; the launches were then sunk in line across the dredged navigation channel at the mouth of the river, which was otherwise crisscrossed by innumerable sandbanks, considerable hazards to shipping. The ships zigzagged across the Bay of Bengal for four days, escorted on the last stage by the aged Indian Navy sloop, which had left Rangoon some days earlier. Hostile submarines had been operating in the Bay and several ships had been sunk off the Indian coast. The congestion of shipping at the mouth of the Hooghli river was massive, all ships' captains waiting for pilots to guide them up the treacherous stretch of water to Calcutta. We had to spend another forty eight hours, anchored at sea, before stepping once again on firm land.

In my wildest subsequent dreams, of these and other wartime incidents in my life, I never envisaged the possibility of setting up a record. In fact, I believe that of all the 'last ditchers' I was the first back in Rangoon. Having left on the 7th March 1942, I was back in town on the 2nd May 1945. I happened to be in the forward Brigade of the Division which assaulted Rangoon from the sea, in the first major combined operation conducted in South East Asia. To boast further, I had actually been ashore the day before, when I had to contact a Gurkha Parachute battalion, which had been dropped at dawn at Elephant Point to 'take out' a strong point set up by the Japanese who had built an elaborate network of connecting underground bunkers there to defend the sea approach to Rangoon. Apart from the information I had to obtain, I acquired an unexpected bonus; a Samurai sword from a Japanese Major who had no further use for it.

Once in Calcutta, I set about trying to find my wife and child. Like many others in a similar plight, I resorted to advertising for information of their whereabouts in the leading English language newspaper, 'The Statesman'; I still have a copy of the insertion in that paper. This method for gaining contact was then commonplace; the pages carried daily such 'cries de coeur' from worried wives, husbands, sweethearts and other relations who had been forced by the war to separate at short notice and without plans for the future. The public in general was extraordinarily kind and helpful in responding to these advertisements. Individuals and organisations, having the slightest information which could prove useful, got in touch by the quickest means. Luckily I have an unusual name and within a day of my advertisement's appearance, I received a telegram from the Chartered Bank in Madras, stating that they had arranged some credit facilities for a Mrs. Tydd when she had called some weeks ago on her way to Kotagiri, a small hill station in the Nilgiri Hills in South India. That was enough for me; trusting to the likelihood that there was no other woman of that name in the place, I sent off a wire announcing my imminent arrival and caught the next train to Madras. I managed to spend ten precious days with the family before I was recalled to Burma.

My wife, her best friend and their two small boys had spent some time travelling around after landing in Calcutta, searching for a suitable haven to await the outcome of events in Burma. Luckily my wife's friend's husband worked for a firm with offices in Calcutta. They very generously agreed to advance funds also to my wife when both found themselves short of ready cash. I gladly repeat my thanks to Messrs. Steel Brothers and Company for their generosity in that adversity. The two families spent some weeks in Nuwara Eliya, the main hill station in Ceylon. They left on advice given by the authorities to European refugees from Hong Kong, Malaya, Singapore and Burma. The guidance arose from the belief that the island of Ceylon was next on the list for invasion, after the fall of Burma. I suppose that a possible reason for this advice arose from the thought that the conquerors would not be slow to use the captive women, in some way, to blackmail their prisoner husbands or other relatives in the occupied territories, to co-operate with the foe.

Our two families continued to remain united; returned to India, where they settled together in a beautifully situated but rather primitive house, built by an Indian with an eye for a view, in the small, unfashionable hill station of Kotagiri in the Nilgiri Hills. The place they had found was 6,500 feet above sea level, with a spectacular long-distance view across the Madras plain to the Palni hills, sixty miles away. The main, fashionable hot weather seat of the Madras Government, Ootacamund, was not far away. To anticipate events, I spent in due course two happy and peaceful months in this home-from-home, recuperating after my trek out of Burma, before joining up for the duration of the war. As a consequence of the wives' close association over so many months, sharing all trials, tribulations and anxious suspense, the two women became and have remained the closest of friends. Whenever they meet, they immediately begin to re-live their eventful days; they never seem to tire of recalling reminiscences from those eventful times, sometimes to the irritation of their other Burma friends at the periodical reunions who had not shared this close relationship over the months. Perhaps also the Celtic bond between Scot and Welsh has added its chemistry to the association but, as Kipling so aptly put it, "Betty and Mary are sisters under the skin".

When I got back to Calcutta, I found that half a dozen of my 'last ditching' companions had also been recalled at the direct request of the Governor of Burma. We sat around for two days waiting for air transport before flying back in one of the few passenger planes set aside for the evacuation of civilian refugees from Burma. On the 30th March 1942, we landed at a make-shift air strip near the north Burma town of Shwebo, once also one of the royal capitals of the country.

Evacuation of Rangoon, 7 March 1942; Sule Pagoda wharves demolition.
(Picture taken from one of the launches evacuating 'last ditchers' and military personnel left
behind to carry out demolitions after evacuation of population)   Note height of smoke compared
to Port Trust Clock Tower – at extreme right – which was over 100 feet high.

29
Exodus

Shwebo had become a rallying point for evacuees who hoped to leave by air. In fact, a pitifully small number were eventually air-lifted out of the country. An Army truck was waiting to take us all to Maymyo for further orders. On the way we passed through my beloved Mandalay, now looking decidedly part-worn. Chinese troops had been billetted on the town and they looked a ragged, indisciplined lot. I saw one soldier ride his small shaggy steed right up the front steps and into the main room of an unoccupied Burmese house in the town. In Maymyo, I called first on the Inspector-General of Police; he seemed surprised to see me so soon after the fall of Rangoon. He told me to report to Army Headquarters as he had released me from further Police duties.

The next morning, after some shunting around, I was eventually directed to the Military Intelligence department. The senior staff officer there (the G.I(I), in military parlance) was an old acquaintance from my Rangoon Police days when I had some official contacts with him after the outbreak of the European war. He was the only Japanese speaker in the Burma Army; he told me that he had requested my services after the evacuation of Rangoon. He gave me a short grim outline of the military situation to date, told me to have a good night's rest and to report for duty on the following morning, Good Friday the 3rd April 1942.

When I reached Headquarters on the next day, I was told that a hitch had developed about my transfer to military service. Apparently, after the initial consent for my release from civil employment, someone had objected on the grounds that I had been earmarked for some specific job. I was never told who the objector was or what kind of work I was to do. I felt sure that I could now be better employed in the Army, which was short of Burmese speaking officers with some knowledge of the country. I knew that hard-pressed formations in the field were crying out for officers with those qualifications. Nevertheless, even my friend in Intelligence could do nothing but wait for the controversy to be sorted out.

The Civil Administration was in disarray and collapsing fast. Lower Burma was already in the hands of the enemy. Most indigenous civil officials had been given leave of absence for an indefinite period; or had, not unexpectedly, anticipated similar instructions and had just quietly faded away to look after their families hidden in remote villages. The few British officials, still at their posts, could do little else but wait for their inevitable turn to withdraw with or just ahead of the retiring armed forces. Added to all the confusion and uncertainty, was the evacuation problem of thousands of Indian refugees; the majority from Rangoon and other parts of southern Burma, all clamouring for escape to India. The problem was formidable and, considering the short time in which arrangements could be made, had been energetically tackled with the pitifully few means available. Collection centres had been set up in the north, food dumps were being arranged on escape routes and some were being air-lifted to India. Nevertheless, many endured great hardships and numbers perished on the way, from exhaustion or disease, mainly in the final stages when those who had been gradually pushed into the far north of the country had no choice but to try their luck on unprepared and unexplored tracks, leading over mountain ranges into Assam.

My anticipated short stay in Maymyo dragged into a full week, during which time I did nothing at all whilst my fate was being debated by others. During this waiting period, Mandalay was largely destroyed by fire after a severe air raid, due to the preponderance of wooden buildings in the town. Maymyo received two successive air attacks in force, whilst Generalissimo Chiang Kai-shek was conferring with the Governor of Burma and the Army Commander in this hill station; proving that enemy intelligence was receiving accurate information from their numerous secret agents in the country.

Eventually, the Secretary of the Home Department appeared one morning, riding rather incongruously on a bicycle, with orders for me to proceed at once to Myingyan district on special duty. The Home Secretary explained the absence of precise instructions by stating that nobody here knew what was really happening there, except that the main oil fields in Burma, at Yenangyaung, were about to be blown up. These fields were situated on the border between Myingyan and Magwe districts. The signs were that Myingyan district was next on the list for total evacuation.

So, without much of a brief and against my personal inclination, I reverted to civilian status after my short spell as a local Major in 'Rangoon Fortress'. My sojourn in Myingyan district was brief, fourteen days. To my pleasant surprise, the Deputy Commissioner turned out to be a contemporary of mine from my early Rangoon days. When I had been Superintendent of the Western Division, he had been Western Divisional Magistrate. He invited me to share his newly built comfortable, official residence. We spent a harmonious but anxious fortnight together. We decided that the best role for me was to act as his general dog's body and, since he was tied to headquarters because most of his subordinates had already left, I should also liaise with the various Army units in, or about to arrive in, the district.

On the following day, realising that time was short, I went off on a swift reconnaissance by road to the southern half of the district where the troops, now in the adjacent oil fields' area, would be arriving after the final demolitions. A few days later, I was more than glad that I had familiarised myself with the lines of communication. I had been to Divisional Headquarters for consultations on the day following the withdrawal from the oil fields and had then gone on to the important military centre at Meiktila, to gather news from the eastern front. On the way back, I nearly ran into a road block set up by the Japanese after I had left the Divisional staff. Without my recently acquired knowledge of the local topography, I could have been caught or shot if I had stayed on the main road. The unpleasant incident happened near Mount Popa.

Mount Popa (in effect a large hill surrounded by flat country) was a famous landmark in the area; mainly because its slopes were infested with the infamous king-cobras. The local inhabitants, men and women, would go into the bush to catch these dangerous snakes, keep them as sort of house pets for a while and then release them for a new batch. They would entertain visitors with displays of their familiarity, amounting to contempt, for these reptiles. The favourite piece of showmanship, and a very spectacular one, was for the person to kneel in front of the half-erect, swaying body of the cobra and then very gradually draw his or her face nearer and nearer to the venomous fangs. Both opponents would sway their bodies in unison as if in a trance, getting their heads closer and closer together until it looked as if they were about to kiss. People did die of snake-bite in the place, but fatalities did not seem to be more numerous than elsewhere!

When I got back to district headquarters after my round trip, bringing nothing but bad news from both fronts, the Deputy Commissioner informed me that my bicycling friend, the Home Secretary, had rung up from Maymyo just after I had left, to recall me at once for duty with the specially appointed Commissioner for Civil Evacuation. My reaction was to point out that the rapidly deteriorating military situation around the southern border of the district meant that civil evacuation was imminent and would have to be swift when it happened. I offered to stay on under the circumstances, if I could be of further use. The Deputy Commissioner seemed glad of my offer, so I telephoned Maymyo, but was told that the Home Secretary was not available; I informed the underling that I could not leave Myingyan as evacuation was imminent. I did not hear anything more after this terse exchange of words over the telephone. I learnt later that my call had been made as the remaining skeleton Secretariat staff was, in fact, getting ready to move that day to my old haunt, Myitkyina, in the far north.

On the 15th April, we were told about the imminent destruction of the oil fields and of the further withdrawal of our forces. I spent the following days dashing around from pillar to post on a multitude of diverse jobs, conveying and receiving information, issuing instructions on evacuation or destroying records and equipment. One of the most difficult tasks was to burn wads of bank notes in the district treasury. I realised that the expression 'money to burn' must have been coined by someone who had tried it! The Deputy Commissioner and I left together, in separate cars, on the 25th April, bringing to a close over fifty years of British administration in the district.

We decided, on leaving Myingyan, to make Sagaing, across the Irrawaddy, our next stop. To our surprise, the local Burmese ferry was still plying at a place called Sameikon, thus saving us a long detour via the

Ava bridge near Mandalay. I had been down to the ferry jetty a few days earlier with some staff officers to assess the possibilities for a crossing by the retreating Division from the oil fields. Returning with the batch of staff officers to Myingyan, it did cross my mind that the sight of so many uniforms had probably unsettled the ferrymen and would cause their departure. In fact, the Army did use this crossing after us, obtaining crafts from Mandalay with Royal Engineers' crews; which was as well, as the local men had gone.

We arrived in Sagaing on the following day and spent the night with separate friends; that was the last I saw of my Myingyan companion until we met years later at a Burma reunion party in London. The next morning, I started my road journey to Shwebo; on the way, I had to dive into a road-side ditch to take cover from a sudden air attack on road traffic. In amongst the other crouched bodies in this natural trench, I unexpectedly observed the Commissioner for Civil Evacuation in person. He was my old friend the Deputy Conservator of Forests, who had organised the famous Christmas camp in Pegu district. He told me that he was on his way to Army headquarters and asked me to join him in the discussions, since I was going to be attached to him. We arrived at our destination soon after the raiders had flown off, having failed to hit the building used by the headquarters' staff. The long and the short of this conference was the decision to evacuate at once all civilians from the refugee camps in the area. My new chief asked me to supervise the clearing of three camps; at nearby Yeu, at Kyaukmyaung on the Irrawaddy and at Okma on the Chindwin river, whilst he proceeded to another concentration area in the north, where his wife had been performing outstanding service amongst the Indian refugees. I did not see him again, until many years later at another London Burma party.

To cut the rest of the story short, we managed to clear the three camps in record time. We had a stroke of extraordinary good luck at the furthest one, Okma, which looked as if it could present considerable problems, being isolated and without lines of communication, except the river. Having cleared the other two camps, which were on motorable roads, a party of volunteers accompanied me for the final evacuation operation at Okma. We motored a few miles down the road from Yeu to Monywa, then had to face a walk across country for two days to reach the camp. Having destroyed the vehicles at the roadside, we set off on our forty mile hike, mostly through teak forests, which gave us some shade and coolness. Indeed had the circumstances been different, I would have enjoyed the walk, as of old. We reached the camp early on 1st May, having force-marched through the night. During the morning, rumour reached us that Monywa, uncomfortably close to the camp, had been evacuated by our troops and had been occupied by the Japanese. Towards dusk, whilst we were still busy sending off parties of refugees in boats and on foot, one of the Irrawaddy Flotilla's purpose-built sternwheeler steamers appeared round the bend of the river, from the direction of Monywa. The craft appeared empty and in a hurry; we hailed her to draw in but no notice was taken of our shouts, until I told one of the escort to fire a burst from his tommy gun across the bows. The serang (native captain) was in a great state of terror and excitement and could hardly answer our questions. It transpired that he had only just managed to get his boat away before the Japs arrived to board. Indeed he had been obliged to cut his ropes and, fortunately for us, had no time to cast off the flat tied to his vessel's side. So instead of having to trek or paddle upstream in country boats, we completed the journey of fifty miles to Kalewa in relative comfort in the company of several hundred Indian refugees of both sexes and all ages, packed tight into every nook and cranny on the boat and the barge alongside.

I had now completed my official duties and devoted the following days to getting myself to India on foot, as countless others were doing, trudging through the dreaded, fever-infested Kabaw valley to Imphal in India which I reached on the 9th May 1942. Eleven days later, I was once again reunited with my family in Kotagiri in South India. The one redeeming feature in this final exhausting trek was the absence of the monsoon. Mercifully, the rains broke late in this fateful year.

Even amongst all the misery and heartbreaks endured during those last weeks, there were some comic incidents to relieve the universal gloom. I feel it appropriate to conclude this dismal chapter with two short stories to illustrate less tragic happenings.

When still in Myingyan district, and as the Army were coming through from their grim fighting in the oil fields, the Divisional General came to the Deputy Commissioner's house for a few hours. In the course of conversation, he asked if there was any news about the Japanese thrust towards the smaller oil field at Chauk, even closer to the district border. On the spur of the moment, I picked up the telephone, got through to the local police station at Chauk and enquired if there was any sign of the enemy. The policeman on duty reacted quite normally and politely, he said that they were expecting the conquerors shortly and, to my utter surprise, offered to ring back when he had more definite news! Sure enough, about an hour later, the telephone rang, it was the policeman from Chauk; he reported that the Japanese had just arrived in the deserted town. The speaker was quite unemotional and polite, calling me even 'Thakin Gyi' (big master!).

The other story refers to an event which happened later. A group of us, civilians and military, were standing by the roadside watching a long column of men and vehicles passing slowly, part of our general retreat out of Burma. Suddenly, an Army staff car with pennon flying, drew up sharply with a screech of brakes. "You there", shouted th red-tabbed occupant of the car, leaning out of the rear window, "arrange for twenty bullock-carts to be assembled here in an hour". The astonished civilian, who had been so curtly addressed, began to argue about the difficulties in trying to meet the order. The staff officer waved him impatiently aside, summoned one of the uniformed spectators and repeated the order. The young captain drew himself smartly to attention, saluted impeccably and replied, "Very good, Sir". The car then drove off, again at high speed, tyres squealing. The young officer turned to us and said, "The bloody old fool", then disappeared in his turn.

Epilogue

My services with the Indian Police did not end with the events in 1942. After the Japanese surrender in August 1945, British officers in the Indian Army could again apply for furlough. Leave was granted on a priority basis, according to the date of the previous long vacation out of India. Thus, at the end of 1945 I arrived in Edinburgh to join my family once again. My wife had preceded me by more than a year; she had travelled in war-time discomfort, in a blacked-out, overcrowded troopship. I, on the other hand, by luck of the draw, returned comfortably, nay in near pre-war luxury, in a capacious Sunderland flying boat with a normal complement of passengers.

During this Army leave, I was offered and accepted an appointment in the Allied Control Commission for Germany, at the dazzling rank of Lieutenant-Colonel. Before I could take up the post, my departure was postponed until further orders. Once again, the delay was caused by the intervention of the Civil Authorities. The Secretary of State for India and Burma had requested my release from military service. After many weeks of waiting for a decision, I was finally ordered to return to Burma, at the end of September, 1946, much against my will.

The new British Government was engaged in negotiations to bring about the independence of India and Burma, at the earliest opportunity. Both countries had been promised complete autonomy by progressive steps, begun before the war. Now, conditions in the two countries differed in one important respect. Unlike India, Burma had been fought over recently, twice in succession, by two powerful adversaries provided with great weapons of destruction, devastating the land, demoralising the population and, leaving in their wake, large armed and lawless gangs. Some of these armed bands operated now under the guise of new political labels; each aiming to wrest power from the others by force of arms. All of them, whether plain dacoits or so-called political followers, were living off the meagre resources of the impoverished and powerless law-abiding inhabitants. In short, the country was in a worse state than after the collapse of the Burmese monarchy in 1885 when law and order ceased to exist in many areas. The then new rulers, the British, by a lengthy process of pacification, restored order, peace, prosperity and the rule of law.

I was no rabid imperialist; indeed, like many of my expatriate colleagues in pre-war Burma, I had accepted the need to implement a gradual process towards self-rule and had played my small part to assist the progress. My objections now were of a practical nature; I believed that the programme for rehabilitation was not only insufficient but impossible of achievement within the contemplated time-limit. No doubt, the timing for Burma had been influenced by the date proposed for India's independence, but then conditions were very different in that country. My worm's eye survey of the situation gave me a very different point of view. I had lived contentedly for more than a decade in that once happy, prosperous and peaceful land of Burma. I wished to see it restored to those same conditions before we handed over power to future rulers. I felt strongly that the British Government had an overwhelming moral obligation to pursue this practical aim before dealing with the political ambitions of the new, young, untried Burmese politicians, not interested in the economics of the situation.

The war was directly responsible for the deplorable state into which the country had been plunged; the people had neither sought nor wanted that war. It seemed to me that our new political leaders in London, and some of their advisers, just did not seem to appreciate the immense size of the problem or the great difficulties under which re-construction and rehabilitation would have to be undertaken. The proposed inadequate measures seemed doomed to failure, resulting in mutual bitterness between the two nations on the day of parting. Alas, so it proved in the end, despite all the well-meant efforts and goodwill.

I was, on my return, appointed District Superintendent of Police, Yamethin District; the very same place where I first tasted executive power in what now seemed another age. Things were going from bad to worse in the country as a whole; my district was no exception; in fact, it had the doubtful distinction of being near the top of the league for lawlessness. I hardly spent any time in my office at headquarters during my few months of duty. The Police and the Army (an Indian infantry battalion was stationed in the area for internal security duties) were constantly on the move, chasing after large, well-armed gangs, intent on pillaging and maiming wherever and whenever the opportunity arose. Some of these armed bands aped the prevailing fashion for new political name tags; white communists; red communists; peasants' army, and so on, declaring themselves followers of this or that local politician currently in fashion; they looted under the guise of political levies for the cause. What it really all boiled down to was plain dacoity on a vast scale.

To cap it all, certain political leaders in the capital had decided to subvert the Civil Police force, by encouraging the rank and file to go on strike. I forget now the spurious factors trotted out for the occasion. My old force, the Rangoon City Police, now without the steadier contingents of Karens, Indians and Gurkhas, were the first to succumb. The strike, or rather the mutiny, spread soon from one district to another. When news of these happenings reached us, I visited at once all the Police stations in the district. I warned all concerned that every police striker would be arrested immediately and held for trial as a mutineer under the Police Act. This warning seemed to hold the force together for a while. Yamethin was one of the last, if not the last, district in which some of the

Police went on strike.

I managed to carry out my threat swiftly and effectively; firstly, because only a minority of constables mutinied, the rest and all the higher ranks remained on duty. Secondly, the Commanding Officer of the internal security battalion co-operated readily with all my requests. He also offered to supply all the guards needed to keep the culprit policemen under lock and key, so that loyal members of the force were spared the shame of guarding their late comrades. Once this hectic punitive action was over, I discovered, to my great satisfaction, that nearly all the prisoners had been recruited into the Police hurriedly by Civil Affairs officers of the Military Administration, set up temporarily immediately after the end of hostilities in Burma. With the help of all ranks in the district force, members of the pre-war Police establishment who had not rejoined were traced and interviewed. As a result of these contacts, many of these overlooked trained policemen returned to the fold. In the end, we had managed to replace a substantial number of the mutineers and, what was just as important, had restored morale; law enforcement was looking up once again. The Law Courts were not yet fully functional and there was no immediate prospect of swift trials for the incarcerated mutineers; I was not unduly worried about this temporary delay in the judicial process.

The acting Inspector-General of Police, George Chettle, had been kept informed of the policy in the district and how the striking policemen had been replaced to a great extent. Quite suddenly and without any prior indication, I received a wireless message (telephone and telegram facilities were not yet available over long distances) informing me that the Government had decreed that all police strikers were to be re-instated at once unconditionally and without punishment. The administrative message made it clear that the orders emanated directly from the young, newly appointed Burmese Minister of Home Affairs. In our district, the order also meant the summary dismissal of the re-engaged pre-war constables, as surplus to establishment. This political interference in a matter of internal police discipline was not only bad for the executive authority but was against the law as it still existed. Although I was not as surprised as I should have been by this new situation, I was not prepared to accept it.

I signalled back to the Inspector-General that it was impossible for me, in view of the corrective measures I had taken to deal with the police strike, to carry out the Minister's instructions. I requested to be relieved of my appointment and to be allowed to proceed on leave preparatory to retirement on proportionate pension. My application was accepted by the Governor of Burma, Major-General Sir Hubert Rance, and I was instructed to hand over at once to my Assistant Superintendent, pending the appointment of a Burmese successor. The district force was upset by this abrupt and puzzling outcome for what had seemd to them a satisfactory solution to the shaming strike. I decided that even at this late stage in the impending handing over of power, I had to avoid further unnecessary weakening of executive authority for my successor; so I did not broadcast the real reason for my departure. Nevertheless, the force got to hear about the main facts on the 'jungle telegraph'. I was greatly moved by the number of individual officers and men who came to bid me personal good-byes and good wishes before I took the road to Rangoon. I had only been in the district for five months but it seemed much longer before I was again on my way home, this time for good, in March 1947.

By one of those curious coincidences, the name of the ship in which I made my final sea voyage home, bore the same name, 'Herefordshire', as the vessel in which my then recently widowed mother and her two small children, had gone home for her last time in January 1914.

There was a saying in Burma that anyone going away, whose last glimpse of that land was the tall gold-glittering spire of its largest Pagoda, the Shwe Dagon, was surely to return. I had always observed this charming superstition on previous departures; even on the unusually sad one for the 'last ditchers' in 1942. This time, I did not turn round for the proverbial last look, as the steamer rounded the bend in the Rangoon River.

Postscript

My personal gesture of protest had a negative practical effect. I was on leave, and thus still officially on the books when the compensation terms for loss of career were promulgated for all expatriate officers employed before the date of Independence. I sent in my claim for this benefit but my application was turned down on the grounds that I had retired voluntarily. Red Tape won in the end! Greed makes me regret the loss of a tidy sum of money (for those days) but I am still glad that I made what seemed to me then, and now, the right decision.

Salt p.139